Power Teams

Power Teams

The Complete Guide to Building and Managing a Winning Real Estate Agent Team

By John Featherston and Ralph R. Roberts

RISMedia

Norwalk, CT

ISBN 978-0-9800341-1-0
Printed in the United States of America.

Introduction

Being a real estate agent just isn't what it used to be. In the past, the playing field was fairly level and stable. An honest, hard-working professional could earn a pretty good living as an independent real estate agent.

Recent advances in technology and changes in the industry have dramatically changed our industry. Today's real estate consumers are more sophisticated and knowledgeable than ever before and tomorrow they will be even more advanced than today. Computers and the Internet have made it possible for sellers to market their own homes locally and nationally and have simplified the process of searching for homes. Consumers can also tap the Internet to find plenty of real estate agents offering bargains—flat-fee MLS listings, low-cost title commitments, free appraisal estimates, and so on. Some industry analysts believe full-service real estate brokers are now at risk of going the way of full-service gas stations, as consumers are empowered to serve themselves.

While neither of us believe this is really going to happen, we both believe that in order to remain competitive, agents have to do much more—place more phone calls, ramp up their marketing efforts, offer additional services, spend more time with their clients, and better understand the needs of today's real estate consumers. As a result, many agents are feeling the strain. They are working 80+ hours a week, neglecting their families, and suffering burnout in record numbers.

What's the solution? While there isn't just one singular solution, many agents have found that forming an agent team is the perfect solution for their own business. Simply by hiring an assistant to answer the phones, process the paperwork, and manage other office chores, agents can reclaim their lives, offer superior customer service, and generate enough revenue to more than cover the cost of their assistant. By bringing on additional personnel—buyer's agents, listing agents, accounting assistants, closing managers, and marketing managers, you can generate even more revenue and possibly transform your team into a salable asset.

The problem, however, is that most agents are fiercely independent. They are afraid that if they hire an assistant, they will lose control—that certain tasks will not be done or done correctly, and their relationships with their clients will suffer. Others simply worry about the cost—how will I manage to pay team members when the market is slow? Some agents avoid the agent team approach simply because they believe it will further complicate their business.

Well, welcome to *Power Teams: The Complete Guide to Building and Managing a Winning Real Estate Agent Team*. In this book, we help you overcome the obstacles that may be discouraging you from forming your own agent team. Here, we explain the agent team concept, reveal the various styles of agent teams, help you decide whether the agent team solution is right for you, and then lead you step-by-step through the process of building your own agent team from the ground up.

To write this book, we interviewed dozens of agents who have formed their own teams. These real estate professionals have blazed the trail for you. They have already made the most common mistakes, recovered from them, and designed systems that have a proven track record. By reading this book and learning the strategies and tips presented here, you will be able to steer clear of the most common pitfalls and begin reaping the benefits of having your own agent team.

We hope you enjoy the book and look forward to becoming your source for information and motivation.

Author Bios

John Featherston founded RISMedia (**www.RISMedia.com**) in 1980 as the premier source of news and business-development information for the residential real estate and home services industries. Under Featherston's leadership, RISMedia has become the leading media organization for breaking news and analysis, educational and networking events, and marketing and branding solutions for the leading real estate and home services companies throughout the United States. RISMedia's flagship publication, *Real Estate* magazine, is distributed to some 40,000 brokers and leading agents nationwide, and RISMedia's Daily e-News is circulated to upwards of 300,000 real estate professionals each day. A longtime proponent of the agent team concept, Featherston launched the monthly *Power Team Report*, a publication targeting the specific needs of agent teams, in 2006. He quickly realized the need for a comprehensive guide to creating and running a successful agent team and spearheaded the formation of this book, the only publication of its kind to provide practical information and guidance on how to take a real estate business to the next level with a team-based approach. For more information about RISMedia's print and online products, and its educational events, please visit www.rismedia.com.

Ralph R. Roberts' (**www.AboutRalph.com**) real estate sales success is legendary. He has been profiled by the Associated Press, CNN, and *Time* magazine; the latter dubbed him "the bestselling REALTOR® in America." In addition to being one of the most successful salespeople in the country, Roberts is also an experienced mentor, coach, and consultant, and he's authored several renowned books, including *Flipping Houses For Dummies, Foreclosure Investing For Dummies, Advanced Selling For Dummies*, and *Foreclosure Self-Defense For Dummies* (Wiley Publishing, Inc.); *Sell It Yourself* (Adams Media Corporation); *Walk Like a Giant, Sell Like a Madman: America's #1 Salesman Shows You How To Sell Anything* (Collins); *52 Weeks of Sales Success: America's #1 Salesman Shows You How To Close Every Deal!* (Collins); *REAL WEALTH by Investing in REAL ESTATE* (Prentice Hall); *Protect Yourself from Real Estate and Mortgage Fraud* (Kaplan); and *Mortgage Myths: 77 Secrets That Will Save You Thousands on Home Financing* (Wiley). Roberts was one of the first agents in America to embrace the power agent team concept, taking this approach out of necessity; he simply couldn't handle all the phone calls and paperwork himself. Now, he's a leading advocate of the team-based approach and a successful sales coach who teaches the benefits of teams to all his clients.

Authors' Acknowledgments

All books are a team project, but this book was more so than most, and we would like to acknowledge some of the key team members who contributed their efforts and expertise into making this book an engaging and informative guide on power team building and management. Special thanks to writer Joe Kraynak, who was instrumental in taking our loose collection of notes and interviews and transforming them into a cohesive whole.

Special thanks also to: Darryl MacPherson for his invaluable partnership in this project; Maria Patterson for managing the process and ensuring quality; Christy LaSalle and Susanne Dwyer for lending their design and production expertise; and project editor Eva Brennan for her comprehensive development of the entire manuscript.

Thanks also to Lois Maljak, Ralph's second-in-command; Paul Doroh, foreclosure specialist; Jerry VanGoethem, a specialist in small-business accounting; and all at Ralph Roberts Realty, for their significant contributions to the development of the manuscript. Contributor Nate Martinez would also like to thank his second-in-command, Sarah Bliss, for gathering the materials and drafting his contributions to the project.

Power Teams:
Building and Managing a Winning Real Estate Agent Sales Team

Chapter 15: Identifying New Opportunities and Adding New Teams

Chapter 16: Overcoming the Top Ten Challenges of Operating a Successful Agent Team

Appendix: For Brokers Only: Supporting Agent Sales Teams in Your Office

Part I

Uncovering the Agent Team Concept:
How It Can Help and What It Requires

Chapter 1

Grasping the Power Agent Team Concept

By definition, a *team* is a group of people working together for a common purpose, but the true essence of a team is really much more than that. A team is an entity with diverse skills, talents, and personalities. It is a whole that is greater than the sum of its parts, enabling each individual to accomplish more than he or she could do alone. A team's diversity makes it more capable of meeting challenges, and its flexibility enables it to quickly adapt to changing conditions. In a field in which progress is rapid and competition is fierce, a team enables far more success than the independent approach.

In a way, assembling an agent team is easier than hiring people to work for you. When you hire people, you often end up with employees who have little stake in the health of the business. They are primarily working for a paycheck and benefits. Of course, they want the business to survive, because it represents job security, but their pay probably is not directly linked to how much revenue your business brings in. When independent contractors decide to team up, they do it voluntarily, making a conscious decision to join forces. It is by choice, not by chance or necessity that professionals go into business together.

Despite the many benefits of teams, real estate agents often choose to fly solo, and if they achieve any level of success, they eventually find themselves overworked and unable to take their business to the next level. As a result, they lose a sense of balance in their lives and ultimately become rather unhappy and unfulfilled. Enter the solution: an agent team. With an agent team, you focus on what you are best at and most passionate about and then delegate the rest to other team members, such as a personal assistant, a listing coordinator, and an office manager.

Building and managing an agent team can be quite a challenge, but the potential benefits almost always outweigh the drawbacks, and most agents who opt for a team-based approach are usually very satisfied with the results. In this chapter, we introduce you to the agent-team concept, homing in on the differences between operating independently and leading a team of agents. Keep in mind, though, that an agent team isn't the right choice for everyone. More on that topic in Chapter 2—here, we explore the benefits of agent teams as well as the various ways you can structure your team so you can begin to envision the possibilities.

What Is an Agent Team? Traditional Real Estate versus the Team-Based Approach

The traditional model of running a real estate business—the model that most agents follow—consists of working independently for a broker and performing the thousand and one tasks required to serve your clients all by yourself, such as:

- Answering phones and voice messages
- Filtering through and responding to e-mail
- Marketing yourself and your business online and off
- Networking
- Managing leads
- Meeting with clients and prospective clients
- Assembling and delivering marketing packets
- Delivering listing presentations to prospective sellers
- Coaching sellers on how to properly stage their homes
- Scheduling showings
- Showing homes to prospective buyers
- Obtaining feedback on showings
- Tracking and processing closing papers
- Calling past clients to keep in touch

With a team-based real estate business, on the other hand, after you get the business up and running you can clear the most time- and mind-consuming chores from your desktop and focus on marketing yourself, serving clients, and growing your business. The other members of your team manage the details such as answering phones, processing paperwork, scheduling appointments, and so on, so you can focus on the bigger picture. For example, you can whittle your responsibilities down to these tasks, depending on what type of client you serve:

- **As a buyer's agent**, your four primary responsibilities may be to meet with prospective clients, show homes, negotiate the purchase price and terms, and follow up with Internet and phone leads. With the right systems in place, assistants can handle everything else, including researching homes in the area that meet your client's specifications, scheduling appointments, and drafting your daily itinerary. You may spend the morning showing homes, but after your clients find a home and reach agreement on their offer, you simply call back to the office and pass your clients along to another team member, who schedules the closing and begins assembling the necessary paperwork. Other than attending the closing to watch your clients sign the papers and congratulate them on their new home, your job is complete, and you can focus on other clients.

• **As a seller's agent**, you can save even more time per client, because you have more administrative work you can offload to assistants, such as assembling and delivering marketing packets, researching comparable properties, creating Microsoft® PowerPoint® presentations for prospective clients, taking photos or videos of homes, posting listings, and dealing with all the other details involved in marketing homes. Your job, then, is to work closely with the homeowners to make sure their properties are in marketable condition, obtain feedback from buyer's agents on showings, pass that feedback along to the sellers, field offers and assist through the negotiating process. When negotiations are complete, you pass each transaction along to another team member, who ties up all the loose ends. After a brief cameo appearance at the closing, you're ready for your next clients.

Identifying the Parts that Make the Whole: Types of Team Members

What exactly constitutes a team, and who qualifies as a team member? Some people claim that a team is any two or more people working together to achieve a common goal. Others insist that team members must be partners in the team, sharing the risks and rewards. They argue that hourly employees don't count as part of the team, per se, because they're paid the same amount regardless of the team's success; employees risk very little and do not stand to reap greater rewards if the business is highly successful.

We prefer to take a broad view, with a team comprising any two or more people working to achieve a common goal and sharing in the risks and rewards.

A team often consists of several types of team members, generally classified according to their involvement and compensation:

• **Team leader:** The team leader is obviously a key member of the team, assuming the greatest risk and standing to receive the greatest potential benefit from the team. The team leader is responsible for generating sufficient business and revenue to support the rest of the team.

• **Commissioned Agents:** By any definition of "agent team," agents qualify as bona fide team members, because their financial success is tied directly to the success of the team. They are the ones who work directly with clients and generate the most revenue.

• **Salaried Employees:** Salaried employees are often professionals who work in administrative capacities, such as office managers, department managers, and supervisors. These are not your nine-to-fivers, so they are usually considered part of the team.

• **Hourly Employees:** We believe that hourly employees count as part of the team, as long as they are not your average nine-to-five clock watchers, and especially if they have bonuses tied to the team's success. After all, if the team does not produce, hourly employees can feel the pain, too—in the form of lost employment, pay, benefits, and bonuses.

• **Contractors:** Like hourly employees, contractors (including virtual assistants, home stagers, and consultants) may or may not be part of the team. Again, it depends on the person. If the person frequently contracts with the team and is sincerely committed to the team's success, then he or she may be considered a team member.

Note: We generally don't consider vendors as part of the team because they are just selling a product or service, but you can certainly establish mutually beneficial relationships with vendors that foster a team spirit.

The Agent Team Structure: Roles and Responsibilities

Although every agent team is unique, most start out as a fairly simple two-person team, with just an agent and an assistant. The agent does what he or she is best at and performs the most dollar-productive activities—activities that drive business and generate revenue. The assistant fills a supporting role—scheduling, processing paperwork and performing other tasks to free up the agent's time and resources so the agent can focus on generating business. When agents realize how much more productive and profitable they are with an assistant, they usually decide to grow their team. In fact, agent teams can become small businesses unto themselves.

Agent teams vary in size and structure, with some complex teams comprising numerous members who play the following roles (Note: Sometimes one person can play more than one role):

• **Team leader:** Usually the most experienced and energetic agent—the one who puts a face on the team—promotes it, networks, builds relationships, and generates the most business.

• **Team manager (second-in-command):** The person who keeps the team on track, oversees operations, double-checks the accounting, and runs the team meetings.

• **Listing agent or listing partner (seller's agent):** One or more agents who specialize in listing properties for sale, representing sellers during negotiations, and delegating other tasks to the support staff.

• **Showing agent (buyer's agent):** One or more agents who specialize in finding the right homes for buyers and representing their interests during negotiations.

• **Closing manager (transaction manager):** Someone who works with the title company to manage the transaction from sale to closing.

• **Client care specialist (customer service representative):** The front line team member who meets and greets clients, answers most of their questions, and refers clients to others when he or she does not know the answer.

• **Listing coordinator:** The person who supports the listing agents, creates marketing materials, updates clients monthly, obtains feedback from agents who show the listed homes, handles the listing transaction, makes sure all documents are signed, and sends out "just listed" and "just sold" postcards and company mailers.

• **Office assistant(s):** One or more people who manage daily activities, such as assembling marketing packets, updating Web sites and blogs, researching comps and homes for sale, fielding general questions from clients, and so on.

• **Virtual assistant:** A freelancer who conducts business primarily online and can handle various responsibilities, from lead management and listing coordination, to transaction management and Internet marketing. For more about virtual assistants, check out the nearby sidebar, "Discovering Virtual Assistants Online."

• **Photographer or videographer:** This person takes photos of the home for the MLS and other marketing materials and may produce a video (virtual) tour of the home for placement on the Web.

• **Professional office organizer:** The office organizer makes sure everything has a place and everything is in its place. Although this job may seem fairly mundane, far too many teams waste far too much time looking for misplaced documents and supplies.

• **Relocation expert:** The relocation expert is responsible for generating relocation business by networking with corporations and relocation businesses.

• **Courier (delivery person):** The courier is basically in charge of running the team's shipping department, making sure all packages reach their destinations. Duties can entail dropping off packages at the post office or delivering them in person.

• **Cash-buy agent (guaranteed sales agent):** Some teams have a cash-buy agent who has cash on hand to purchase homes below market value from homeowners who have to or want to sell their homes in a hurry and don't have time to place them on the market. Sometimes this person is referred to as a guaranteed sales agent, because the agent can list the home with a guarantee to purchase it for a certain agreed-upon price if it doesn't sell by a certain date. For details on setting up a cash-buy department, check out Chapter 16.

• **Real-estate-owned (REO) agent:** An REO agent can list homes for banks and other lenders who take possession of the homes by way of foreclosure.

• **Foreclosure/preforeclosure agent:** Foreclosure/preforeclosure agents specialize in working with distressed homeowners. These agents educate the homeowners about their options and then offer them several choices, including listing their home for sale, buying their home for cash, or buying their home for cash and then selling or leasing it back to them. For details on setting up a foreclosure department, check out Chapter 16.

• **New-construction agent:** A new-construction agent lists and sells homes for builders and refers buyers who need to sell their current homes to the listing agent.

• **Property manager:** A property manager is responsible for taking care of properties that the team owns and may even take care of client properties. This person is responsible for hiring contractors to perform repairs and renovations, securing insurance, making sure all taxes are up-to-date, leasing out rental properties, handling collections and evictions of past-due tenants, and working with the listing department to place rehabbed houses on the market as quickly as possible.

• **Receptionist (director of first impressions):** The receptionist is in charge of answering the phones, meeting and greeting clients, and handling other office chores.

• **Public relations/marketing manager:** The PR person or marketing manager is in charge of generating positive press through as many media outlets as possible, including the Web, e-mail, TV, radio, print (advertising and articles), podcasts, and videocasts. This person may also function as the team blogger or ghost blogger. For more about blogging and other marketing efforts, check out Chapter 14.

• **IT (information technology) specialist:** This person provides technical support for the office and may also create and manage the team's Web sites and blogs.

• **Staging specialist:** If your team chooses to add staging to the list of services it offers, a staging specialist can help prepare homes for sale, which typically allows you to sell the homes for more money and in less time than it takes to sell unstaged homes.

• **Cleaning crew:** In addition to maintaining the cleanliness of the office, the cleaning crew can clean the team's investment properties and also help clients clean their homes in preparation for a showing or open houses.

• **Land-acquisition agent (land development):** A land-acquisition agent is particularly useful if your team has a new-construction agent working with builders. The land-acquisition agent can help builders find and acquire land for building new subdivisions and other projects, which creates even more business for the new-construction agent.

Take a Lesson from Your Dentist

Most dentists don't work as their own receptionists or clean patients' teeth. They hire a receptionist to answer phones, greet patients, process insurance information and bill patients. They hire dental hygienists to clean teeth, take x-rays and prepare patients for their dental inspections.

If your dentist runs an efficient office, he or she probably spends about five or 10 minutes with you for your six-month checkup, primarily to find out how you're doing and quickly examine the inside of your mouth for any potential problems. Your dentist offloads all the lower-level tasks and then focuses on higher-level tasks, such as filling cavities, capping teeth and referring patients to specialists.

To maximize your own efficiency as a real estate agent, take a lesson from your dentist and learn to delegate tasks. Apply the assembly-line approach to selling real estate.

Discovering Virtual Assistants Online

When you are building a team, remember that team members don't necessarily have to work right alongside you in the same office. With the development of the Internet and a host of other technologies, you can have team members that work all over the world, processing transactions, handling your accounting, designing and maintaining your Web sites and blogs, designing your marketing materials, and much more.

Although these team members are real, live people, they are referred to as *virtual assistants* (VA), because they market their services and do most of their work online. The good news is that because they're freelancers, you simply buy as much work as you need and pay a flat hourly fee or by-project fee. You don't have to worry about paying taxes, offering additional benefits, or offering paid vacations. Following are some of the many benefits that virtual assistants offer:

- You pay only for the time the VA works for you
- You don't have to create work to keep the person busy
- No payroll taxes or payments into worker's compensation insurance
- No insurance or other benefits
- No paid sick days, holidays or vacation days
- VAs come fully equipped, so you have no overhead
- No relocation costs
- No hiring or firing—if the person doesn't work out, you just find another VA

Tip: Because the real estate business tends to cycle with the changing seasons, VAs are a particularly attractive option. They enable you to scale up or scale down your team at a moment's notice. Scale up when you have more work to do and scale down when sales taper off.

Most virtual assistants specialize in a certain field—writing, editing, Web design, transcription, database management, accounting...you name it. Many specialize in serving the real estate industry. Here is a short list of what a qualified real estate virtual assistant can do for you:

- Build an online transaction-management system
- Design feature sheets and postcards
- Implement a drip e-mail program

- Create CMAs
- Update Web sites with new listings
- Design and maintain your blog
- Provide sellers with feedback from showings
- Manage leads
- Manage e-mail
- Record IVR listings (800#)
- Enhance listings on REALTOR.com®
- Prepare holiday mailers
- Order closing gifts
- Screen phone calls
- Assemble prelisting packages
- Design and personalize listing presentations
- Research properties
- Update calendars and schedules

Whether you have more work than you and your current staff can handle or are simply looking for ways to save time and money, a virtual assistant can be the perfect solution. Virtual assistants provide you with the resources you need to scale up and scale down your staff at a moment's notice.

Remember: Virtual assistants are not the best solution for everyone. You have to decide whether virtual outsourcing is right for you. Are you a person who needs to oversee the process? Do you like to have all your team members working in the same physical location? Do you need to see your fellow team members come into work every day? If you answered "Yes" to any of these questions, VAs may not be right for you.

Identifying the Benefits of Agent Teams

Real estate agents who successfully make the transition to a team-based system rarely regret their decision. What they regret is not having done it sooner. They often tell us about how frustrated and overworked they were prior to building a team. Working over 80 hours a week, having insufficient time and resources for their clients, they often found themselves making costly mistakes and having little time for themselves and their families.

After establishing a team, their lives improved. These agents were able to focus on what they do best—dealing with clients and selling homes—and could outsource the rest to other team members who had the time, resources, and energy to take on those tasks. Sure, they had to share their profits with the rest of the team, but the increase in commissions more than covered the added expense. Perhaps best of all, these agents had more time and energy for themselves and for their families, friends, and communities.

Team-based agents are overwhelmingly more satisfied with their careers and with their lives than are agents who work alone, and in the following sections, we explore some of the reasons why.

Increasing personal productivity and boosting sales and profits

Imagine removing from your daily schedule every task you perform that keeps you from doing what you do best. Imagine having someone sift through incoming e-mail messages, calling your attention to only those messages that you really need to see. Consider how much more efficient you'd be if someone kept your office organized so you didn't waste time looking for misplaced files. How much more time could you devote to clients if someone answered the phone for you and took messages, or handled all the paperwork after a sale?

As an agent, you generate revenue through commissions. The more you sell, the more you earn, so you should be focusing on talking with clients and prospective clients and selling properties. Everything else you typically do in a day—promoting yourself, designing and producing marketing materials, researching properties, updating your Web site or blog, answering general questions over the phone, and so on—is simply distracting from your ability to generate revenue.

Even if your team consisted of only you and one trusted assistant, you could more than double your production. If you had one assistant along with a closing manager, you could more than triple your production. And if you had other agents working with you, you could boost production even more.

For example, say you pay an assistant $20 an hour, which equals about $800 per week or $40,000 a year. That $40,000 could be a real mental roadblock for you unless you shift your thinking a little. Instead of thinking about the sticker price, think about how many hours of your day that person would free up for you, how many more clients you could tend to, how many more transactions you could close, and how many more referrals you would receive from those additional clients now that you're able to provide them with better service. As you can imagine, the commissions you'd earn by having more time to serve more clients would likely exceed your assistant's salary. And in addition to the financial gains, you'd be less stressed. It's a win-win situation.

Launching a Team Out of Necessity

Since my entry into real estate, I have been part of a team. The reason for this decision was simple—I don't spell well, and my handwriting looks like Egyptian hieroglyphics.

In my case, necessity was the mother of invention; I needed a teammate to help me accomplish my daily tasks—answering phones, jotting down notes, scheduling appointments, and keeping everything organized. Many colleagues thought I was being uppity by having an assistant, and I was too embarrassed to correct their false impression of me. Consequently I was never a Lone Ranger; I've always had a Tonto, and it has made all the difference in my career. *–Ralph R. Roberts*

Improving office efficiency

Generally speaking, the more transactions you handle, the more inefficient you become. Every time you have to stop what you're doing to attend to a detail on another transaction, you lose momentum (and you create more opportunities for errors on account of distractions).

With a team-based approach, you can delegate more tasks to others who are better equipped to perform them. A team enables you to create an assemblyline of sorts. Each person on the team handles certain tasks required to process each transaction. Instead of having to stop what you're doing to take a phone call or follow up on paperwork prior to closing, you can hand off those chores to a teammate who has the time needed to perform those tasks.

In turn, the division of labor makes each team member more efficient at performing particular tasks. With the right training and resources, a great system, and detailed procedures manuals in place, a team should operate like a well-oiled machine.

Staying Out of the Office

Jean Shine of the Shine Team (www.shineteam.com), Coldwell Banker, in Central Texas figured out that everyone on the team benefits by letting Jean make rain—actually torrential downpours—and keeping her out of the office, where she tends to cause chaos.

According to Rodney Shine, Jean's second-in-command: "The

best way to keep the team functioning is to have everyone focus on what they are good at. Jean is awesome, especially outside of the office, where her skills really pay dividends. The team prepares files and makes appointments. Jean simply calls into the office ahead of time, and then drives into the parking lot where another team member meets her to hand over the schedule and files. When Jean is done, she drops off the files to be processed and picks up another batch. It took awhile to figure out the best systems, but now that they have them in place, the team operates on automatic and reaches new levels of success each year."

Generating new opportunities

A team-based approach packs your business with what we like to refer to as TNT—time 'n' talent, both of which are great at generating new opportunities. If your team has an excellent writer, for example, you have an opportunity to generate more marketing buzz and perhaps even some revenue by writing articles, books, and press releases. Another team member who is technically savvy may open your business to new opportunities on the Internet or expose you to productivity software that saves you time. You may be able to find inroads to an entirely new market through a team member who has foreign language skills or sensitivities to different ethnicities and cultures. And don't forget the networking aspect: You also have access to all the team members' contacts.

Tip: As your team grows, continue to recruit new talent so you're constantly growing your talent pool and adding fresh perspectives.

Increasing scalability

More and more businesses are finding value in scalability—being able to scale up when business is brisk and scale back when it drops off. In the real estate business, seasonal and market shifts can cause significant swings in the volume of business you do, and having one or more teams in place can help you ride out these swings. With a scalable team, you have more flexibility to trim overhead when needed and then quickly ramp up your staff when business picks up.

Tip: One way to increase scalability is to staff your team with virtual assistants, as discussed in Chapter 4. Another way is to create separate divisions within your team. For example, you could add a foreclosure and/or REO division to generate business and add another revenue stream; when the market is strong, you could divert resources from the foreclosure division to sales, and when the market weakens, you can divert more resources to the foreclosure division and/or REO.

Improving customer service

A major component of long-term success in any business is the ability to deliver quality customer service. The personal aspect of customer service is why so many real estate agents are reluctant to embrace a team-based model—they feel that they must attend to every detail of a transaction themselves. But their fear of losing control is often based on the myth that the individual agent can provide superior customer service only by attending to everything personally.

The fact is that most teams provide superior customer service. When a team has two or more agents, one agent is always on call to handle customer questions and concerns. In addition, the agent can focus on top-level issues while the support staff handles lower-level issues. This setup increases the customer service efficiency quotient, which is better for everyone.

Tip: You can expect many of your clients to be reluctant about signing up with a team. They believe that the commission they pay makes you responsible to personally perform every task related to the transaction. To allay their concerns, assure them that your team is staffed by the top professionals in the business and that you're committed to serving their needs. Knowing that someone is always available to answer their calls can put them at ease. You can easily reassure potential clients by having a listing/buyer presentation that introduces the members of your team and reminds clients that everyone on the team is working to get their house sold.

Focusing on the work you find most rewarding

Nothing can sap your motivation more than having to perform chores that you find boring or frustrating. You probably got into the real estate business because you enjoy working with people and selling properties. That is the sort of work that wakes you up in the morning and keeps you pumped up throughout the day.

Other parts of your job may actually drain your energy. For most agents, these chores include pushing paperwork, running errands, answering phones, and tracking down misplaced records. These tasks are the ones you need to delegate.

Tip: Always keep the three Ds in mind: Do it, Delegate it, or Ditch it. Do what you enjoy doing and what will generate revenue, delegate all other essential tasks, and then let everything else go. This system is great for just about anyone who feels as though 24 hours isn't enough time in a day to get everything done.

Maximizing your free time

Success includes much more than your career. It encompasses your own happiness and self-fulfillment, your relationships, your family, and your community. In other words, success requires balance, and when you're working 24/7, all other aspects that factor into the success equation begin to suffer.

A team can help you bring balance into your life. You can begin to take vacations and days off, knowing that your partners and other team members are there to take care of your clients and keep the business running. You have more time and energy to pursue your other interests and find fulfillment outside of your career. And you can begin to focus more resources on what matters most to you.

Manchisi Real Estate: A Case Study

Domenic Manchisi (www.domenicmanchisi.com) of Prudential Town Centre Realty is an accomplished REALTOR® working out of Milton, Ontario, and is recognized as leading one of the top three teams in all of Canada in 2006. He has also received numerous awards, including the Top 1/2 percent in the Nation and Top 100 out of 30,000 agents on the Toronto Real Estate Board—the largest board in Canada.

Although Domenic was a very successful agent right from the start, he quickly realized that if he had any hopes of managing a successful career and having a life at the same time, he needed to build and manage his own agent team. We talked to Domenic about his experience in building a successful agent team, and here's what he had to say:

"I entered the real estate business at the age of 20 with very little direction. Within the first week, I developed a simple script and made phone calls every night. Within the first six weeks, I sold two homes and listed four new properties. Within a year, I sold 28 homes—not bad for a rookie. By my third year in the business, my sales were up to a respectable 40 units per year, but I was working day and night, and by the age of 23, I was already beginning to feel burned out, but I was determined to achieve even higher sales volumes.

"I knew I couldn't possibly work any harder or work longer

hours, and as I saw it, I was already working as efficiently as I possibly could. I couldn't clone myself, so I tried the next best thing—I decided to hire my first administrative assistant. Now I realize that I should have hired an assistant after my first year, but I'm a high "D" personality (direct, decisive, and driven)— the nobody-can-do-it-like-I-can personality. Unfortunately, the 'D' doesn't stand for 'delegate.'

"Prior to hiring an assistant, my wife, Jody, and I sat down and drew up a list of everything I did. When we had a comprehensive list in place, I reviewed it and highlighted all the tasks that I really didn't need to do and that an assistant could handle. From these lists, Jody and I developed detailed procedures manuals, providing complete instructions on how to perform each task. I believe this preparation is essential in ensuring success; otherwise, you end up hiring someone who has nothing to do and has to keep asking you questions on how to perform certain tasks.

"After a short period of training, my assistant was well schooled on her exact role and her daily responsibilities, and I began to notice an immediate improvement in both my attitude and my conversion rates. My assistant answered the phones, gave vendor feedback, put listing packages together, and personally delivered them on my behalf—all the tasks I didn't need to be doing. She also managed the listing paperwork and handed it to me all filled out and ready to be signed by prospective clients. In the first year of having an assistant, my sales jumped from 40 to 78 units.

"With my assistant taking on much of my workload, I was able to invest more time and resources in building my business, and my sales and commissions increased. I invested 15% of my earnings for that year in marketing (a critical component of my team). I began spending more money on Web sites, postcards, newsprint, and branded and nonbranded marketing.

"Jody and I also invested plenty of time and energy implementing systems to manage the business more efficiently in preparation for adding more team members. We designed and built our own management systems for following up with both sellers and buyers. These systems would generate automated mailings and e-mails and notify us when we needed to place personal phone calls to clients and prospective clients.

"We also built systems on how to follow up with sign calls, ad calls, e-mails, and open houses. We built these systems in order to monitor any agents we might decide to add to the team later and to ensure that they were making calls, going on appointments, and following up with clients.

"We held off on hiring any new agents until I began receiving more leads than I could possibly keep up with. At that point we hired our first buyer's agent, who is still with me today and is a 20-year veteran in the business. I gave her the tools and training on how I wanted her to work with clients. I provided her with sample scripts, and we role-played and rehearsed buyer presentations on a daily basis. She also shadowed me once a week to observe how I handled follow-ups.

"Personally, I had a tough time giving my buyers to another agent. I enjoyed working with buyers, showing homes, and negotiating offers on their behalf. But if I wanted to increase production, I had to focus on my true gift—working with sellers—and refer buyers to someone who could provide them with specialized service and individual attention.

"By the end of that first year with my buyer's agent, we had sold 103 homes and were third in Canada for unit sales for Prudential Real Estate. We now have three buyer's agents, an office manager (Jody), an onsite assistant, and a virtual (offsite) assistant, who will take us to the next level. In 2007, we were on track to close somewhere between 170 and 180 units.

"When do you know that you need an agent team? When you come to realize that you can't possibly achieve your career goals and still give yourself and your family the required attention. Don't get me wrong—building and maintaining a team is hard work, but the pros far outweigh the cons."

The Various Types of Team Structures

Many real estate professionals are on teams and they do not even realize it—they simply call it something different or have their team structured in such a way that it does not have a team feel. In this section, we attempt to expand upon whatever preconceived notion you may have concerning agent teams by introducing a variety of team types. Keep in mind, however, that teams are constantly evolving and what works for one team may not work for another.

In the course of the past five years or so, our own definition of agent team has expanded to include teams that consist almost entirely of virtual assistants working out of their homes.

Some agents who build teams choose the type of team they want, but in most cases, the team type chooses the agent. In other words, the type of team that is right for you depends a great deal on who you are, what you hope to accomplish, and what human resources you have at your disposal. If you have a spouse, for example, who is passionate about real estate and can serve as your assistant or office manager, you would probably choose to start a team with your spouse. If you have a colleague you enjoy working with, forming a partnership would be a more logical choice.

Because every team and every agent is different, we can't tell you which team style will work best for you—that depends on your needs and the human resources you have at your disposal. In the following sections, however, we introduce you to several common team types, so you can choose the type that suits you best or assemble pieces of each to develop your own unique organization.

Tip: Seize every opportunity to talk to someone who is part of an agent team about how his or her team is structured and how it operates. A brief conversation can often reveal options that you would never have dreamt up on your own.

Spouse teams

Some of the best agent teams begin with "I do." Two agents get married, and they instantly form both an intimate and professional partnership, or one partner marries into the real estate business with little or no experience and learns along the way.

Is a spouse team right for you? Well, that depends on you, your spouse, and the lifestyle that you desire. *Warning:* Don't enter into such an arrangement without making the following considerations:

• Do you and your spouse share a passion for real estate?

• Do you work well together? If you can't wallpaper a room together without getting into a War of the Roses, then you probably can't run a business together.

• Do you both have sufficient time to devote to running a successful business? If one of you has to (or wants to) stay home and raise children, then that person may not make the best business partner.

<u>Spouse Team Case Study: Ralph and Kathleen Roberts</u>

After several years of growing a successful real estate business, I married Kathleen and took on my best business partner at the same time. She had been working in a closing department and understood the business, so she didn't require a great deal of training. I was acquiring property and needed a property manager. Fortunately, she agreed to join me. She was excellent.

After our first daughter, Kolleen, was born, Kathy continued to serve as wife, mother, and property manager. Soon after Kolleen turned five, we adopted our son, Kyle. The following September, we hosted an exchange student in our home.

Kathy went from being the mother of one to the mother of three. She fell behind in the property management arena, and her passion changed. She wanted to be a full-time mother and no longer wanted to deal with the issues of property management. Later, she opened a title company and worked there a few times a week—a personal choice that we made together. She opened the title company because of the amount of business we had, and it was an instant profit center.

I know of several other romantic partners who are also very successful working and living together—sharing both their personal and professional lives. John Featherston and I believe that one of the most famous and successful teams consists of Dave and Gail Liniger, co-founders of RE/MAX International.

Keep in mind, however, that we are not recommending that all married agents team up with their spouses. Some spouses simply can't work together; it wouldn't be healthy for their relationship and shouldn't be forced.

If you decide to team up with your spouse, pay close attention to the warning signs. If you're bringing too much of the office home with you at the end of the day, make other arrangements. Maintaining the balance between your professional and personal lives can be very tricky, but it's imperative. *–Ralph R. Roberts*

<u>No One-Size-Fits-All Team Style</u>

We asked Teresa Strohmeyer of The Teresa Team (www.homes-database.com/teresastrohmeyer) at ERA OakCrest Realty in

Winchester, Virginia to share her experience in building and managing an agent team, and here's what she had to say:

"The important thing to remember about real estate teams is that one size does not fit all. Just as you have different types of agents, you see different types of teams. Each team is unique, reflecting the personality of the team leader and other team members, capitalizing on their strengths, and overcoming their weaknesses. However, successful teams seem to have one thing in common: They are solidly built around a top-producing agent who continues to produce year in and year out.

"My team is solidly built around me. For many years, I worked alone without assistance. I then tried working with a partner for awhile, but realized that I like having my own team so much better. It's rare for a partnership to be fair and equitable. It's also difficult for two different, strong-minded personalities to work together over the long haul without conflict or resentment.

"To be successful, one has to be single-minded. Not selfish, but centered and focused on the goal, which, in our case, is excellent service and sustained high production. To achieve this, the person at the head of the organization must be free of other vital obligations that can be handled by others just as well, if not better. That way, he or she can focus intently on sales and service and leading the team.

"Everyone is born with one head for a reason. No matter what the form of government or organization, nations and businesses are comprised of a leader supported by numerous vice presidents, advisors, and assistants. And so it is for teams. It's as simple as this: The queen bee's survival depends upon her worker bees, and the worker bees' purpose within the organization is to support the queen bee. When the system is working as it should, the relationship is symbiotic and synergistic and is based on trust and mutual respect.

"I pay salaries or hourly wages to my three full-time employees. I do not have any commissioned salespeople working for me. My husband, Joe Strohmeyer, works in real estate full time as The Teresa Team's marketing coordinator and as the leasing agent and property manager of our 17 rental units. While I would love to call our organization The Joe and Teresa Team and have it be more of a visible partnership, it does not fit into Joe's wishes or personality. Joe prefers to play a supporting role.

"Although Joe is a licensed agent and does an excellent job when he assists me in showing property, he mainly works other aspects of our business. He takes all our photos, compiles our ads, and places them on the Internet and in the home magazines. His excellent photography and eye-catching brochures have become a key component of the unique selling proposition that we offer to our clients. He also does less glamorous work that frees me to work on the front lines directly with clients. He puts up all our signs and keeps the flyer boxes full. And he keeps our personal investment properties rented and running smoothly.

"Joe works mostly from our home office while I work at our office in town along with our other two full-time assistants. Although he has a place to work at our office and stops by frequently, he does the majority of his work at home because he finds it easier to be creative in an environment with fewer distractions. By working from home, he is also the one who oversees our household. He takes care of the pets and makes sure that we have groceries and clean clothes. While we have delegated our lawn care and cleaning to outside services and hire out all the maintenance of our rental properties, Joe is the one who handles the logistics and oversees the work.

"Joe also helps me market myself. Between the radio ads that run two weeks out of every month on two radio stations, and sending out calendars and seasonal postcards at various times of the year, Joe periodically also sends out Just Sold direct-mail pieces.

"My good friend Brenda Snider joined us several years ago as The Teresa Team's office manager, transaction coordinator, and bookkeeper. Brenda was an agent when I entered real estate. In fact, she trained me, and we partnered on some of my earliest real estate sales. I learned a lot about customer service from Brenda. In addition to supervising our office and overseeing our finances, she monitors every transaction from contract to closing, making sure that the trains run on time, so to speak. She obtained her real estate license again and also occasionally assists in showing property, opening doors for inspectors and hosting broker open houses.

"Ann Craighead joined us recently. She is not a real estate licensee but she worked as a receptionist and assistant in another real estate office in our town. She also has banking experience. Her title is Client Services Coordinator. She assists in managing and monitoring our listings and buyer prospects.

"An important aspect of Ann's job is communications. She keeps buyers updated with new listings and sets my showing appointments. She compiles feedback reports from agents who have shown my listings and mails or e-mails the reports to our sellers. She monitors our Web sites to be sure that all the photos are uploaded and the information is current and correct. She also does research, looking up plots and septic permits, so that we have all the supporting documentation that buyers might need to make a decision. Ann also clips and mails to our sellers any ads of their houses that appear in the home magazines.

"In time, as my business grows, I will hire additional assistants and spin off some of Brenda's and Ann's duties to them. As I grow older and approach retirement age, I hope to hire one or more buyers' agents so that I can concentrate mainly on listings and working with repeat buyer clients. But hiring a buyer's agent is tricky. I prefer someone who would stay with me for a number of years and who will not use me merely as a springboard to launch his or her own career."

Producer + Staff

A Producer + Staff team is what we discuss in general throughout this chapter: it comprises a front person (the team leader) and the team members who allow the team leader to do what he or she does best without having to be bothered with all the day-to-day chores of running the business and processing transactions.

For example, you may have a top-producing agent/broker who is great at bringing deals together but horrible at dotting the i's and crossing the t's. The rainmaker establishes a team of individuals who can carry the load and make sure all the details are taken care of. This setup may look like an employer/employee situation, but it's often more than just that. Yes, the paper pushers are probably hourly or salaried employees, but they're also crucial for the team's success. The rainmaker can't function without them, and they're unemployed if they don't enable the rainmaker to be free to perform or if they fail to complete all paperwork correctly and on time.

On teams like this one, the rainmaker often ties performance bonuses to the team's success and productivity. This monetary incentive gives everyone a stake in the team—something that people who are simply employees often miss. The most successful teams are success oriented—individual compensation is based on the team's success.

Family businesses

Some real estate teams expand with the family and may even include several generations of family members.

The Fairbanks Team (www.brandonfairbanks.com) of Montecino & Associates in California began with Brandon Fairbanks and his mother Patty. Brandon Fairbanks began exploring the team concept in 2002. As his business was expanding, he found less time to market, develop leads, and work with buyers and sellers. He convinced his mother, Patty, to get her real estate license and join him, with the expectation that Patty would handle the paperwork and Brandon would work the leads. Since then, several other agents have joined the team.

Other family teams contain multiple family members, including brothers, sisters, cousins, uncles, aunts, and even in-laws. Like any family business, a family-based agent team faces unique challenges. Disagreements over money, workload, and other issues can threaten to damage relationships among family members, so everyone needs to be prepared for this. Of course, nothing is more rewarding than working together as a family to achieve a common goal.

The Crockett Team (www.thecrockettteam.com) of Howard Hanna Smythe Cramer REALTORS® in Concord and Painesville Townships, Ohio started with Mom Crockett (Judie) at the helm. Her husband later joined her, assuming the role of second-in-command. Now that the kids have grown, they all have joined the team in various capacities.

Partnerships

Teams often begin when two successful agents discover that they have a good deal in common and get along well. How these partnerships unfold can vary depending on the skills, talents, and passions of each partner. Sometimes, a listing agent will partner with a buyer's agent to complement one another. Other times, two listing agents may form a partnership and then scout for assistants and buyer's agents. An agent may even partner with someone who has absolutely no experience in real estate—perhaps someone who specializes in marketing and public relations or is a great office manager.

Like a good marriage, a partnership requires outstanding communication skills to survive and thrive. Partnerships often crumble when partners disagree about the division of work and money. Choose your partner as carefully as you choose your spouse, and work together to communicate your visions, dreams, ideas, and any problems you may have that could negatively affect your partnership. Being open, honest, and understanding can keep your partnership on an even keel.

Partnership Team Case Study: Nate Martinez

Nate Martinez (www.nateshomes.com), a RE/MAX Professional working out of Glendale, Arizona, runs his team as an equal partnership with his colleague Frank Russo. We asked Nate to share his experience of forming a partnership team:

"My company is a little different from the average real estate office setup. Frank Russo and I co-own our RE/MAX Professionals franchise as well as a joint business venture with Wells Fargo Home Mortgage, Professional Financial Services of Arizona.

"Within our company, each of us operates our real estate teams independently and separately from RE/MAX Professionals. Neither Frank nor I are the designated broker or the manager for the company. Frank's team is set up much like my team, and we have a separate staff of people to run the franchise. We currently have four offices, and each office has its own Director of First Impressions (what we feel is a more accurate description of our 'receptionists'). We also have a recruiter, office managers for two of the locations, a general manager, who also manages two of the office locations, three transaction coordinators, a human resource person, a designated broker, a broker assistant, and an IT person. Our RE/MAX Professionals franchise has a total of 27 employees and 160 agents.

"My best advice about creating your own team is to surround yourself with good people who complement your weaknesses. I am the one with the vision, and Frank is the one who keeps things in perspective, while the rest of the team performs all the important tasks that bring our vision to life."

Conglomerates of equals

Just as a team can form out of a partnership of two equal parties, it can include more than two equals. Several agents and other skilled individuals can get together and decide that they'll all contribute their unique skill sets and share the proceeds fairly equally (or however they decide to split them).

Although we rarely see the conglomerate teams in action, they do exist. Remember, though, that when you begin sharing the power and decision making "equally" among people, the more people you bring in, the more complications usually arise, especially when strong egos are involved.

Corporations

Some teams are set up as a separate business entity, with all the members owning part of the entity through stock or membership interest. This setup is a great way to limit liabilities and spell out exactly how the team operates and who is responsible for every facet of the corporation's success. The team has its own articles of incorporation, or articles of organization, bylaws, operating agreements, and so on.

Note: The start-up costs for corporation teams may be a little higher than for other team types, due to legal fees for setting up the corporation properly, but once it's up and running, a corporation is a great way to create a team that has a feeling of being involved in a common enterprise. For more about corporations, refer to Chapter 4.

Associations

Many people envision an agent team as a group of professionals working under the same roof, but that is not necessarily the case. Some loosely structured teams may consist of several independent real estate professionals, each of whom runs his or her own separate business. The agents simply agree to share clients by referring business to one another.

This is the old-school way of running a team—before the term "agent team" ever existed—and it still plays a role with how agent teams operate today. Most independent agents and agent teams, for example, have a preferred lender, title company, home inspector, termite inspector, and so on. All these vendors perform tasks that the agents are unable or unwilling to perform and can help grow the business through referrals.

Tip: Association teams are informal. Some people refer to them as referral networks or networking, while others consider it team building. The association setup is probably the most common way that real estate professionals work together.

Virtual teams

In this modern era of real estate, you barely need an office to run a successful agent team. We know of at least one agent whose entire team (except for himself) consists of virtual assistants who work out of their homes. They do everything from developing his marketing materials to researching properties and processing the paperwork for closing. This type of setup really cuts down on overhead and allows the agent to quickly scale his workforce up or down in response to changing market conditions. The main drawback is that good virtual assistants may be serving other clients when you need them most. For more about using virtual assistants, check the "Discovering Virtual Assistants Online" sidebar, earlier in this chapter.

My Team

Although Nate Martinez, whom you met earlier in this chapter, has structured his business as a partnership, he runs his own agent team separate from his partner's team. We asked Nate to describe his team to us:

"Right now, I have seven licensed associates and one field technician, Larry, who drives my service truck, installs signs, takes photos and does small handyman jobs. My licensed associates include: my marketing manager, Jessica; my listing manager, Brandi; and my office manager, Sarah. My sales team, or what we used to call 'buyer agents,' includes three full-time licensed agents—Danielle, Brandon and Kristy. (We changed the title of 'buyer agents' to 'buyer specialists' because of our focus on the luxury market—it conveys to our clients that they are working with an extension of me or a business partner.) I also work with the company transaction coordinator, Janice, who handles all our closings once they go into escrow.

"Everyone on the team has a clear understanding of the role they play. Brandi handles all the feedback and communication with the sellers, and Jessica prepares all the market materials."

Understanding the Evolution of a Team
By Marylyn B. Schwartz, President of TEAMWEAVERS

There are many tremendously successful real estate teams around the country. Some are as small as three members, while others number more than 20.

Each one of these teams succeeds because it follows the predictable stages of development, coined by Dr. Bruce Tuckman in 1965: forming, storming, norming, performing, and where needed, adjourning (added in 1975). (For more about Tuckman's model, visit www.businessballs.com/tuckmanformingstormingnormingperforming.htm). By following the steps in the process, avoiding the temptation to take shortcuts, continually checking to ensure that the team isn't showing signs of spiraling downward, dealing with challenges as they arise, displaying zero tolerance for divisive behaviors, and maintaining the presence of the common goals and purpose clearly in the forefront, the teams' sponsors (team leaders) are far more likely to be successful in creating a team destined to thrive.

Forming

Placing the successful real estate professional as the sponsor of the team, consider the predictable actions that sponsor would need to take:

1. Determine that his/her business would benefit by forming a team.

2. Create a business plan that includes the growth potential as a result of the team's formation. The plan should be very specific so potential team members can see the business's vision and purpose as clearly as the sponsor does.

3. Create job descriptions for team members. If the sponsor wants the team to include a personal assistant, buyer broker, and perhaps another agent who will handle spillover tasks for the sponsor as well as list and sell real estate, the sponsor should clearly delineate the tasks for each team member through job descriptions. However, the individual job descriptions are a part of the overall objectives and purpose of the team. So, the team has a business plan (job descriptions), and then each person has specific tasks within the overall plan.

It is crucial for each team member to have knowledge of all job descriptions in order to support each other if and when coverage is necessary. The sponsor is responsible for ensuring that team members know how to handle absences, illnesses, unforeseen emergencies, and so on. Although teams must have the power to make appropriate decisions in emergency situations, guidelines are essential for times when a problem arises (if at all).

Storming

After the team is formed, it goes through the inevitable storming phase, where emotional issues surface, egos get in the way, unforeseen challenges crop up, and the team begins to doubt its ability to thrive. The sponsor plays a crucial role at this time. He/she must be clear in the business' mission and support-ive, strong, and intolerant of power struggles, all the while maintaining sole focus on the team's purpose and goals. During this phase is when adjust-ments may be required; perhaps the sponsor revises time lines, tweaks job descriptions, and reviews communication methods, for example. In general, the team members are working toward consensus.

Norming

The norming stage is all about perfecting problem-solving skills and putting the collective power full force toward the achievement of the goal(s). The in-dividual team members align their roles in unison with one another as well as with the sponsor. This is the adjustment period, when everyone is getting up to speed on the system and working together as a unit. This coming together with greater clarity and commitment is required for the team to enter the performing stage.

Performing

In the performing stage, the team is rocking and rolling! They have coalesced into a body that understands each member's strengths and weaknesses and maximizes the former, working to eliminate the latter. They are proud of each other and what they've achieved as a unified body instead of being focused on individual accomplishments. The sponsor is able to look toward continued growth and expansion knowing that the team is able to function with little oversight. In addition, the foundation is well laid to increase the size of the team, if desired.

Adjourning

With all the planning and care that a sponsor might put into the initial for-mation of a team, sometimes the group doesn't coalesce into a team, and the sponsor must dissolve one or more of the relationships. (Even teams that have done well will find it necessary to adjourn.) Sounds like an easy task? Think again.

Dissolving partnerships between/among real estate agents who have teamed together can be like navigating that proverbial slippery slope. Teams formed with all of the above caveats and processes in place, yet with no consideration given to creating an exit strategy at the time of forming the relationship, run into problems when they dissolve.

Being cognizant of the following when forming a team and getting written agreements as to how you'll resolve issues if the team disbands will make the breakup less stressful. Here are the questions to ask yourself:

1. When new leads are brought into the team, to whom do those leads belong upon dissolution?

2. If a transaction occurs while the team is together, who continues to prospect that client/customer going forward?

3. If the team shares the income from each transaction based on a date the team is officially formed, but the transaction is the result of a relationship with a past client or customer, how is the income split? Is the split even for the current team members and the former team member? Does that past client/customer then go into the team's database to be handled as the team's client/customer?

4. Does the team share or begin client databases based on an agreed-upon date in time?

5. How are the proceeds from pending transactions handled?

6. If the team was marketed as a unified entity and appears as such, how do the former team members market themselves going forward?

7. If the team used a name, who "owns" the future use of the name, if anyone?

8. How will you handle outstanding liabilities of the team at dissolution? If any invoices are outstanding, who pays them? How? When?

9. If technology equipment, office materials, furniture, and so on, were purchased while the team was intact, who owns those items? Do they have to be sold, or does one agent have to buy the other out? Who determines their value?

10. If the team breaks up due to issues of integrity or as a result of accusations of impropriety from outside sources, is the whole team held liable, or are the innocent members protected by a prior agreement? How does the company's errors and omissions insurance view the team arrangement?

Warning: Although working with teams in ugly situations isn't the most pleasant way to earn a fee, I've been involved with several teams that didn't pay heed to the preceding issues when they teamed up. If things didn't go as planned, tensions rose and a breakup was inevitable; then it was time to hire an expert to create an after-the-fact exit strategy. Be assured that the process was akin to a four-star divorce. The old adage that the best time to handle an objection is before it comes up holds so much truth!

Chapter 2

Taking Stock: Is an Agent Team Right for You?

When you've been flying solo for a good part of your career, you may be reluctant to team up with someone else; you may not realize the advantages of forming a team, such as increased productivity, profitability, and job satisfaction. Forming a team can even improve your relationships outside of work by affording you more free time and, therefore, a better attitude toward life.

But how do you know when the time is right to start building a team? Some agent team enthusiasts will answer that question by saying, "Yesterday." They believe that you should always at least have one assistant, making for a two-person team. Other experienced team builders recommend that the conditions have to be just right before you should even consider assembling your own team. If you do not have enough business to keep everyone busy (and paid), for example, then adding personnel just doesn't make sense.

In this chapter, we reveal the most common signs indicating that the time may be right for you to form a team. We help you honestly assess your abilities as well as your available resources to determine whether you're truly agent-team ready.

Recognizing the Signs That You Need a Team

Just about every agent who has built a team has experienced a unique epiphany that clearly revealed why forming a team would be the right move for them. Some have come to this realization through careful soul searching, discovering their weaknesses in certain areas—areas that were critical in order to reach the next level. Many agents realize they need a team when they find themselves working 80 hours a week and still not getting everything done. A few others stumble into the team approach by partnering with a family member or a friend who is also in the real estate business.

Hopefully, you have already found your inspiration to create a team or perhaps you will find it in this book. If you haven't quite reached this turning point, consider some of the most common signs indicating that a team approach could significantly improve your business and your life:

- You have more clients or leads than you can handle. You're actually referring surplus prospects to your competitors.

- You're experiencing an increasing number of missed opportunities due to time and resource constraints.

• You find it more and more difficult to meet deadlines, or you're chronically missing deadlines.

• You see an increasing number of mistakes and miscommunications in your work.

• You feel as though you never have enough time to do what you need or would like to do.

• Family members are complaining that you don't spend enough quality time at home.

• You skip vacations to catch up on work.

• You feel alone and frustrated. You want to share ideas and get feedback before bringing those ideas to life, but you have nobody to bounce those ideas off of.

• You have great ideas for improving your business, but you're missing the key skills and talents to implement those ideas.

How many listings can you imagine yourself juggling before you become disorganized and start dropping the ball? Whenever you can't handle your workload, customer service starts to slip because you're too busy, or your quality of life is suffering under the strain of your career, consider lightening your load by bringing a new team member on board.

Considering the Requirements of Supporting a Team

Although we're strong advocates of the agent team approach, we strongly recommend that you prepare yourself and your business thoroughly before diving in. Think about what you're about to get yourself into—the added expenses along with your ability to collaborate effectively with another person—before taking on a teammate.

Agent teams aren't for everyone. In the following sections, we address two fundamental areas you need to consider before implementing a team-based system.

Assessing your financial resources

Financial speed bumps often discourage many agents from exploring the agent team option, which is somewhat ironic. Agents who are most in need of a team are usually strapped for both cash and time. On their own, they simply can't handle the sales volume required to be truly successful, so they end up in a self-defeating cycle—no money, no team, no money, no team... ad infinitum.

The fact is that most agent teams, if managed well, generate far more revenue than it costs to run the team. What makes teams so affordable is the fact that core team members share expenses, risks, and profits. Launching the team business doesn't require a huge amount of start-up capital, because everyone knows that you can't share profits until you have profits to share. The question of whether you have sufficient funds and other resources to build and manage a team is often a moot point. If you're asking the question, "Can I afford a team?" you may be better off asking yourself, "Can I afford to not build a team?"

Remember: We don't mean to downplay the costs of running a team, particularly the cost of paying team members, but if you have more work than you can handle yourself and enough work to keep an assistant busy full time, starting a team is almost always the best way (and often the only way) to take your business to the next level.

Of course, the "money is no object" approach to building a team may be a little unrealistic, but you can work the team concept into your existing budget. If you are having trouble making ends meet, consider hiring a part-time assistant to get started. This enables you to cut your teeth on the agent team approach and realize the potential benefits of having more people as a part of your team.

Tip: If you're truly strapped for cash, explore options for borrowing the money you need. You're essentially launching your own business, so consider contacting the Small Business Administration (www.sba.gov) for assistance. You may also consider taking out a bank loan, asking family members or friends to lend you the money, or perhaps split the costs with a partner.

Whatever you do, don't let money get in the way of your dreams. Sometimes you have to bite the bullet, trust what other people are telling you, and try a particular approach for yourself before you're fully convinced that it can deliver the benefits it promises. Start slowly and build over time; you won't be disappointed.

Assessing your management capabilities

Although real estate agents tend to be control freaks, they're also experts on building relationships. Many agents, therefore, already have all the qualifications required to build and manage an agent team—as long as they're ready and willing to relinquish some control and certain responsibilities. The following list covers the key ingredients you need to head up your own agent team:

- **Positive attitude:** As team leader, a positive attitude is one of the most important qualities you should possess. The energy you exhibit at the top is contagious, whether negative or positive, so make sure you maintain optimism.

• **Motivational skills:** You don't necessarily have to be a motivational speaker in order to successfully encourage your team members. If you find team members and other personnel who tend to be self-motivated, and then offer them an attractive incentive package based on performance, you should never have to worry about motivating your team. However, an added incentive always helps. Be sure to recognize and praise those team members who go above and beyond the call of duty. Money is nice, but it's usually not enough—people need recognition as well. For details about motivating team members, refer to Chapter 13.

• **Controlled ego:** A strong ego can be a valuable asset for a team leader, especially if you're the designated rainmaker. You have to love the public exposure you receive, but keep that ego in check. Teams function best when every member of the team feels like an equal part. You may be in the spotlight, but other team members working behind the scenes to serve clients are just as important in generating business and revenue. When recruiting, find that special value in each player and focus on it. Remember, the team is more than the sum of its parts—the team is bigger than you.

• **Vision:** Although your team develops its vision together over time, the team leader develops the initial vision and functions as the driving force that fuels its future development. With a clear, unified vision, team members can coordinate their efforts and have a greater impact.

• **Ability to delegate:** If you feel as though nobody can do something better than you, you need to get over it. Teams function best when each member focuses on his or her specialty, and you need to delegate so you can focus on the most dollar-productive activities—generating business that keeps all team members productive and well paid.

Building an Agent Team: A Case Study

We asked Julie Vanderblue of The Vanderblue Team in Westport, Connecticut (www.vanderblueteam.com), several questions related to the early stages of building a team. Here are the questions we asked, followed by Julie's replies.

What led you to the decision to form an agent team?
To me the decision was about not only needing a team (which I did), but also wanting to share in the joy, hardships, ideas and

camaraderie with others whom I trust and feel comfortable with. Real estate can be a very lonely business, and sharing the joy doubles the goodness, while sharing the hard times divides it tenfold.

Personally, I was very good at turning open house lookers into buyers, so I quickly had more clients than I could handle on my own. My creative energy was increasing listings rapidly, and the only way to truly service the sellers' needs was to assign two agents to each client. One agent is never available 100% of the time—that expectation is simply impossible to meet—yet clients deserve 100%. Two agents (with a solid team backing them up) are the only way to truly offer that.

How much money do you need to start a team?
I didn't have much when I began my team, and you really don't need a lot if you have realistic goals and creative ideas. You have to remember that the other team members are generating revenue, saving time, and working together to increase productivity. They're more than paying for themselves.

As our team began to take off, I began putting about 50% of my own income back into the team. Each team member pays a 6% marketing fee to help us grow. We are very, very creative and will always put a large percentage of team funds back into the business. You have to invest in yourself if you want to be successful.

What is the key to successfully managing a team?
I believe the key to building and managing a successful team is instilling confidence in the team members from the beginning. If they believe that they're capable and valuable, then they will be. The law of attraction rings true—feel good about yourself, and others will, too.

In the beginning, each team member works with me on three listings I have for sale. He assists me with the walk-through, joins me at the marketing presentation, brainstorms and helps with the comparative market analysis (CMA), offers ideas and comments, helps with marketing materials, listens to how I handle feedback, hears me negotiate...everything. His name and face are on the brochures with me, he does the brokers' open, public open, and so on.

I pay each team member a significant servicing fee; although I do most of the work on these listings when the agents are new, the shared commission is more than worth the effort involved in getting to that point. In the agent's mind (and in the mind of buyers and other agents), the listing is hers. She has succeeded. She has accomplished the goal, and when she goes to her own marketing presentations, her confidence level skyrockets. When she starts doing her own listings, she brings me or another team member along to her presentations. We all help each other on every listing. I also attend at least one public open with each member before she goes at it alone.

I have created a way to soft sell that works, and although each partner has his or her own style, we help each other by sharing what works for us. They listen and watch what I do, take what works for them, and tweak it to make it their own. The agents on my team have told me they learned the most in their first few months just by listening to me negotiate, talk on the phone, call leads, turn buyers around, and so on. There is something to be said for having a small office in the beginning! It can actually be helpful...new team members learn through the opportunities they have to listen and watch.

Identifying What You and Your Business Are Lacking

When choosing members for your team, it's tempting to choose people who are just like you. After all, you want your business to be a reflection of who you are and the way you do business. Choosing too many people like you, however, can be a big mistake. It can create a stagnant workplace void of creativity. It can hinder your ability to appeal to diverse clientele and markets. Perhaps worst of all, it can leave you with an entire team of people who dislike all the same activities and tasks. Who's going to fill out all that paperwork if nobody on the team wants to do it?

An effective team consists of people with complementary skills and talents and different personalities. In the following sections, we show you how to assess your own skills and personality and take inventory of the tasks you're most able and willing to perform, so that you can identify the gaps you need to fill.

Assessing your own skills and weaknesses

Initially, your team is likely to consist of you and an assistant. You take on the tasks that you are best qualified to perform and that you enjoy most, and then you assign the remaining tasks to your assistant. Take some time and jot down a list of your skills—the skills that generate revenue. For most agents, these include the following:

• Meeting with clients and prospective clients

• Listing homes for sale

• Showing homes to prospective buyers

• Researching properties

• Negotiating prices and terms

• Solving problems

• Marketing your services

After identifying your strengths, focus on your weaknesses—your weaknesses are typically tied to the time-consuming chores you dread. Ask yourself what you like best about your work. Working with customers? Working in the background (devising strategies, thinking, and writing)? Managing the office? Marketing? Generating leads? What do you like least? In general, you want to be doing what you love, what you're most passionate about—and then delegate the rest.

Highlight the areas where you can use some help—areas where you're lacking, where you'll never get up to speed, and where you have absolutely no interest in trying to develop the skills yourself, such as

• Filling out paperwork

• Answering phones

• Stuffing envelopes and handling mailings

• Updating your Web site or blog

• Paying bills and reconciling accounts

• Managing your e-mail accounts

Tip: If you are thinking of adding an agent to your team, you should also consider the area in which you would like to specialize. If you consider yourself to be a better listing agent and you enjoy it more than representing buyers, you should think about bringing a buyer's agent on board. If you want all the buyers to yourself, add a listing agent to your team.

My First Assistant

I began my real estate career in 1976. I was fresh out of high school and wanted to take over the world. Some folks would tell you that I was the class clown, while others referred to me as the Most Likely Not to Succeed. Like all agents, I was assigned floor time ("opportunity" time). This time was my chance to take calls from people who were actually interested in listing or buying a home, as well as my chance to play receptionist for the broker and other agents.

The problem? I can't spell, my handwriting is horrid, and in my haste I often wrote down the wrong information or phone number. (I even needed assistance writing this sidebar!) Needless to say, my frequent errors didn't go over too well with the other agents in the office, who were soon complaining about my incompetence. I think they thought that I was doing it on purpose.

To remedy the problem, I hired my first assistant—a co-op student from the local high school. She accompanied me on my floor time and wrote down everything, so that everyone received correct information. Thirty years later, I still have an assistant to manage e-mails, phone calls, and messages. In my case, ineptitude was the mother of invention.

When I coach agent teams around the globe, I tell them over and over again that if you don't have an assistant, you are one—you are your own assistant. It seems very simple, but you'd be surprised how many agents don't recognize this truth. I had a real problem when I started in the industry and probably wouldn't have lasted long had I not hired an assistant to overcome one of my weaknesses. The office was more successful, and I was more successful because of this arrangement. I didn't have the luxury of saying that I just couldn't afford to pay an assistant; I had to have one, and I had to work hard enough to make sure that I could pay her (and pay her on time so that she would come back each week!). *—Ralph R. Roberts*

Analyzing peer assessments

Another way to identify the gaps you need to fill is to have your peers assess you. Although peer assessments are designed to help in staff development (later, when you have a team in place), they're also helpful in identifying areas where you could use some help. For example, if assessments show that you're a lousy manager, you can start looking for someone who's better suited to playing the management role on your team.

Several companies offer peer assessments, referring to them as "360-degree feedback"—perspectives from your customers, your peers, your boss (or broker) and yourself. You e-mail notices to the people you'd like to assess you, along with a link to a site where they can log in and complete the assessment anonymously. By seeing yourself from different perspectives, you can build a skill set that enables you to improve relationships with all those individuals who have a vested interest in your success.

The Booth Company at www.boothco.com offers several assessment programs and can even produce customized assessment forms based on the criteria you specify. We highly recommend that you use an experienced company, like The Booth Company. With the growing popularity of peer assessments, many new companies that are less qualified to provide accurate assessments have popped up on the landscape.

At Ralph Roberts Realty, we asked the agents and staff to rate the agents by category. We then averaged the scores and inserted them into the spreadsheet shown in Figure 2-1. (The first four names are real; we changed the rest.) Something as simple as this system can help you identify personal achievement gaps or gaps in your team where you (and your team members, eventually) could use some improvement.

	A	B	C	D	E	F
1	Agent	Professionalism	Reliability	Knowledge	Experience	Sales Skill
2	Lois Maljak	5	5	4	4	5
3	Ralph Roberts	4	4	5	5	5
4	Joy Santiago	4	4	4	4	5
5	Paul Doroh	5	5	4	4	3
6	Bill Smith	3	4	3	2	4
7	Sally Fields	4	4	2	2	1
8	Mike Shaulk	1	4	4	4	4
9	Patty Dion	3	3	3	3	3
10	Jennifer Jones	3	3	2	2	2
11	Phil Specter	3	2	4	4	4
12	Sally Brown	3	2	2	2	3
13	Kathy Tootle	1	1	4	5	4
14	Jimmy White	3	3	2	2	2
15	Andy Stettler	2	2	4	4	3
16	Harriet Stowe	3	4	2	2	2
17	Dave Kostka	2	1	4	4	2
18	Jimmy Smits	3	3	2	2	3
19	Randy Wolman	4	2	2	2	2
20	Marisa Vital	4	1	1	1	2
21	Don Johnson	4	2	4	4	3
22	Gary Player	3	3	1	1	1
23	Melissa Johnson	2	2	2	3	2
24	Kelly Fairbanks	3	2	2	3	2
25	Ken Huston	1	1	1	1	3
26	Jessica Wheel	3	1	1	2	2
27	Merv Griffin	2	1	1	1	2
28	Averages	3	2.653846	2.6923077	2.8076923	2.846154
29						
30						
31	1 poor					
32	2 fair					
33	3 good					
34	4 very good					
35	5 excellent					
36						
37	Most PtsAvail 65					

Sheet1 Sheet2 Sheet3

Ready

Figure 2-1: Sample peer assessment ratings.

Figuring Out What Fits Your Needs: Common Team Members to Start With

After you identify your strengths and weaknesses, you can start working to fill the gaps. You have three options: Obtain the training you need to do the job yourself, hire someone who already has the skills, or partner with someone who can fill those gaps. If you decide to bring others on board instead of trying to do everything yourself, now is the time to start listing the team-member roles you need to fill in the gaps and balance your team for maximum productivity.

Agents are frequently part of a team without ever realizing it. They may partner with a spouse, another family member or a colleague and simply consider it "working together." They may hire an assistant to work for them or collaborate with another professional to exchange referrals without ever thinking that they are really functioning as a team.

Think of the people you work with on a daily basis? Do you have an assistant who answers the phone and takes care of the office? Do you have someone processing transactions for you? Are you part of a referral network? If you are already part of a team, expanding your team to include other members is that much easier.

In this section, we show you how to start building your team by adding an assistant. We then reveal other areas where agent teams commonly add personnel.

Starting slowly with one assistant

When most agents hear about agent teams, they automatically jump to the conclusion that we're talking about groups the size of baseball teams. The fact is that a team can be as small as two people—you and an assistant. You take care of your clients, and your assistant takes care of you by handling all the phone calls, paperwork, and other chores that you don't have the time, talent, or inclination to handle yourself.

Tip: When hiring a personal assistant, avoid the temptation to simply place an ad in the newspaper. If you do, you're likely to end up with someone who is ill prepared to handle the stress and workload of a high-powered real estate office. Instead, ask colleagues if they know of anyone who has the qualifications and track record of a promising candidate:

- Energy
- Enthusiasm
- Intelligence
- Talent

- Eagerness to play a supporting role
- Communications skills, both verbal and written
- Loyalty

Avoid hiring a nine-to-five clock watcher. You want someone who's going to assist you for as many hours a day as you need assistance. Make sure any new assistant is well aware of what he or she is getting into. Consider having the person shadow you for 30 days. This gives you both a good sense of what you can expect from one another.

Adding new team members

Having a qualified assistant can make you feel as though a tremendous weight has been lifted from your shoulders. You can now focus on what you really love to do and even have extra time to spend with family and friends.

However, as you have more time to devote to your clients, business will naturally pick up, and you'll soon find yourself feeling like you did before—overworked, stressed out, and at risk of burnout. These are great signs that you need to add another member to the team. You already have an assistant, so start looking for people who can manage transactions and handle the increased paperwork load and other tasks, as explained in the following sections.

Listing coordinator

A listing coordinator can manage a file up to the point at which a prospect signs the contract. In this role, the listing coordinator is in charge of the following activities:

- Setting appointments
- Dropping off prelisting packages
- Developing CMAs
- Preparing all documents for signature
- Confirming appointments
- Creating files for clients and listings
- Ordering For Sale signs put up and taken down
- Posting Sold signs
- Managing listings on the MLS
- Preparing weekly updates
- Communicating to the office about the listings
- Preparing disclosures for the front desk

Closing coordinator

A closing coordinator picks up the file when the home sells and manages the closing from start to finish. The closing coordinator is responsible for the following tasks:

- Handling contract-to-close activities
- Managing files
- Communicating with the broker, agents, title and appraisal company
- Managing transactions
- Scheduling the closing

Office manager

Keeping the office running smoothly can be a full-time job that requires someone who is very well organized and works well with others. An office manager fulfills the following job duties:

- Making sure someone is available to greet clients and answer the phones at all times
- Personally greeting clients who call or visit
- Ordering and monitoring supplies
- Entering real estate transactions into the MLS system
- Logging, tracking, and assigning leads to agents
- Scheduling team meetings
- Working with agents to ensure that they've supplied all the necessary documentation
- Documenting office tasks and providing training to new staff and team members
- Proactively identifying tasks that need to be done to keep the office running

Note: On a small team, your office manager may be responsible for many more tasks than those listed here, including bookkeeping, producing marketing materials, and keeping Web site and blog content up-to-date. As your team grows, your office manager may be able to delegate these tasks to new team members and take on more of a managerial role.

Accounting assistant

Many agents report that accounting is one of the most time-consuming areas of their work. When you have to manage accounts for multiple agents, accounting alone can take up to 15 to 20 hours a week, and if you aren't very good at it, you can create a real mess that costs you even more time and money.

An accounting assistant can help you manage your internal accounting system and work with your team's outside CPA to prepare taxes and deal with bigger issues. This assistant typically juggles the following responsibilities:

- Creating and managing client accounts
- Collaborating with team members to create a budget
- Tracking revenue and expenses
- Calculating and paying out commission splits
- Paying outside vendors
- Reimbursing agents and other team members for eligible expenses
- Preparing weekly, monthly, and quarterly reports, including profit and loss statements, income and expense reports, and commission statements

Marketing manager

Generating revenue streams is the primary focus of the team leader/rainmaker, but it often requires the assistance of someone who's devoted solely to marketing the team. The team's marketing manager is typically responsible for the following tasks:

- Designing and producing marketing materials, including flyers, brochures, and business cards
- Generating positive press through as many media outlets as possible, including the Web, e-mail, TV, radio, print (advertising and articles), podcasts, and videocasts
- Maintaining content on the team's Web sites and blogs
- Scheduling special events for clients
- Producing a team newsletter or e-newsletter
- Managing the team's drip e-mail campaigns
- Transforming the team into a brand

For more about marketing, check out Chapter 14.

IT (Information Technology) specialist

In the high-tech world of modern real estate, a team usually requires an IT specialist to make sure the entire computer system and the team's Internet service and communications networks are properly set up and remain up and running. Smaller teams may not need a full-time IT specialist on staff, in which case they can hire a contractor to install and maintain the equipment. Larger teams may need and be able to afford a full-time IT specialist. The IT specialist is typically in charge of the following tasks:

- Recommending technology solutions that are appropriate for a real estate team, including both hardware and software
- Installing new hardware
- Setting up, securing, and maintaining the network
- Troubleshooting technical problems
- Educating team members on how to use new technologies
- Building and maintaining the team's Web sites and blogs

Tip: When searching for an IT specialist, look for someone who has experience in real estate. Such a candidate will be much more aware of the types of hardware and software that other real estate agents and teams find most useful.

Client care specialist

A client care specialist or "director of first impressions," as REALTOR® Nate Martinez likes to refer to this position, is the frontline team member (receptionist), who handles

- Meeting and greeting clients
- Answering most of the clients' questions
- Referring clients to others on the team when he or she does not know the answers they need

Tip: Your client care specialist should have an engaging, energetic personality, a friendly and professional telephone voice, and the ability to take accurate, detailed messages.

Chapter 3

Transitioning from Independent Agent to Team Leader

When you're flying solo as an independent real estate agent, you feel good about being able to handle everything on your own, and you're constantly rewarded for your self-reliance. After all, you're a self-made individual, you run your own business, and you're solely responsible for your success—all achievements that you should certainly be proud of.

When you become a team leader, however, all of that changes. You're no longer the one-man band. You begin to rely on other team members for your success, and you take on several new roles—CEO, visionary, facilitator, coach, trainer, cheerleader, and role model, to name a few. These new roles require an entirely different skill set and often a change in attitude or approach. You can't afford to be as tough on others, for example, as you are on yourself.

Many agents who are first starting a team find the transition to team leader quite challenging. In writing this chapter, we consulted with team leader Wayne Turner (www.wayneturner.com) of the Wayne Turner Real Estate Company in Hendersonville, Tennessee, to gather techniques and strategies that help smooth the transition to team leader. The insights presented in this chapter will benefit not only you but also your team and clients.

Honing Your Team Management Skill Set

When you become a team leader, you suddenly make the move from employee to manager, and as manager, you have an entirely new set of clients—your teammates. Although you may still work directly with home buyers and sellers, your primary clients are the people who work with you. By ensuring their success, you ensure the success of the home buyers and sellers you service, your team as a whole, and yourself as team leader.

Recognizing your target: What a remarkable team leader does

Becoming a top-notch manager—someone your team members respect and love but someone who also runs a profitable business—is a lifelong process. Before you can get to that place, though, you need to recognize the major responsibilities of an accomplished team leader. As team leader, your team depends on you to do the following:

- **Create and communicate a clear vision.** As leader, you need to see where the team is heading and what each member of the team needs to do to get there. Formulate a clear vision for your team and then make sure everyone knows what that vision is and the role that each individual needs to play.

• **Plan the work, and then work the plan.** You need to put the systems in place to accomplish every task that needs to be done—from marketing your business and homes you've listed, to processing transactions and expanding your business.

• **Create an enjoyable workplace.** Enjoy the people you work with and the activities that you're involved in on a daily basis. Feel free to break the routine every once in awhile. You don't need to turn each day into a wild party (nor should you, if you ever want to be successful), but don't lose your soul in pursuit of success. Crack a smile. Crack a joke. Celebrate accomplishments.

• **Be a positive role model.** All other team members follow your lead, so model the behavior you expect from them. If you're ripping people off, coming in late to work and leaving early, or complaining all the time, your teammates will view that behavior as appropriate and acceptable. Instead, remain positive, even when times are rough. Act with integrity. Demonstrate how much work it really takes to be successful. Replace the words "bad" and "problem" with "challenge" and "opportunity"— remember, challenges are simply opportunities to grow. Master these habits, and watch the positive results flow.

• **Commit yourself to the success of your teammates.** Hire great people and give them everything they need to be successful—resources, technology, training, coaching, and so on. Invest heavily in their success, especially early on, and then give them the freedom and responsibility to take it to the next level. When your teammates know that you're committed to their success, they'll be committed to yours. The likelihood is that they'll also tell others about the great team they're part of. Money can't buy the type of genuine, positive PR this relationship generates.

Tip: Produce high-quality business cards for everyone on the team and encourage them to distribute them to everyone they meet. This extra step makes your teammates proud to be affiliated with you and is a constant reminder that they're team players.

• **Consistently hold and manage productive meetings with team members.** According to almost everyone we talked to during the writing of this book, team meetings and individual meetings were key tools in enabling team leaders to build and manage a successful agent team. New team members should have a mentor to get them up to speed and answer any questions they have. Team leaders and others who are in management roles should meet individually with the people they manage, and the team should meet as a group once a week to clarify team goals, share information, and celebrate one another's achievements.

• **Delegate and let go.** Don't hover over team members to make sure they get their work done. Hire people you can trust to do the job you're hiring them for, provide them with the training and tools they need, and then let them perform. When you recognize a new revenue-generating opportunity, build a profit center, put the right self-starter in place to run it, and then move on to more business development. Foreclosures, REOs (Real Estate Owned or bank-owned properties), new construction, land development, probate, divorce, and so on are all possibilities. For more about delegating effectively, see the section "Discovering How to Delegate Well for Maximum Profitability," later in this chapter.

• **Create a system of accountability.** Make each team member accountable for his or her own success or failure, so you don't have to step in and take disciplinary measures. Your team members should know your expectations of them upfront, as well as what will happen if they fall short of those expectations, and what rewards they'll receive if they meet or exceed those expectations.

Tip: Encourage teammates to form personal partnerships to set goals and hold one another accountable for achieving their goals. With the Personal Partnering Process, developed by speaker and coach Terry Wisner, partners meet regularly to discuss their priorities and plans and keep one another on track. For more about the Personal Partnering Process, check out *Advanced Selling For Dummies.*

• **Communicate clearly.** As an agent and team leader, communication is essential, and we don't mean simply expressing yourself clearly; we also mean listening to what your teammates have to say. You have two ears and one mouth, so use them proportionally. Remain in constant touch with your team, with past customers and clients, with colleagues, and with vendors. Nine times out of ten, problems arise due to miscommunication. As team leader, you become a communications hub, monitoring communication and stepping in to clarify issues when needed.

• **Deal with issues immediately.** Don't let problems fester. If your team has some internal strife, investigate the problem, identify the root cause, and then address the problem with everyone involved. The longer you allow a problem to exist, the more damage it can do.

• **Manage your team's growth.** Make sure your team has the infrastructure in place to support new team members before you add a new member to the team. In other words, you should have a clear idea of a position you need to fill before bringing a new person on board. Also, as your team grows, don't lose sight of what made you successful as a smaller team. When teams grow too quickly, team leaders often overlook the basics, such as weekly team meetings, which can result in the entire team falling apart. Whether your team consists of two people, eight people, or more spread among multiple offices, you should be careful to maintain steady and manageable growth.

Reading up on managerial tips

In addition to all the great tips and techniques presented in this book on building and managing an agent team, you can find dozens of books that cover the basics of human resource management and office management in greater detail. Read up on those topics, put your findings into practice, and soon you'll find that you're becoming a better manager with each passing day.

Following are some excellent books on how to be an effective manager:

• *Who Moved My Cheese? An A-Mazing Way to Deal with Change in Your Work and in Your Life*, by Spencer Johnson, M.D.

• *The Three Signs of a Miserable Job: A Fable for Managers (And Their Employees)*, by Patrick M. Lencioni

• *Peak: How Great Companies Get Their Mojo from Maslow*, by Chip Conley

• *Fish! A Remarkable Way to Boost Morale and Improve Results*, by Stephen C. Lundin, Ph.D., Harry Paul, and John Christensen

• *Co-Active Coaching, 2nd Edition: New Skills for Coaching People Toward Success in Work and Life*, by Laura Whitworth, Karen Kimsey-House, Henry Kimsey-House, and Phillip Sandahl

• *Motivating Employees For Dummies*, by Max Messmer

Attending management seminars

Many agents who eventually become team leaders seem to forget how they became top-producing agents in the first place. When they first started out as real-estate agents, they read books, listened to tapes, shadowed other top producers, and attended conferences and seminars to learn the tricks of the trade. When they first start out as managers, however, many of them try to jump in without any preparation or education. Remember, as a team leader, you are launching a new career that requires an entirely new set of skills—managerial skills. Just as you needed additional training when you first started out as an agent, you now need additional training to bring you up to speed on how to be an effective manager. As you take on the role of team leader, shop around for seminars that can help you learn the management skills you need to be effective.

Learning management skills from others

Top agent-team leaders are usually very willing to share what they know with others in the industry who are committed to building their own strong agent teams. We strongly recommend that you take advantage of those opportunities to network with other agent team leaders. You may have to drive (or fly) somewhere outside your market to learn from the best team leaders, but the investment is usually well worth the time and effort. Contact one of the team leaders of the top agent teams and ask whether you can shadow the team leader or one of the top agents for a day. If you're working with a coach, ask your coach for ideas about people to shadow, and always offer to pay the person for his or her time. You might be surprised at just how giving these people really are—sure, they're busy, but they know the value of networking and building productive relationships.

Tip: I have had many superstars of the industry shadow me, spending an entire day watching me work. The funny thing is, while they're learning from me, I think I learn more from them. I'm like a sponge, and I try to take in everything I possibly can. In order to take, however, you have to give. You can't be afraid to share your secrets. The more you give, the more you get. You can only improve your industry with this mindset. If you are approached by salespeople who want to learn from you, share with them! You'll be amazed at what you might learn. *–Ralph R. Roberts*

Also, keep up with industry trade publications that regularly profile and interview successful teams. RISMedia's *Power Team Report*, for example, highlights at least six agent teams each month, detailing their success strategies and their best tips for leading a profitable team.

Tip: Success leaves big footprints, so you should have no trouble finding the most successful agent teams. Once you do, follow the path that they have already blazed for you, customizing it along the way to suit your own specific needs and style.

One Realtor's Transition to Team Leader, One Step at a Time

Faye Rispoli of the Rispoli Team (www.ffrispoli.com), RE/MAX and Associates of Latham, New York, started in real estate as an independent agent over three decades ago. In 1991, Rispoli joined RE/MAX and almost immediately recognized her need for an assistant and additional team members.

Rispoli started growing her business with a part-time assistant. The assistant concentrated on inputting information into databases, listing paperwork, and performing other light administrative duties, which freed Rispoli to spend more time in the field. However, Rispoli soon realized that she wasn't always actively selling when she was out in the field. Before long, she found herself out at 5:00 a.m. trying to keep up with things like putting up For Sale signs, installing lockboxes, taking room measurements, and testing keys. To further free up her schedule for selling, she hired a high-school student to handle all those remedial tasks, except taking room measurements.

To further conserve time and energy, Rispoli outsourced the task of gathering information about the listings to the homeowners. In her listing packet, she included an advertising packet that homeowners could complete with such information as room sizes, taxes, fuel costs, amenities, and so on. According to Rispoli, "Homeowners are generally happy to provide this information themselves. After all, who knows their home better than they do?"

Rispoli also discovered that with quick accessibility of information on the Internet, sellers demanded immediate progress reports. The office staff was spending an inordinate amount of time fielding phone calls from anxious new sellers wondering when their signs would be up, when their homes and photos would appear on the Web, and so on. In order to alleviate many of these premature questions, she developed a marketing timeline to help manage expectations. The phone calls eventually tapered off.

Rispoli now has a full-time assistant who handles almost all matters related to writing contracts, setting up appointments, scheduling inspections, channeling information to and from attorneys and banks, producing marketing materials, answering client questions, and so on. Rispoli has also outsourced other duties to professionals, including hiring a professional photographer to take pictures and create virtual home tours. Rispoli can now spend her time doing what brings in the business and income—selling.

Rispoli believes in rewarding team members to both retain and motivate them. "Early on, I was told to surround myself with quality people, and I learned early on that you get what you pay for, so to speak." She gives her buyer agents a higher percentage on commissions than some in the area and hires assistants who have more experience and naturally command higher salaries. "I want someone I can trust and not have to spend a lot of time managing. By rewarding them for being a part of achieving the goals for the year, they have more reason to take ownership of the results of the business, rather than simply doing what is required by rote."

Discovering How to Delegate Well for Maximum Profitability

Many real estate agents tend to shy away from teams. Although they are people-persons by nature, they also prefer to act quickly and decisively without having to check in with someone else, stop to answer questions, or take time out to offer guidance to a peer. In general, most agents would prefer to do everything themselves. The problem with that approach, however, is that it can seriously limit your upside.

People who can effectively delegate tasks to others are able to get more done. Even better, they can do less and get more done. Sound good? Well, you can do it too. The only requirement is a willingness to make the up-front investment—putting in the time and effort to hire the right people, provide them with the right training, and build a system in which you can manage the decision-making process, so that the right people are in charge of making the most critical decisions. In this section, we reveal the fine art of delegating.

Tip: The goal of delegating is to create a team that can operate on a daily basis without the need for constant direction from the team leader. How do you achieve that goal? By assigning responsibilities and putting systems into place that empower team members to do their jobs independently and efficiently.

Unfortunately, most agents—particularly the best agents—tend to be control freaks. We often assume that nobody can perform a particular task better than we can do it ourselves, so we hesitate to let go and delegate. To be a successful team member, however, you need to focus on doing your job and letting others do theirs.

Separating the tasks: What you MUST do, and what others CAN do

One of the easiest ways to grasp the art of delegating is to imagine that you have three boxes near your desk for all the tasks you need to perform. The boxes have the following labels:

- **Do it!** Everything you, personally, need to attend to in order for your business to succeed and everything you love to do, should go in the Do it! box…and then you should do it.

- **Delegate it!** Everything that needs to be done in order for your team to achieve its goals or that you would like to see done but neither need nor want to do yourself, goes in the Delegate it! box.

- **Ditch it!** Anything that's not absolutely necessary for your business to succeed and that neither you nor any other team member has time to do goes in the Ditch it! box.

You can discover your own personal path to productivity and profitability by spending some time analyzing everything you do in a day and identifying which of those activities makes you the most money. And when we say "analyzing everything" that means everything—at work and at home:

1. Jot down what you figure you earn in an hour. Is it $200, $350, $500? Whatever it is, write it down.

2. Create a list of all of your typical daily activities at work, home, and wherever else you spend time.

3. Review your list, placing a check mark next to any activities that you could hire someone else to do for less than you currently earn per hour. For example, if you can earn $250 an hour selling houses and you can hire someone to clean your house for $150—a job that normally takes you three hours—you could save about $600 by hiring someone else to clean your house.

Tip: Do not place a check mark next to activities that you feel you need to do or that you really enjoy doing, such as coaching your daughter's soccer team. You don't want to delegate your life, only non-dollar-productive work activities. In addition, if you simply love to clean your house, or you find it therapeutic, then we wouldn't want to discourage you from participating in this enjoyable activity.

You should now have a pretty clear idea of the tasks that you need to perform yourself and those you need to delegate.

Leveling the workload fairly among team members

Although you should pass as much of your workload as possible to others on your team, be sure to distribute the work equitably to avoid creating any animosity or conflict, especially when you're first starting out. Monitor everyone's workload carefully and try to observe whether any of your team members or other staff members seem overwhelmed. You may need to make adjustments or even bring another person on board to handle the extra work.

Tip: Account for the learning curve when you bring a new person on board. The person may be overwhelmed for the first week or so and then do just fine. Don't assume just because a new person is stressed out that you have overloaded the person with responsibilities. Be patient and understanding as the person gets up to speed.

Delegating Case Study: The Virginia Realty Group

In January 2007, RISMedia, publishers of *Real Estate* magazine, named The Virginia Realty Group (TVRG) one of the top 25 most innovative real estate teams in the country. This team has managed to reach beyond the team itself to partner with local businesses to offer discounted services to their members, further solidifying their relationships with clients.

We asked the TVRG to provide us with some insight on how their team is structured and how they manage to effectively delegate the tasks that need to be done. Here is what team leader Bryan Felder had to say:

"Our team consists of the following:

Team leader: The main function of the team leader is to set goals, guide the team, and assist them in achieving their goals. Constant analysis and evaluation (monthly, quarterly, annually) is necessary to keep the team running efficiently. The team leader constantly asks, 'What are we doing now that could be done better?' The team leader also delegates sales responsibilities to our agents.

Agents: Our agents deal primarily with clients in the field. Their primary objectives are to know their market and serve the needs of their clients in that market. Our agents are our revenue generators. The more agents we can bring on board, the more revenue we generate, and revenue is the fuel that powers the train.

Operations: Our team leader delegates daily operational tasks to our director of operations. This takes the burden of running the office, paying the bills, ordering supplies, and so on off of the team leader. This also creates a work environment where everything that is needed to do an accurate job is readily available. Our director of operations is responsible for the following:
- Ordering supplies
- Addressing IT issues
- Pipeline reporting
- Bill paying
- Managing our internal rewards program
- Recruiting new agents
- Coordinating our monthly team meeting and keynote speaker
- Handling oversight of transactions and marketing
- Overseeing office design and property management
- Managing our client care program (ordering flowers or gift cards for clients and partners)
- Overseeing the management of investment properties
- Creating processes to make the office run smoother
- Conducting weekly one-on-ones with agents and transactions and marketing

Transactions: Our team leader and agents delegate the processing of all transactions to the transaction coordinator. This frees up time for the agents so that they can focus on selling and generating new business. Almost all paperwork that needs to be processed through our office goes through our transaction coordinator. Our transaction coordinator is responsible for the following:
- Managing sales transactions from start to finish—from processing listings on the MLS system and other online databases to coordinating the transaction all the way to closing
- Ordering homeowners association and condominium documents
- Scheduling home inspections, walk-throughs, and closings
- Coordinating all paperwork, addendums, other documents, including obtaining applicable signatures and sending cop-

ies to all appropriate parties
- Coordinate closings through proactive touchpoints to lenders, title companies, appraisers, inspectors, and agents
- Maintaining weekly contact proactively with TVRG clients
- Creating and maintaining daily spreadsheets that are sent to the TVRG team on a daily basis to keep them updated on pending listings and closings
- Assembling applicable paperwork and presentation packets for new listings appointments and buyer appointments
- Ordering signs for homes
- Linking all of our Web sites to the MLS
- Assembling listing items for agents on listing dates, including lockbox, brochure box, riders, property disclaimer, and brochures
- Maintaining inventory for listings including brochure boxes, signage, and lockboxes

Marketing: Our team leader delegates all marketing responsibilities to our marketing coordinator. The marketing coordinator not only educates our clients about what TVRG can do for them, but also creates high quality marketing materials that will help sell their property. Once again, the agents are freed up to focus on selling. Following is a list of our marketing coordinator's responsibilities:
- Coordinating appointments with clients to take pictures of their property
- Designing and distributing professional brochures
- Coordinating home buying seminars
- Meeting with vendors and partners for joint promotion
- Coordinating client-appreciation parties
- Coordinating our monthly client-appreciation program
- Answering phones and transferring or taking messages when applicable
- Coordinating the printing and delivery of marketing materials with vendors
- Managing details for all broker and public open houses

All five groups of the TVRG team (Team Leader, Agents, Operations, Transactions, and Marketing) work closely together to ensure the overall success of our team. Everyone understands the critical role they play on our team and is ready, willing, and able to carry out their responsibilities."

Balancing Your Personal Life with Your Professional Responsibilities

One of the greatest benefits of forming a team is that it enables you to establish balance in your life, but that is not what always happens. Some agents form teams and still can't let go. They're so accustomed to hard work that they continue working to the point of burning themselves out, not to mention burning out their families and friends. Don't get us wrong—a strong work ethic is something to be cherished, but working too much at the expense of your most intimate relationships is not the definition of success.

Long-term success hinges on your ability to balance work with your private life. If you're highly successful in business but your marriage fails and your children grow up despising you (or even worse, not knowing you), then you can't consider your life a success. To be truly successful, you must take into account all aspects of your life.

Consider the following strategies for establishing and maintaining balance in your life:

• Meet with your family and schedule some time every week that you can be together, focusing on each other. Schedule it on your calendar, if necessary, just like every other important appointment.

• Schedule date nights with your spouse or significant other. Your team at home begins with you and your partner, so give it the time and attention it requires.

• Schedule at least one family weekend per month and one or two weeks per year for vacation.

• To free up your evenings, Wayne Turner (www.wayneturner.com) of the Wayne Turner Real Estate Company in Hendersonville, Tennessee, recommends that before you leave work at the end of each day you leave a greeting on voicemail stating that you have chosen to spend time with your family and that after a certain time (say 8:00 p.m.), you won't be checking your voicemail, but that you will return phone calls promptly at 8:30 a.m. the next day. Finish by saying something like, "Thank you again for your call and the opportunity to help you." (According to Wayne, as long as you let people know that you have a family and value your family time, they will respect it. After all, they probably have families, too.)

• Clue in your clients. According to Faye Rispoli, "A key benefit in taking the time to put a good team in place should result in the team leader being able to confidently leave the business in the hands of her team. Educate clients early on about how your team operates so that they feel comfortable asking other team members for assistance. Just as team members take vacation days, the team leader should be able to do the same. For small business owners, allowing themselves time off is probably one of their biggest challenges. Remind yourself that even heads of large corporations take time for themselves, and that time for regrouping plays a role in their success."

• When you have a client who doesn't respect your need for family or personal time or is simply wasting your time and energy, Wayne Turner recommends that you simply say, "Next," a word that has become a huge force in his life. Whenever Wayne senses something toxic infecting his life—a client who feels as though he doesn't return phone calls fast enough, someone who doesn't like him or how he does business, or someone who's overly negative—he simply says, "Next," as in "Next client, please."

Although you've heard time and time again that "the customer is always right," that statement is simply not true. Clients can be wrong, and when they're wrong and wasting your time and energy, and sapping your enthusiasm, they can drag you so far down that you have nothing left to give to your better clients and prospects. In such cases, you need to cut the client loose. Remember, though, that cutting a client loose doesn't necessitate being offensive or ill-mannered. Simply tell the client that you're having trouble servicing his or her needs and recommend another agent who may be a better fit. If you're experiencing difficulty with a particular client, bring it up at the weekly team meeting. Don't be negative about the client—you don't want to poison their relationship with the next agent who may be better suited to working with this client.

Safeguarding Your Own Profitability as Team Leader

When you have a team, you're almost acting as a broker, providing your agents with the tools and resources they need to be successful. You invest in their success, and, in return, they generate revenue and pay you a portion of their commissions.

What sometimes happens is that team leaders become so focused on making everyone else successful that they lose sight of their own success and their own need to earn a profit. As team leader, you certainly want your team members to meet their goals and earn commissions, but you also have to safeguard your own profitability. Here are some suggestions on how to ensure that your business thrives:

- Do the math. You must have a team budget and a personal budget to guide you. Although a CPA and accounting assistants can help you draw up a budget and track income and expenses, as team leader you need to oversee the business finances. See Chapter 8 for details.

- Pay yourself a salary (and a portion of team commissions). To rein in any impulse to spend all your commissions as they come in, pay yourself a small salary to start. Later, when you have a better understanding of the team's finances and have built up a reserve (more on reserves later in this list), you may consider increasing your salary as you're able to. As team leader, you'll spend more time managing the team, mentoring individual team members, strategizing, planning and running meetings, and so on. You'll spend less time actually selling homes. To replace the income you'll lose by giving up some of your sales, other agents need to contribute a portion of their commissions to your salary.

- Build a reserve for lean months. The real estate business is often feast or famine, so make sure you have sufficient funds to keep the business up and running when the market is slow. We recommend starting with a surplus that's sufficient for covering all the bills for one month and growing it to cover an entire six months. At the end of the year, you can take out any excess reserve as a bonus.

Tip: Put the reserve in a high-interest-bearing savings account to generate even more income.

- Charge transaction fees at closing (to both sellers and buyers). This charge is another way to generate revenue. Rather than having these fees paid to you, you can have them paid to your broker to cover monthly fees and expenses, so you don't have to write a big check at the end of the month.

- Base agent splits on production. This approach ensures that you're not paying agents who aren't selling, and it motivates your agents to close more deals. For more about paying commissions, refer to Chapter 6.

According to Marsha Waddelow of The Waddelow Team, RE/MAX Associates of Arlington, Texas (waddelowteam@hotmail.com), the agents on her team pay administrative fees on every transaction (the higher the split, the higher the fee). The Commission Structure, shown in Table 3-1, illustrates how the agent split increases in relation to the agent's level of production. Following the commission structure is a numbered list that highlights important details in how commissions and payments are calculated and explains the processing fees that agents are responsible for paying back to the team. "These fees help cover my administrative costs," says Marsha, "The fee increases as does the split, which offsets some of the split increase. For example, when the split rises from 65% to 70%, the processing fee increases from $150 to $200."

COMMISSION STRUCTURE FOR THE MARSHA WADDELOW TEAM

Production Level	AGENT EARNINGS	ASSOCIATE LEVEL
1.	$0 to $14,999	50%
2.	$15,000 to $21,000	55%
3.	$21,001 to 32,000	60%
4.	$32,001 to $45,000	65%
5.	$45,001 to $63,000	70%
6.	$63,001 to $78,000	75%
7.	$78,001 to $150,000	80%
8.	$151,001 to $250,000	82.5%
9.	$250,001 and up	85%

1. Associate receives a percentage of gross commission income paid to Marsha Waddelow, Inc., in accordance with the above schedule. Concessions agreed upon between associate and team leader (i.e., home warranties, incentives to buyer/seller, etc.) will be deducted prior to establishing the level of percentage paid to the associate.

2. Associate's commission level is based on net commission paid to associate. The increase in percentage of commission paid to associate is based on closed sales. All commissions are disbursed at the rate effective at the time the transaction is closed.

3. The commission structure is based on the calendar year from January 1 through December 31.

4. Associates revert to level #1 of the commission structure on January 1 of each year (at discretion of team leader).

5. A processing fee of $150 is charged to the associate on each transaction closed up to production level #4. From production levels #4 to #6, the processing fee is $200 per transaction closed. Level #7 and above pay $250. This fee, which is for administrative and operating expenses of the team, is deducted from associate's commission check.

| Associate | Date | Marsha Waddelow | Date |

Figure 3-1: Sample commission structure showing splits.

Part II

Taking Care of Preliminary Details

Chapter 4

Drawing Up a Business Plan

Agents are often too busy doing business to think about building a business. They end up working 80-plus hours a week just to maintain their existence and often must continue working well into their retirement years. Why? Because they didn't think ahead. They didn't create a business entity that they could sell or from which they could continue to draw a steady income. Instead of creating a business, they did business, and doing business requires constant effort and energy.

One of your goals as a team should be to create a true business entity that continues to thrive even when team members and team leaders move on. You want to create an entity that has true value, something you could sell or pass down to the next generation of top producers.

In this chapter, we show you how to build a true business entity and salable asset by drawing up a solid business plan, composing a mission statement, and establishing a well-defined organizational structure for your team. We then discuss how you go about defining and communicating your corporate culture, managing the team's collective assets, and building a legacy for future generations.

The Components of a Solid Business Plan

The first step in transforming a loose collection of team members into a bona fide business entity is to draw up a business plan. A business plan is an essential tool in formulating a vision for your team, setting goals, and developing a strategy for moving from point A to point B. It sends a clear message to you, other team members, and anyone outside the team, that your business is bigger than any one individual. In addition, if you need a business loan, your plan shows banks that you have put some thought into your business and have a strategy in place for turning a profit.

Your business plan doesn't have to be intricately detailed, but it does require a substantial amount of thought and foresight. It needs to address the structure of your business, where your team wants to go, how it's going to get there, and what it's going to do once it is there. A business plan establishes early on that what you are creating is an entity unto itself—something that is bigger than the sum of its parts—in this case, the individual team members.

Familiarize yourself with the key areas that your business plan must address in order to be effective:

- Describing your business
- Defining your market

- Analyzing current issues and existing resources
- Communicating your vision
- Projecting revenue
- Budgeting for expenses
- Identifying sources of investment capital

Tip: Many books provide excellent advice on developing a solid business plan; for more detailed guidance than we offer here, we recommend the following books:

- *How to Write a Business Plan*, by Mike P. McKeever
- *The Ernst & Young Business Plan Guide*, by Brian R. Ford, Jay M. Bornstein, Patrick Pruitt, and Ernst & Young LLP
- *Business Plans Kit For Dummies*, by Steven Peterson, Ph.D., Peter E. Jaret, and Barbara Findlay Schenck
- *Anatomy of a Business Plan: A Step-by-Step Guide to Building a Business and Securing Your Company's Future*, by Linda Pinson

Note: A business plan can range from a few pages to 30 or 40, depending on the complexities of your business model and the size of your business. What's important is that you have a detailed plan in place. As you begin to implement your plan, it is likely to change and will usually grow.

My First Business Plan

I am a little ashamed to admit it, but I didn't write my first business plan until many years after I had created my first team. It was handwritten on a pad of yellow legal paper, fewer than ten sheets. At the time, I was running a business in excess of $50 million a year, scribbling my business plan on a legal pad.

When I went to the bank to get a line of credit to buy some foreclosed homes, the banker asked for a copy of my business plan. When I gave it to him, he responded, "Well, it's good, but is this how you keep your business plan?"

I quickly replied, "Well, that's the written copy; I could show you the typed copy, but we keep it back at the office in a safe." I didn't have a typed copy, and the staff didn't know what I was going to do or where we were going. When I approached my banker for a loan, I had to tell him that this was my original copy—the typewritten copy was stored back at the office.

Although I joke about it now, I have become much more serious about developing business plans before pursuing new opportunities. My team and I meet several times to draw up the plan (and type it), and we review it thoroughly to ensure that it's logical and realistic. I strongly recommend that you do the same. *—Ralph R. Roberts*

Describing your business

Every business plan should start with a brief description of the business—its name, where it's located, what it does, and the types of services it offers clients. Your description may change as you work on other components of the plan, but describing your vision on paper can act as a catalyst for developing the rest of your plan. Following is a sample business description:

Destiny Building Company is a Macomb County builder that will specialize in land development and the construction of neighborhood sub-developments, individual homes, and mental-health group homes. Through its relationships with Ralph R. Roberts Real Estate, The Loan Source, Inc. and Summit Title, Destiny will offer customers one-stop shopping under one roof—a service unique to the new-construction industry.

As you can see, the description is relatively brief (59 words), yet it sets out exactly what the business will do and what it offers clients.

Defining your market

After you describe the services your business will offer, your business plan must establish your market, and by that, we do not mean "the housing market." The market definition focuses on the need for your team's services in the area you choose to service. When composing your market definition, try to focus on a relatively narrow niche market. This may seem illogical at first, because you want to serve as broad a range of clientele as possible, but focusing on a niche market allows you to become an expert in that market, which eventually gives you a higher profile. You can always expand your business into new markets later, as your team develops and you acquire new talent.

Instead of taking aim at the entire residential real estate market, set your sights on a specific niche market. If your team lives and works around downtown Des Moines, Iowa, for example, you have several options—downtown housing, rural acreage, suburban neighborhood housing, downtown commercial office space, and so on.

Let's assume you chose the suburban neighborhood market. Great—off you go to make your fortune, right? Well, not exactly. You're probably still not focused enough. Which of the suburban markets are you going to focus on? Do you want to be the expert on affordable housing? If so, pick the location around downtown Des Moines that offers the most affordable housing. Do you want to specialize in upscale professional type housing? If so, focus on where the doctors and lawyers live.

Following is a sample market analysis included in the business plan for Destiny Building Company:

Macomb County is currently among the top 10 markets in the nation for land development. This trend should continue as Metro Detroit, which has the highest percentage of suburban dwellers of any metro area in the U.S., expands further outward.

Fortunately for Destiny, no single builder in Macomb County currently controls more than 5% of the total Macomb County new construction market. Not a single company owns more than 1% market share in Destiny's primary niche— affordable ($100,000 to $199,000) new construction homes for first- and second-time home buyers.

In this example, the analysis shows that the market supports a new construction company that focuses on affordable homes in the suburbs of Metro Detroit. It identifies a need in the marketplace that is unmet. Once that has been established, the business plan can go on to explain the strategy for capitalizing on the opportunities in that market.

Analyzing current issues and existing resources

Businesses are never created in a vacuum, so your business plan needs to address the realities of where you plan on doing business. It should address questions, such as the following:

- What resources do you have that make your team uniquely capable of achieving success in this venture?
- What relationships can you tap for additional leverage?
- What can you expect in the way of competition?
- Are you facing any challenges as a result of current market conditions?
- How is the market likely to change in the future?

The business plan for the Destiny Building Company has an entire section devoted exclusively to situation analysis:

Destiny Building Company has all the tools necessary to be a highly successful venture. It has more than 100 years of combined experience in land develop-

ment, building, real estate, mortgage, and title work in Macomb County. It has great relationships with all the companies essential to its success—real estate, mortgage, and title—making it the market's only true one-stop shop.

Additionally, it has an advantage over other start-up builders in working with subcontractors, which has traditionally been one of the most difficult areas to manage. Ralph R. Roberts, the company owner, has built significant relationships with many area trades during his 20-plus years in real estate, property management, and land development. Ralph E. Roberts, one of the company's licensed builders, has more than 40 years of alliance-building with Macomb County subcontractors. Also, with an attorney on board, Destiny can sign agreements with contractors to ensure performance, a step that only the largest builders typically take.

One of the biggest threats to other builders—a recession—could actually be an opportunity for Destiny to grab more market share. With its one-stop-shopping concept, Destiny has eliminated several middlemen from the new construction process, thus increasing profitability. In a recession, Destiny has more room than its competition to cut prices and remain profitable. Additionally, recessions always hurt higher-end new construction ($200,000 and up) long before affordable housing is affected.

As this example illustrates, situation analysis looks at the business from all sides to ensure that the proper resources are in place to capitalize on the target market. Destiny's obvious strengths are the experience of its team members and the relationships it already has in place. The analysis also accounts for a potential recession (a negative change in market conditions), and explains why a recession could possibly improve the long-term success of the business.

Communicating your vision

When you close your eyes and see your business operating on a daily basis, how do you envision it? This vision should be included in your business plan. Your vision is likely to touch on other components of your business plan, including your market, the consumer you're targeting, and the unique combination of products and services you have to offer. In your vision, you crystallize everything in your business plan, summing up everything in a brief paragraph of two to five sentences, as in the following example:

As more and more people flee the Metro Detroit area in search of better homes and schools for their children, the demographic of suburban Detroit is destined to change. More buyers will be seeking affordable new construction, and Destiny will deliver with high-quality, affordable housing that's readily available, and one-stop shopping that places buyers in their dream homes in a matter of days or weeks instead of months.

Projecting revenue sources and amounts

Focusing on revenue is usually a poor way to run a business, because it draws your attention and resources away from what really generates revenue—serving and satisfying your clients. Your primary focus should always be on customer service. Forget about the bottom line, and serve your top line—your clients. When you are developing a business plan, however, you must pay some attention to that bottom line so you can effectively manage your team's income and expenses.

To keep your team in the black, you need to know your break-even point for each month. How much does your team need to earn in order to cover the monthly expenses? When you know your break-even point, you can use it to determine minimum monthly sales goals for everyone on the team. You can also use your budget to help generate your P&L (profit and loss) reports.

Remember: When creating a budget, don't forget to account for tax bills. You can pay your taxes online, so it is actually pretty easy. Work with your accountant to pay taxes monthly or quarterly so you don't fall behind. Playing catch-up on overdue tax bills is often a losing battle. Stay ahead of the game.

Your business plan should include the following:

• **Break-even point:** Gross revenue you must generate in order to break even, both annually and monthly. (After you calculate your expenses, as we discuss in the following section, you will have a clearer idea of your break-even point.)

• **Projected gross revenue:** The gross revenue your team plans to earn, both annually and monthly—your revenue goals.

• **Projected number of transactions:** The number of transactions your team needs to complete in order to generate that revenue.

Remember: Set realistic goals. If the total number of homes sold per year in your market area is 200, a goal of selling 200 homes per year is unrealistic. Identify the biggest player in your market. How many homes does your biggest competitor sell annually? What percentage of the market does that competitor control? Can you realistically expect to control 30%, 40%, or 50% of the market?

• **Average commission:** The average commission from each transaction.

A good portion of your business plan is going to unfold from these initial estimates. For example, if you currently command 5% of the market and want to build a team that controls 25% of the market, your business plan must include the various strategies you will use to accomplish that goal, including the number of team members you need to add, how you're going to ramp up your marketing efforts, the steps you're going to take to improve customer service, and so on.

After you establish the percentage of the market your team is pursuing (as explained earlier in the section "Defining your market"), calculating your projected gross revenue is fairly easy. For example, if the average home in your area sells for $100,000 and 200 home sales close annually, that's $20 million. Let's say you can capture 40% of the market. That's $8 million in gross sales. If your team was handling only the listings and the standard agent commission is 6% in your area, your team is getting half of the commission or 3%. That represents $240,000 in gross revenue.

If your goal is to earn more than $240,000 in gross revenue, then you need to adjust your plan accordingly. Perhaps adding one or more buyer's agents would help. If your team can successfully sell the houses it lists, then you can nearly double the team's revenue without having to control a larger percentage of the total sellable market simply by servicing both sellers and buyers. Other options would include ramping up your marketing efforts to command a higher percentage of the market or adding new revenue-generating departments, as discussed in Chapter 15.

Budgeting for expenses

In order for your team to remain solvent, you have to create a business plan that sets you on a course of bringing in at least enough revenue to cover expenses. Your business plan needs to show how much money your team needs to get going and to keep going on a monthly and yearly basis.

Consider breaking your expenses into three categories:

• **One-time expenses or start-up costs:** These expenses include the cost of equipment, such as a building, car, computers, and office furniture. What do you need to get your team up and running?

• **Fixed monthly expenses:** Your fixed expenses are hard expenses that will change little if at all each year and are therefore easy to calculate. They'll be a line item on your budget. Some of them might include

- Rent or mortgage payment on your office building

- Taxes on your building

- Employee salaries (if any)

- Utility payments

- Phone service

- Internet service

- Office supplies

• **Fluctuating monthly expenses:** Your team is also likely to have expenses that are extremely difficult to pin down, such as the following:

- Marketing/advertising expenses

- Seminar and continuing education opportunities

- Thank you gifts

- Miscellaneous

Items here might be just as important as the items on your fixed list, but the budget can fluctuate. If you want to ramp up advertising in a given year, or given quarter, for example, then this will create a larger than usual expense. Plan for fluctuations as much as possible.

Tip: Although you may not be able to eliminate fluctuating expenses, you can usually cut back on them if necessary. For example, you may not be able to afford to advertise less, but you can, in fact, advertise less. You can't, however, decide not to pay rent on your office building.

Identifying sources of investment capital

As you take on new team members and begin to build a business, you need some sort of funding—cash. In most cases, you need enough investment capital to get your team up and running. Once the team starts producing enough revenue to more than cover expenses, it can begin to pay back any loans.

Where are you going to obtain that cash? Are you investing your own capital? Requiring new team members to contribute? Taking out a business loan from the bank? In your business plan, identify each and every source of investment capital; you can include more than one.

Note: As we discuss in Chapter 2, launching a team doesn't require a great deal of start-up capital, so this may be one of the briefest sections of your business plan. You should, however, account for how you are going to handle the added expense of a personal assistant or any other team members you decide to bring on board.

Fleshing out your business plan with additional sections

A business plan can be very detailed and robust. We covered the most important sections of your business plan, but if you would prefer a more detailed plan, you may want to consider additional sections, including the following:

• Management

• Ownership

• Market segments and growth potential

- Customer profile
- Competition
- Market share
- Geographic market factors
- Barriers to market entry
- Marketing strategies
- Team member biographies

Composing a Mission Statement

A mission statement is a vital component of any business entity. It sets the business apart from any and all individuals that contribute to the business and sends a message to every team member that "this is what we need to be doing and working toward each and every day." It also sends a message to clients and prospective clients, showing them what they can expect from your team.

In many ways, the mission statement is identical to the vision described in the business plan, but even if you choose not to have a business plan, your mission statement can help to unify your team and provide a sense of direction and purpose. Think of the mission statement as your vision communicated in a way that speaks more directly to fellow team members and to your clientele.

A mission statement should consist of carefully chosen words that establish

- Who you are as a team
- What you're trying to accomplish
- How you're going to accomplish it

The wording should form one or more action statements, which are personal to you and to the clients you serve.

Remember: A good mission statement is broad enough to allow some flexibility but narrow enough to keep the team's focus on the target. A statement that promises to provide all services to all clients in a huge geographical area is too broad.

Consider this example for a four-member team focusing on the affordable housing sector around downtown Des Moines:

Our mission is to provide a complete range of full-time quality and professional real estate services to first-time home buyers and sellers in the suburban Des Moines area. We pledge to treat each customer with dignity and respect and to always uphold our professional duty in servicing their real estate needs.

This mission statement is short and sweet, but it does the trick. Let's break it down and analyze the various statements it is making:

Q: Who are your customers?

A: First-time home buyers and sellers.

This phrase identifies your clients. You are not focusing on people who are looking to buy or sell high-end properties, second homes, or investment properties. Your sole focus is on first-time buyers and sellers who have homes that appeal to first-time buyers.

Q: What are you going to provide?

A: A complete range of full-time quality and professional real estate services.

This tells you what you intend to do for your clients. You're not going to provide budget real estate services or part-time services. That means you're going to list and sell homes and advise and counsel buyers and sellers in your marketplace. You're going to focus your attention on them and on their desire to secure or sell a home.

Q: Where is your focus?

A: The suburban Des Moines area.

Notice that this phrase doesn't mention commercial landlords, upscale waterfront homes, or the Des Moines farming community. It focuses specifically on your market of affordable homes in the suburban Des Moines area. This doesn't mean that you can't work with others, but remember: You're establishing a niche market that you can dominate.

Q: How will you accomplish your mission?

A: By treating each customer with dignity and respect and always upholding our professional duty in servicing their real estate needs.

This phrase sends a clear message that your team is committed to acting with integrity and treating your clients with dignity and respect. Prospective clients can read this mission statement and approach you with confidence and trust, knowing that you'll treat them right.

Tip: Your team's mission statement is important to include in your business plan, but avoid adding it to the plan and then forgetting about it. Include your mission statement on your Web site and blog, in outgoing e-mail messages, in newsletters, and when you communicate with fellow team members. You should also consider posting it in a prominent location in your office. A good mission statement keeps you focused on your goal when the everyday muddle drives you off course.

Here's a sample mission statement from the Destiny Building Company:

Destiny Building Company is dedicated to providing new construction options to Macomb County home buyers searching for affordable homes. Realizing that a customer's time can be as valuable to them as their money, Destiny is committed to working with its team to offer consumers great value for their investment as well as a hassle-free, one-stop-shopping program that saves time. Destiny will encourage customers to take an active role in each phase of the new-home building process, ensuring that potential problems are addressed and resolved quickly, producing 100% customer satisfaction.

Your mission statement may be followed by a section on objectives and strategies, as discussed in the following sections.

Stating your objectives

Your objectives are whatever you envision your business accomplishing. Think of objectives as very specific goals you set for your business. Following are some examples from the Destiny Building Company:

- Establish a one-stop-shopping service for new construction homes.
- Maintain an 11–19% net profit on every home built.
- Capture at least 25% of the market share within the first year.
- Achieve 100% customer satisfaction.

Formulating your strategies

Your strategies are the tasks you need to accomplish in order to achieve your objectives. Think of strategies as your plans for getting from point A to point B. For example:

- Hire a personal assistant to answer phones, take notes, and process paperwork.
- Hire a transaction coordinator to track transactions from sale to closing.
- Hire a buyer's agent for additional revenue and to generate more listings.
- Place all noncommission team members on a bonus program, so every team member works to lower costs and raise profits.

Creating an Advisory Board

Whenever you create a business and place yourself in the position of being "the boss," you set yourself up for failure in a way. The people working "under you" may hesitate to offer their honest opinions, and you end up working in a vacuum. To prevent this situation from occurring, consider setting up an advisory board, whose members are free to speak their minds and encouraged to do so. Your advisory board might consist of the following:

- Your attorney
- Your CPA
- Key community leaders
- A family member
- One or more key staff members

Tip: At Ralph Roberts Realty, my advisory board consisted of my personal attorney, my personal assistant, my mother (who has a good mind for business), a good friend (who's also a savvy business person), a stockbroker, my CPA, and a different guest speaker for each meeting. We met once a month for a business dinner, in which we discussed the evening's special topic—land development, mobile home parks, building specs, a possible new department, new construction, foreclosures, and so on. It was a great way to bounce off ideas or solve problems with the best businesspeople in our community. Prior to the meeting, I sent any applicable documents to the board members so they could prepare their thoughts about the evening's topic of discussion.

Building Your Team's Organizational Chart

To establish a team as a business entity that can thrive even when individual team members leave, it's important to have a structure in place. You would never put together a baseball team, for example, without assigning people to different positions. If you had three people playing third base and nobody in right field or playing first base, your team would probably find itself on the losing end of most games.

An organizational chart gives your team the structure it needs to operate efficiently and effectively. It identifies each position and the person responsible for that position, and provides you with a starting point for developing job responsibilities for those positions.

In the following sections, we show you how to create meaningful job titles and descriptions, establish your corporate hierarchy, and draw up a plan of succession.

Creating meaningful job titles and descriptions

When you start looking for someone to fill a position, you'll draw more and better candidates by advertising an elite title than a simple, no-frills one. Advertising a position for Executive Office Manager, for example, sounds a lot better than advertising for an assistant or receptionist. In addition, when a client calls and wants to talk to someone in charge, that person would probably rather talk to the Customer Service Supervisor rather than your "receptionist."

In addition, if you call everyone you add to your team an "assistant," that doesn't do much in terms of motivation. Everyone on your team should feel important and project an image of confidence to your clients and prospective clients, which starts with a meaningful job title that conveys a sense of importance. Here are some suggestions:

- Second-in-Command or Personal Assistant (rather than simply Assistant)
- Public Relations Liaison
- Director of Sales
- Director of Marketing
- Director of Operations
- Senior Sales Manager
- Client Care Manager
- Executive Assistant
- Business Manager
- Senior Business Developer
- Customer Service Supervisor
- Director of First Impressions (aka "Receptionist")

For more about common positions on a team, refer to Chapter 2. In Chapter 11, we offer guidance on how to choose and add new members to your team.

Establishing your corporate hierarchy

Just as your team needs a business plan to give it focus, it usually needs a single leader to keep the team on track—a person who can hold all other team members accountable and ultimately make the tough decisions.

Smaller teams may consist of a team leader and an assistant or a team leader and several employees, none of whom really holds an executive role—the team makes decisions and acts collectively as a unit. Larger teams may function as mini-corporations, complete with a president, vice president, CEO, CFO, and several department managers, as shown in the following organizational chart in Figure 4-1, contributed by Steve and Nancy Whitfield of the Whitfield Properties Team (www.whitfieldproperties.com) of Burlington, North Carolina.

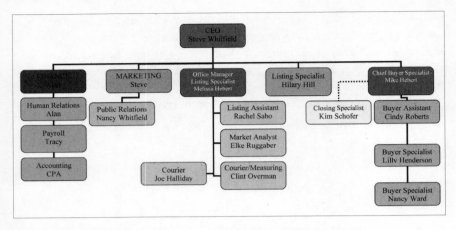

Figure 4-1: A sample organizational chart for a large agent team.

Tip: If you decide to incorporate your team, as we explain in Chapter 7, make sure that your incorporation papers include wording on who will serve as the team leader and how the leader will be chosen, especially if team members are given the power to vote for team leader.

Drawing up a plan of succession

When you're drawing up plans for your team-to-be, the last thing on your mind is the possibility that a team member will eventually leave or become disabled to the point of not being able to fulfill his or her responsibilities, or perhaps even die. However, your business plan needs to account for such possibilities, both in the short-term and in the long-term:

• **Short term:** Which team member or members are going to fill in temporarily? Who is going to take on the person's job responsibilities or how will the responsibilities be divided among team members?

• **Long term:** Who will replace the key team member if replacement is called for? Who is in charge of choosing a replacement? If no single member is in charge of choosing a replacement, what procedure will be followed?

Chapter 5

Establishing Office Policies and Procedures

In Chapter 4, we focus on various strategies to establish your team as a business entity on paper. Your business plan, mission statement, and organizational chart all function behind the scenes to define your team as an entity that exists above and beyond all individual team members. In this chapter, we shift your attention to the team members themselves, helping you create a lucrative environment for them and, ultimately, for the team. To start your team's business on firm ground, you need clear guidelines and procedures.

Tip: Keep backups for your handbook and procedures manuals on CDs or DVDs as well as on more than one computer. These files are too valuable to lose.

Defining and Communicating Your Corporate Culture: The Employee Handbook

When you assemble a team of professionals, you may assume that everyone on your team understands the concept of conducting themselves in a professional manner, but that is not always the case. What is considered professional for one team member may not be considered professional by another team member's standards. As such, every agent team should have an employee handbook or at least a list of workplace policies. Having written policies in place can benefit your team in several ways:

- Creates a uniform standard that everyone can follow

- Allows you to bring new team members quickly up to speed

- Protects the team legally in the event that a team member claims to have never been informed of a particular policy

- Establishes a system in which all team members can be treated fairly

Whenever you add new team members, hand them a copy of the employee handbook and ask them to sign a statement indicating receipt of the handbook. Every year, you and your team should review the policies and make any necessary adjustments.

Remember: Having an employee handbook or a list of policies is only the first step. You must enforce the company policy consistently and fairly. If you don't, you may be viewed as condoning the action or giving certain team members preferential treatment, which could expose both you and your team to liability. In a sexual harassment suit, for example, if you aren't careful to protect yourself you (as employer) may be named in the lawsuit just because you have deeper pockets than the person who actually committed the act.

Tip: Have an open-door policy so team members can notify you anonymously or talk with you directly about any issue without fear of retribution. The earlier someone notifies you of an issue, the faster and more effectively you can address it and prevent it from becoming a legal battle.

Establishing a dress code

Maybe appearance shouldn't matter, but the fact is, it does. Clients, knowingly or unknowingly, judge you and your team on appearance, and when you are in the real estate business, you are well aware of just how important first impressions really are.

However, the individuals are key, too—your team needs to project itself to clients and prospective clients as a business entity. Some teams go so far as to purchase clothing with their team logo embroidered on it. That may not be right for you and your team, but you should establish some sort of policy that governs your team's dress and conduct.

Having a dress code in place can immediately improve your team in several ways:

- Fosters a sense of commonality
- Eliminates office distractions
- Creates a more favorable impression

In the late 1970s, John Malloy wrote a book called *Dress for Success* that prescribed a uniform of sorts for success in corporate America. In today's more casual corporate climate, you may be tempted to think that the days of dressing for success are over, but what has actually happened is that the wardrobe has simply changed clothes. Blue suits and red ties have been replaced with khakis and button-down shirts...with or without the ties.

When determining your team's dress code, let your market be your guide. In some markets, you almost have to wear a suit in order to be considered professional. In other areas, even in high-end markets, a pair of nice slacks with a team logo polo shirt is sufficient. Have a team meeting to decide on the type of image you want to project to clients and establish your dress code accordingly.

Creating a professional office environment

Although you want your office to be a fun place to work, you should have policies and practices in place to ensure that the office appears and functions as a professional work environment devoted to serving clients. Make sure your office policies and practices cover the following areas:

• **Organization:** The office should be neat and well-organized.

• **Cleanliness:** Hiring a janitorial service should address most of this, but team members should be encouraged to keep the office clean between cleanings.

• **Phone duty:** If team members are expected to share phone duty, spell out how the sharing will work and what happens in the event that a client calls for an agent who will be unavailable for an extended period of time. You don't want to lose business just because a particular agent cannot promptly return the call. On that note, you should also instruct everyone to answer the phone with an upbeat tone and to be courteous to everyone calling in.

• **Internet use:** More and more companies are having to curb Internet abuse by developing policies for instant messaging, blogging, and e-mail. Make sure your team has a policy in place that defines the appropriate and inappropriate use of these communication technologies and how the team will deal with any abuses.

• **Office talk:** Encourage everyone in the office to avoid any discussions or language that may turn a client off. "Innocent" jokes that are a little off-color can offend the sensitivities of some clients, as can any negative talk.

• **Sexual harassment:** Define what you mean by "sexual harassment" and how it will be dealt with. Consult with your attorney to get a clear understanding of exactly what constitutes sexual harassment and then share that information with your team. Clear policies consistently enforced provide the rest of the team with the most protection from the one bad apple.

Explaining benefits and reimbursements

Most people expect to receive benefits above and beyond what they receive as monetary compensation, so your employee handbook should clearly describe any benefits you offer. You should also specify how you will handle reimbursing employees for expenses they cover in the normal course of doing business. Be sure to cover the following areas:

• **Sick days:** Note the number of sick days each employee has per calendar year and define exactly what you consider an excusable illness. Some teams and other businesses require employees to present a doctor's note, but when you're dealing with professionals, this sort of micromanagement can often come across as an insult.

• **Personal days:** If you choose to allow agents or staff members to take additional days off to deal with personal business, note the number of days available and justifiable reasons for taking personal days. Also, specify whether team members are allowed to roll over unused days (and if so, how many) into the following year or years.

• **Vacations:** Note how long a person must be with the team before they can take a vacation and the number of days of vacation they earn each month. You may also require that team members give advanced notice of their vacation plans, so you don't end up with an empty office the first week of August.

• **Benefits:** List any additional benefits that your team offers along with a list of what a person must do to qualify for those benefits. Additional benefits may include healthcare, dental coverage, or profit sharing, to name a few.

• **Reimbursed expenses:** Provide a comprehensive list of expenses that the team will reimburse agents and other team members for. These may include business copies, listing presentation literature, office keys, newspaper and magazine advertising, office rent and overhead, administrative support, For Sale signs, and office supplies. (What your team chooses to cover is up to your team to decide.)

• **Unreimbursed expenses:** These may include personal riders for signs, personal business cards and name badges, board and MLS dues, seminar training and business conference expenses, insurance, cell phone charges, and so on.

Addressing termination and lawsuits

Nobody likes to think about termination and lawsuits, but if you have to fire a team member or the team member chooses to leave, you should have a system in place that provides for a smooth transition out the door. It should also address how any lawsuits will be handled. Make sure your manual addresses the following items:

• **Termination:** Describe the behavior you expect from all team members and list the behaviors that will result in termination. Spend some time to develop a clear and comprehensive list of unacceptable behaviors. You may want to group them by severity—for example, stealing may result in immediate termination, whereas showing up late for work results in warning or a reduction in commission rates.

Your termination clause should also describe everything that the terminated team member must return to the team upon termination. For listing agents, you should also specify what happens to the agent's listings upon termination.

• **Severance:** If and when you do terminate a team member, what sort of severance package, if any, will you offer? You may have different severance packages for team members who own a stake in the company and for staff members who function more as employees.

• **Lawsuits:** Specify how various types of lawsuits will be handled: suit against a team member by third party, member vs. member, member vs. entity, member against third party, and indictments. If the team name and reputation are key (they usually are), carefully spell out the course of action to protect the team's name and reputation in the event of a lawsuit. Consult your attorney for recommendations.

Every team's policies handbook is going to be unique. Yours may not cover all the items we discuss in this section or it may be even more detailed. Marsha Waddelow of The Waddelow Team, RE/MAX Associates of Arlington, Texas (waddelowteam@hotmail.com) shares her policies for buyer's agents in Figure 5-1, below.

Office Policies and Procedures for Team Members
THE MARSHA WADDELOW TEAM
RE/MAX ASSOCIATES OF ARLINGTON

The purpose of this agreement is to outline policies and procedures for the office/team of Marsha Waddelow. All listings taken by any Team Member will be in the name of the Team Leader. All executed contracts will be in the name of the Team Leader and the Team Member who sold the property. Sales will be posted in MLS under the Team Leader's license number with RE/MAX and MLS.

EXPENSES:

The following items shall be the expense of the Team Member:

Personal Riders for Signs (optional)

Personal Business Cards and Name Badges

Board & MLS Dues

Education/Seminar Training and Business Conference Expenses

Supra Keypad

RE/MAX International/Texas dues & renewal fees.

E & O Insurance (Errors & Omission Insurance)

Buyer/Agent fees charged by the company (Currently $395.00 monthly)

Personal Office Phone, Voice Mail, Pager & Cellular Service

(telephone extension and voice mail included in monthly office dues)

Pro-Quest 1-800 Call Capture Service (OPTIONAL to Agent)

($100 one-time charge for RIDERS and $20 monthly service fee.)

CAP Items, Monthly Marketing Pieces and Postage.

The following items shall be the expense of the Team Leader paid on behalf of the Team Members:

CSS Monthly fee

Business Copies

Listing Presentation Literature

Supra Box Deposits

Office Keys

Newspaper & Magazine Advertising (at Team Leaders Discretion)

Office Rent and Overhead

Administrative Support

For Sale Signs

Riders such as Pool, Sale Pending, and Sold

Office Supplies

Any signs, lockboxes, or sign riders provided to Team Members that are missing, lost, stolen, or damaged shall be the sole expense of the Team Member at a cost of $50.00 per sign, $10.00 per rider, and $80.00 per supra box. These figures are subject to change to reflect cost increases. Upon termination of Team Member, any unpaid balances shall be due and will be deducted from outstanding commissions unless other arrangements for payment have been made.

TERMINATION

Upon termination, all signs, riders, lockboxes, and office keys provided to the Team Member shall be returned to the Team Leader within 24 hours. Any unpaid amounts due shall be deducted from commissions unless other arrangements for payment have been made.

All listings belong to the Broker (RE/MAX Associates). Upon termination of Team Member, any listing by Team Member which resulted from efforts of Team Leader will remain with the Team (i.e., sign call from Team Leader's listing, interoffice referral, etc.). If Team Member terminates to become a primary agent or join another Broker, any listing obtained from their direct sphere of influence will be released to the Team Member and a referral fee of 30% will be due and payable to Team Leader upon closing and funding of the property. Any unclosed, pending transactions will be shared between Team Leader and Team Member on a 50/50 split, minus transaction fee.

All office and RE/MAX fees and dues must be current before listings will be released.

It is understood and agreed that Team Member will not terminate for the purpose of becoming a Team Member under another primary agent at RE/MAX Associates.

TEAM PHONE DUTY

Phone duty schedule will be posted for sign up prior to the beginning of each month. In order to receive phone duty calls that day, Team Member shall be in the office or available to receive calls as they come through. If the phone duty agent receives a call on a property listed by another Team Member, phone duty agent will attempt to forward that call to the listing agent. The listing agent will have 15 minutes to respond before losing the call.

PROPERTY CALLS

Any incoming calls generated by signs on properties listed by Team Member shall go to the Team Member handling the property whenever possible. If the designated Team Member is not in the office, a reasonable attempt will be made to obtain the name and phone number of the caller and the listing agent will be contacted immediately. The Listing Agent should return that call promptly. Failure to return the call within 15 minutes could result in the reassignment of the call. If the caller refuses to leave a name or phone number, the call will be assigned to the phone duty agent.

PRO-QUEST CALLS/INQUIRIES

Team Members participating in the Pro-Quest 1-800 Call Capture service will have the opportunity to enter all their listings in the service and monitor their activities on a daily basis. This is an excellent source for leads and has proven to be extremely profitable if inquiries are monitored and follow up calls are made. The Team Member on Phone Duty will receive calls on Team Leader's listings. They are also responsible for checking the Pro-Quest Web site to follow up on buyer inquiries for that day during their phone duty time.

The agent with the 8:30 a.m. shift will be responsible for checking and responding to all inquiries from the night before (Team Leader's Listings).

ADVERTISING

Any advertising paid for by the Team Leader will be assigned to the Team Member listing that particular property. Their direct phone number will be the number listed in the ad. If they are a Pro-Quest Subscriber, the 1-800 with their listing's extension will be published instead. This will enable all calls to go directly to the listing agent. In the event the listing agent is not available to take the call, it is to be transferred to another agent.

Business deemed generated by the Team Member shall be from the following sources:

Cold calls, clients generated by advertising paid for by Team Member, clients/customers from Open Houses, referrals from past clients/customers, and sign calls on Team Leader's listings, personal acquaintances, sphere of influence, or other "leads" or "referrals" generated by Team Leader.

PERSONAL REAL ESTATE TRANSACTIONS

Team Member shall be allowed to waive the real estate commission due to the Team Leader on one personal sale and one personal purchase a year. The Team Member will pay $500.00 fee to cover listing expenses and normal processing fees on the listing at closing. The normal processing fee charged to the agent will be paid at closing on the purchase. The Team Member must be a member of the team for no fewer than 12 months to receive this benefit. This benefit will apply to the Team Member's immediate family only.

Figure 5-1: A sample employee handbook.

Developing Systems and Procedures

Before you even start looking for someone to hire to take on some of your excess workload, you'd better have a system in place, complete with procedures manuals and a plan for training any additional personnel. Otherwise, new hires spend a lot of time with "nothing to do," while you work even harder to pay them for doing nothing.

A system typically includes the following key components:

• Objective: Whatever you need to accomplish. Think of objectives as a "to-do" list.

• Strategy: An overall idea of how your business will achieve the stated objective.

• Step-by-step tasks: Everything that an employee needs to do to achieve the objective. If an alien landed its spaceship in your office and needed to perform each team member's duties, that alien could pick up the manual, follow the instructions, and successfully complete the tasks.

In Chapter 4, we go into detail about creating a business plan for your team, something we consider to be an essential step in building a solid foundation for your business. Likewise, when setting up your team, you should take a systematic approach in building and managing it. All your team members should be aware of the team's goal and mission statement and the tasks they're responsible for. By developing systems upfront, you'll be much more effective and efficient in hiring the requisite talent and then providing them with the training they need to carry out essential tasks.

Identifying objectives

If you wake up in the morning and jot down a list of things you need to accomplish before the end of the day, you're already well aware of objectives. Sit down with a pen and a pad of paper (or at your computer) and generate a comprehensive list of objectives—everything you need to accomplish on a daily, weekly, monthly, and annual basis.

Your objectives are anything and everything that you need to get done, including creating marketing packets, meeting with prospective clients, responding to e-mail messages, creating a Web site or blog, processing a transaction to closing, and so on. When you have a comprehensive list of objectives, you're well prepared to begin the process of laying out the steps to meet those objectives.

Identifying tasks

Once you have a list of objectives, identify the individual tasks that you or someone else must perform in order to meet the objectives. This may consist of writing letters, making phone calls, doing research, meeting with clients, color coding folders, and so on. At this point, you're not going into great detail. You're simply creating a to-do list of what steps each objective requires.

Breaking a Complex Process into Simple Steps

To-do lists are fairly easy to create. You just sit down and think of everything you need to get done. What complicates the to-do list is that some of the items on the list inevitably require days, weeks, or even months to accomplish and often must be performed in several stages, each of which requires a series of steps.

At Ralph Roberts Realty, for example, I decided that I wanted a new business card. I attended an event hosted by a local newspaper, where they passed out mininewspapers (approximately the height and width of an average human hand). This marketing piece was very clever, and I wanted to duplicate the idea. As is usually the case, I wanted to duplicate the idea immediately.

The problem was that we were about to move offices, which meant that our address and fax number were going to change. In addition, we were in the process of producing a series of books and articles we wanted to include in our mininewspaper. We needed to gather articles, images of book covers, and other materials before we could even think about publishing our newspaper. As a result, publication was delayed for several months, and everyone on our production team became disappointed and frustrated. Quite honestly, my expectations simply got out of hand. That's when we took a step back and decided to break the task into a series of steps.

We set a more realistic deadline, assigned more people to the project, and formulated a step-by-step strategy to pull all the pieces together and lay out our own mininewspaper. Although the operation was still a little tense, it went much more smoothly, and everyone involved had more fun.

The moral of this story is that every project needs its own miniplan. State your objective, set a realistic deadline, and break up the process of achieving that objective into the stages and steps necessary to ensure success. (You can even apply this idea to your grocery shopping! Make your trip to the grocery store more productive by planning ahead and having a complete shopping list, so you don't have to go back to the store to pick up items you forgot.) *—Ralph R. Roberts*

Creating step-by-step procedures manuals for accomplishing tasks

Delegating efficiently requires that you provide anyone who becomes a member of the team or works for the team with the training and resources to successfully accomplish their individual objectives. The best way to provide training is to have written procedures manuals that team members and other staff can reference to determine how to carry out any tasks they're required to perform.

Procedures manuals should contain more than simply step-by-step instructions. Provide any illustrations (including screenshots if the task is computer related) that may assist your staff in understanding how to perform each task. In addition, provide information on where to obtain any resources required to perform each task. Your goal is to provide enough detail so that anyone can perform the tasks without supervision and with as few questions as possible, to minimize frustration on your end as well as that of your team members.

Some of your steps will likely be decision steps, and some of the decisions a person needs to make in a real estate office are critical. Make sure your manual contains sufficient information for the person reading it to make the right judgment call or to feel comfortable asking questions without feeling inadequate. You want team members to take initiative and act independently, but you don't want to discourage them from asking the questions required to make good decisions.

Your procedures manuals should constantly evolve. Have another team member try to use each manual and make notes to point out any missing or confusing steps. As other people use the manuals, they should point out any problems they had following the instructions so you can refine the instructions as needed.

Tip: If writing and revising manuals is not your specialty or the specialty of any of your other team members, consider hiring a specialist. Many technical writers have the training and experience to handle the job.

Assembling the manuals

Until the world is completely paperless, you need to employ at least two systems to manage your office—one for the paper that piles up on your desk and the other for the digital "paperwork" on your computer—e-mail and ments. At Ralph Roberts Realty, Roberts' assistant has access to his e-mail in-box and color-codes all incoming paper documents, so they can be efficiently distributed to the team members who are most qualified to deal with them: red for Lois (second-in-command), yellow for Sarah, green for Lisa, orange for Lauren, and purple for Kandra.

Tip: As your agent team grows, you may want to opt for a more structured approach by assembling your procedures manuals into separate binders for specific job titles—perhaps one for your receptionist, another for your mar-keting coordinator, and one for your personal assistant, for example.

Chapter 6

Handling Team Member Compensation

Whenever we hold a session on agent teams and open the floor for the usual Q&A, at least one brave soul asks the question that everyone else is thinking: "How much do you suggest we pay a listing manager, buyer's agent, closing manager, virtual assistant, receptionist (or director of first impressions, as we like to call her), or other team members?"

Of course, this question is an excellent one. Unfortunately, no single answer is correct for all teams and all situations. Compensation can take many forms, including commissions, salaries, vacations, health insurance, retirement accounts, education, status, power, opportunities, you name it. You need to decide on a compensation package that works best for you and your team—a package that motivates and rewards team members accordingly without bankrupting your business.

Although your team's compensation package may include only a few of the many types of compensation available, you should be aware of all the most common types of compensation, so you can cherry-pick the ones you'll offer your team.

Outlining Your Compensation Package: Decisions to Make and Clearly Communicate

The area that tends to cause the most disagreements in any business is compensation. Whichever form(s) of compensation you offer, you need to make sure that all your team members are well aware of how you'll compensate them for their efforts and productivity.

One of the first discussions you should have with all your team members, whether they work in-house or as an independent contractor or on a work-for-hire contract, is how and when you'll pay them. Your discussion should cover the following:

• **Payment amount:** This can be a flat dollar amount per hour, per year, or per project (for independent contractors); it can be a percentage if you are paying the person on commission, or it can be a percentage of the team's net revenue if you are dividing proceeds among partners.

When you are first starting to build your team, we encourage you to keep your compensation package somewhat conservative. Ramping up compensation later is always easier than trying to scale back. Team members usually frown on reduced commissions and salaries.

• **Payment schedule:** Specify the date on which the person can expect to receive payment. For hourly employees, this may be the 2nd and 4th Friday of every month. For independent contractors, you may specify that they will be paid within so many days of your receipt of the invoice.

• **Invoices/reports:** If you require independent contractors to submit invoices for payment, let the contractor know up front the type of information you need in the invoice. If you have agents working for you on commission, you may require that they submit sales reports prior to receiving their commission payments.

Review your payment plan with every member of the team, encouraging the person to ask questions, so you can clear up any potential misunderstandings. Your goal is to establish clear expectations in the minds of all team members, so they do not become confused, disappointed, and disgruntled later by payment amounts or schedules that fall short of what they expect.

Tip: Craft payment plans that are clear and simple. An employee shouldn't have to wade through a convoluted compensation agreement to figure out how and when they can expect to get paid. This would only create an opportunity for misunderstandings. Some compensation schemes are going to be complex, but complex doesn't mean unintelligible.

Remember: When you're trying to develop a compensation package, put yourself in the team member's shoes and ask yourself, "Would I invest the time and energy and take on the responsibilities that this job requires for the compensation I'm offering?" If the answer is "No," then you need to review your compensation package.

Dealing with Monetary Compensation

Whenever we mention "compensation," most people automatically assume that we're talking about money. Money, however, is a very basic form of compensation. If you ask most people what they value most about their job, few will highlight their pay and benefits. Money is not what motivates them. Marsha Waddelow says she discovered through Howard Brinton's Star Power Leadership Retreat that retaining talented team members requires more than just throwing money at them. Employees generally stay put not for money, but because they

- Enjoy their job
- Find value in their work
- Like their coworkers
- Feel as though they're treated with kindness and respect
- Feel needed and appreciated

Still, money is one of the most important forms of compensation. Offer too little, and few qualified individuals will even consider joining your team. Those who do join will leave as soon as a better-paying position comes along.

In this section, we discuss various ways to compensate team members monetarily—through salaries, flat-fee and hourly pay, and commissions (performance pay).

Salary

Long-term team members who are not on the front lines building the brand and generating sales may qualify for a salaried position with benefits. Salaried positions may include your listing coordinator, closing coordinator, office manager, or even your second-in-command.

Tip: When compensating long-term team members, start somewhat low until you have a better grasp of their skill sets, energy levels, and level of commitment. You can always adjust up. Be careful not to start too low, however. If you start too low and promise more based on unrealistic goals, they will soon figure that out. Instead of motivating team members, you will have made them resentful and resigned to doing very little.

The salary-plus-benefits package you offer should be commensurate with

• **The job title and responsibilities:** Team members in managerial positions and those who shoulder more of the responsibility should be paid more.

• **The work load:** Team members who are expected to produce more should earn more.

• **The experience and skill level of the team member:** Generally speaking, those who have more experience and skills require less training and are more productive. They should be rewarded accordingly.

• **The market:** You need to know what other team leaders or brokers in your area pay their team members and employees.

Tip: Find out what others are paying in your area for clerical, administrative assistance and general labor, and then use those numbers as a starting point to determine the salary you'll offer for similar positions. You can research salaries online; for example, www.monster.com has a free salary calculator at http://career-advice.monster.com/salary-benefits/home.aspx. You can also ask other team leaders what they pay team members with similar job titles and then adjust up or down based on pay scales in your geographical area.

Flat-fee, work-for-hire arrangements or hourly pay

You are likely to have at least one or two team members who have no vested interest in the team. Short-term employees usually fit in this category because they aren't integral parts of the team. Paying them an hourly fee for the time they put in or a flat fee for the work they perform is usually enough.

These employees hold positions that are easy to fill and require very general skills, such as answering the phone, doing some light filing, delivering marketing packets and For Sale signs, and so on. Offering commissions or salaries to people who perform these tasks would not be practical, so determine a fair hourly rate or flat fee based on the going rate in your market.

Commissions

The best way to motivate and reward the salespeople on your team is to offer commissions—a percentage of the proceeds from every sale they make. Marsha Waddelow of The Waddelow Team, RE/MAX Associates of Arlington, Texas (waddelowteam@hotmail.com) shares her team's commission structure, which pays a higher percentage commission to the most productive agents. Many teams take this same approach, paying commissions on a sliding scale. As an agent earns more in commissions, he or she gets to keep a larger percentage of the total commissions, as shown below:

Gross Commissions	Percentage Split to Agent
$0–$15,000	50%
$15,001–$21,000	55%
$21,001–32,000	60%
$32,001–$45,000	65%
$45,001–$63,000	70%
$63,001–$78,000	75%
$78,001–$150,000	80%
$151,001–$250,000	82.5%
$250,001 and up	85%

Remember, however you choose to split the profits and pay out commissions is up to you. Some teams pay higher commissions and expect their agents to cover more of their expenses. Other teams pay lower commissions but provide team members with additional tools and resources. Nobody has a one-size-fits-all solution.

Tip: Char MacCullum of the Char MacCallum Real Estate Group of Olathe, Kansas (www.char4homes.com), suggests, "Take into account the expenses you are paying on behalf of each team member. My team members don't have to pay for anything other than the expense of their license and educational requirements for their license, their car, cell phone, and any board dues. They need only to follow up with the leads I give them, show and sell the homes, write the contract, and attend inspections and closings. We handle everything else for them; therefore, their commission is less than that of an agent who works for a broker, but they net a lot more because they incur none of the expenses of running a successful real estate business."

Resisting the Temptation to Overpay Buyers' Agents
By Martin Bouma, Team Leader of The Bouma Group (www.bouma.com), Keller Williams Real Estate of Ann Arbor, Michigan

One of the biggest mistakes rainmakers make is overpaying buyers' agents. At first it sounds great. You're losing leads because you don't have time to follow up with them, so your attitude is—at least I'll get something. With this thinking, many rainmakers will pay their buyer's agents as high as 80% splits. This might work if you are truly doing nothing with the leads, and the buyer's agent processes the transaction through to closing.

As your team grows, however, this model doesn't work any more. As you begin adding staff to handle your business, and you start spending more money on marketing, your expenses go up. Many times, expenses begin approaching 50% of Gross Commission Income (GCI). As you start growing into a large team, Costs of Goods Sold (COGS, including company splits, referral pay outs, splits paid to buyer and listing agents, and so on) and expenses eat up to 70% of GCI. In the perfect world, your business model should consist of COGS at 30%, expenses at 30%, and profit at 40%. However, very seldom is a mega-agent disciplined enough to maintain those percentages.

At this point you need to readdress the buyer's agent split. Why would you pay a buyer's agent a 60–80% split when it costs you up to 60% or 70% of GCI to run your business? Even paying a buyer's agent 50% is a losing proposition over time. You are in business to make a profit. Remember that: make a profit, not break even. If you're paying a buyer's agent anything above a 50% split, you are generally not making a profit. They are getting paid more than what the rainmaker would get paid if he or she sold a house, because the profit is seldom more than 40% of GCI.

This is in a perfect world. I can tell you that by talking with many rainmakers in the real estate industry, many of the large teams have expenses that are out of control, and the money that comes to the bottom line is frightening.

By setting up your model before you grow really large, you can set yourself up to be profitable later. Focus on your value proposition versus splits. Many times our buyer's agents get stuck on splits, versus the rainmaker's value proposition. The Bouma Group pays a 40% split to the buyers agent; however, the top buyer's agent will earn over $150,000, and this is with no risk on their part, no prospecting for leads, no expenses, and total support from the team, including handling the transaction from contract through to closing.

The value proposition at the Bouma Group looks as follows:
• An opportunity in the real estate industry to have "a real job"
• High net income ($60,000–$150,000+), with no overhead or risk
• World-class staffing support to fall back on
• Huge marketing budget and ad campaign, which deliver a constant stream of leads
• A solid track record of real estate production and service
• Predesigned marketing and promotional materials
• A consistent inventory of saleable listings
• A system for holding open houses and meeting active buyers
• Preselected, quality vendor alliances
• The prestige and recognition of a proven real estate team.
• An effective fast-start program for qualified agents
• Prepurchased supplies, signs, business cards, forms and materials
• Mentoring from an experienced and respected professional staff
• Teamwork, encouragement, and support with a family feel
• The entire transaction from contract to closing is handled by first-class, competent staff that only enhances your image with your clients. (This frees you up to work with your next clients as opposed to spending hours of your valuable time bringing your transaction to the closing table).

- Top positioning on all Web search engines
- Use of moving truck for clients
- Error and Omissions insurance paid
- Monthly board dues paid
- Computer and numerous software programs provided (Zipform, eNeighborhood, Top Producer, NetMLXchange, etc.)
- An extensive library of useful resources at your fingertips
- The combined knowledge of the entire team
- Spectacular high-visibility office located in downtown Ann Arbor on the corner of a busy intersection, with 22 parking spots
- No expenses, other than cell phone
- NO RISK (long-term leases, and other fixed costs that have to be paid regardless of whether or not there are closings)

Adding Some Benefits to the Mix

Whether you choose to offer benefits, such as medical and dental coverage, life insurance, retirement plans and paid vacations, in addition to monetary compensation, pretty much depends on your market. If every other team in your area offers these benefits, then you must offer them as well in order to compete for the top talent. Ideas for benefits include the following:

- Flex time
- Sick days
- Personal days
- Paid holidays
- Paid vacations
- Medical and dental insurance
- Retirement program
- Continuing education

Tip: If you do offer benefits, consider tying them to certain milestones. For example, you may offer medical and dental coverage to team members who are in good standing after the first six months of employment or allow team members to earn one vacation day per month. You can also trim the cost of offering medical and dental insurance by requiring team members to cover a portion of the insurance premiums.

Raises and Bonuses

As salaried team members become more experienced and provide more value to the team, consider rewarding them with raises or bonuses. Some team leaders we have talked with rely exclusively on a bonus system—as the team generates more revenue and higher profits, they earn more money in the form of bonuses. Other team leaders choose to reward highly productive and self-motivated team members with raises. The option you choose hinges on the goals of your compensation package and what you feel would most effectively motivate the members of your team. See Chapter 13 for more information.

Warning: If you structure a performance bonus into your program, set very specific guidelines for when that bonus is earned. If bonuses become a gray area, we can almost guarantee that at some point in the future you're going to be dealing with disgruntled team members who feel that they have earned a bonus that you feel they have not earned. This is an almost surefire way to lose a great team member or independent contractor.

Treating Team Members as Clients

One of the first steps in running any successful business is to find out who your clients really are. I once coached an owner of a beauty shop who mistakenly believed that his clients were the people who were coming in to have their hair cut and styled, and their nails done. When I explained that his clients were really the people on the floor doing all the work, he was a little taken aback. I told him that the people on the floor were the ones driving the business. He needed to make his clients happy, so they would make their clients happy, and everyone would benefit. As soon as he made the necessary adjustments, his business really took off.

The president of Southwest Airlines has always practiced this strategy. From the very beginning, he understood that his employees were his clients. He makes them happy, and as a result, they happily serve each other and the flying public. This approach has succeeded in driving more flyers to Southwest Airlines and building a strong base of returning customers. *–Ralph R. Roberts*

Profit Sharing

Some team leaders choose to structure their team as a business entity in which all team members share in the profits. With such an arrangement, everyone on the team is a "shareholder," motivating everyone to do their best for the team's success. If you choose to take this approach, make sure the profit sharing is spelled out in the operating agreement or the corporate papers. Consult your accountant and attorney for details in setting up these agreements, which should answer the following questions:

• What are the splits? Does one team member receive a higher percentage than the others or are proceeds to be shared equally?

• When are distributions paid out?

• Does anyone get a salary or wage in addition to distributions? If a particular team member is paid a salary or wage, what do they need to do to earn it?

• Is there a way to buy out a team member?

• What happens if you need to dissolve the company and liquidate its assets? Who gets what?

These are all issues that you should discuss with your attorney when drafting the paperwork. When you are first launching your team and everyone is excited about the venture and getting along with one another, these issues seem as though they will never come up, but as soon as trouble hits, you will be glad that you have something in writing to guide you.

Other Perks

Although people often think of performance compensation in terms of raises, bonuses, and promotions, other perks can be very valuable and useful in motivating and rewarding team members. Some of these perks can even improve their skills:

• **Continuing education:** Sponsoring and supporting self-development serves two purposes. It helps team members acquire new skills while rewarding them for good performance.

• **Team trips:** Taking your entire team or several members of it to the annual NAR convention, for example, can give the team a much-needed break while providing them with an incredible educational opportunity.

• **Retreats:** Sponsoring a team retreat can reenergize everyone on the team and provide you with another way to show your appreciation to team members.

• **Contests:** Sponsoring a contest that generates some spirited competition can be a great way to motivate team members and reward top producers.

- **Team car:** Consider purchasing a nice car or SUV that your buyer's agents can use to drive clients to showings.

- **Productivity tools:** Equipping your team with the latest technologies, so they can become more productive and earn more, can be a tremendous perk.

Marsha Waddelow adds more ideas to the mix—she says that she likes to show her team members appreciation by rewarding them in the following ways:

- Newspaper recognition
- Company recognition
- Rewards to celebrate success, monthly, quarterly, and annually
- Prizes, including paid travel and gift certificates
- Individual benefits
- Family benefits
- Financial success and freedom

Remember: Help your team members to be successful, and you will be successful. A few years ago, I sent my team at Ralph Roberts Realty to the Franklin Covey Planner program. Some complained that it was going to be a full day wasted. The next day I was anxious to hear what they thought. The whole office was abuzz. Everyone spent time to thank me for the great day. They said that it gave them great insight for both their professional and personal lives. My investment was returned tenfold—communication and follow-through really improved. *–Ralph R. Roberts*

Compensating Your Team

Nate Martinez (www.nateshomes.com), a RE/MAX Professional working out of Glendale, Arizona, shares his strategy for compensating agents and other team members:

"My team is set up with commissioned sales agents, salaried staff and one hourly employee. Larry, our field technician, is hourly but maintains enough hours per week to receive holiday pay benefits. I choose to pay my employees a salary for three reasons: to streamline the accounting (payroll only has to be done twice a month), to give team members flexible hours, and to foster a sense of commitment. For people with children or outside activities, we offer the flexibility of working through lunch breaks or over the weekend to make up for hours missed during the standard work day. I feel that an employee will have more commitment to their job when they have a "salary" versus just getting paid per hour.

"In the past, prior to opening RE/MAX Professionals, I offered profit sharing to my employees. I funded the account, and people who worked for my team for a certain number of years were given a portion of the profits. Now, our company offers health benefits, which include dental and life insurance. They also have paid holidays, sick days and personal time off (PTO). It took us a long time to get to the place where we could offer the benefits package, but now that we have it, I think it sets us apart from our competition. Not all real estate offices can afford to offer the package we have put together for our employees.

"Everyone on my sales team is commissioned, except Sarah, who holds a kind of a hybrid position. When an agent joins my team, the person signs a contract that explains the commission splits and compensations for various scenarios that may arise. The compensation agreement between the agents (not between me and the agent—this is between team members) was created by them. They all sat down and came up with what they felt was fair to receive as compensation from their fellow teammates.

"My agents are on a 50/50 split with a few exceptions. If they buy or sell their own property, there is no split and they get to keep all the commission minus any expenses incurred and the E&O insurance. I do this because I want to encourage them to build their own real estate portfolios and help them to start building wealth with real estate investments. Same thing applies if an employee buys or sells a home, assuming they have a real estate license.

"I also offer an additional 5% on the buyer-side transactions, to my sales agents for certain educational achievements. The 50–55% is for all buyer-side transactions. For any listings they take, they receive 15% commission when it closes and $150 for negotiating any listing-side contracts. If they take a listing that came from their sphere of influence, they receive the 15% plus an additional 25% (total of 40%). If they meet with a seller for me to do the listing paperwork only, when it closes they are paid $150.

"Sarah is my office manager/team leader and also a producing agent. I pay her a salary to help me run the day-to-day functions of the team and to keep me on task. She is the only one who can set appointments for me, and she prepares 90% of my listing appointment CMAs. She does most of the follow-up with seller prospects, and she does the lead accountability for the sales team.

"She also negotiates listing contracts for me if I am not available. Prior to her being my manager, Sarah was a buyer's agent and did sales full time. She built her sphere and client base during that time and now only works by referral. Sarah is great at time management, and she'll make up the work over the weekend if she is out with a client during normal business hours. That was our agreement when she took on the position, and it works well for us. We usually talk first thing in the morning and review my schedule and whatever needs my attention for the day. It helps me stay focused and organized. Her first year as my manager, she sold enough houses to cover her salary expense, so it is a win-win for both of us.

"Another compensation idea we implement, which we learned from the Crockett Team, is the Casino game. When a sales agent has a buyer-side closing, they get to roll two dice at the weekly meeting. Whatever they roll on the dice represents the number of one dollar bills they receive. The administration gets to roll one die for each of their closings. The catch to the game is everyone has to be punctual to the meeting, otherwise the agent who had the closings doesn't get to roll and neither does the administrative team. It adds a spin to the accountability of the sales team to make sure they are taking care of their administration team members."

Chapter 7

Safely Navigating the Legal Minefield

As an independent real estate agent, you are accustomed to running your own business, but as soon as you hire an assistant or take on another agent, you expose yourself to a host of new legal issues. If you hire a less qualified candidate for a particular position just because you prefer the person's appearance over other candidates, for example, you could expose yourself to a discrimination lawsuit. If your teammates feel as though they are not receiving fair compensation, they might file a lawsuit.

Although you can never completely eliminate the legal risks of starting and running a business, you can significantly reduce those risks by planning ahead, having clear and comprehensive policies in place and adhering to the written and unwritten regulations that apply to agent teams and small businesses in general.

Note: Whenever you consult an attorney, your attorney's advice is almost always accompanied with a caveat—a glorified disclaimer that says, in essence, "Here is the advice you asked for, BUT...." We offer this entire chapter with a similar caveat. The information we provide is general in nature and may or may not be applicable in your jurisdiction. It is not offered as a substitute for legal advice. We present it only to touch on topics that you should address with your attorney. Before you implement any policies or practices, consult your attorney.

Understanding the Legalities That Govern Your Team

Your agent team may be subject to an assortment of laws and legal hoops you have to jump through in order to protect your business assets and your team from litigation. Although specific laws vary by state, county, and city or town, the laws generally fall into the following categories:

- **Corporate structure:** The first legal decision you will need to make is how to structure your business—as a sole proprietorship, S corporation, LLC, C corporation, partnership, or limited partnership. How you set up your team influences the laws that pertain to your business—see the section "Establishing Your Team as an Official Business Entity," later in this chapter, for details.

- **Finances:** Certain laws are intended to apply to the financial aspect of your business, including the way profits or shares of the business are divided. Laws will vary greatly depending on how your business is structured. If, for example, you are working as a husband-and-wife team, the laws that apply to you will differ from those that apply to two equal partners or to a group of agents who are sharing in the business. Consult your attorney and accountant for details.

• **Taxes:** For many teams, taxes are the biggest challenge. Because state and local tax laws vary and all tax laws are subject to change, we cannot offer much specific guidance in this area, but we can offer some general advice: Keep good records and make sure you track commissions for every agent separately. We cover the nuances of tax laws and working with an accountant in Chapter 8.

• **Labor:** If you become an employer, you will be subject to labor laws. Refer to the section "Being an Equal Opportunity Employer," later in this chapter, for details.

• **Vendors:** Relationships with vendors are typically based on contractual agreements. You and your vendor will be bound by the terms of your arrangement.

• **Referrals:** Depending on where you do business, you may or may not be able to charge a fee when you refer a client to a particular individual or company. If you are able to charge referral fees and decide to do so, having a contract in place that stipulates the conditions of the agreement is always a good idea.

• **Intellectual property:** You need to focus on two areas here—protecting what you are developing as a team and honoring the rights of other individual agents and teams.

Anyone with $100 and a chip on their shoulder can file a lawsuit, so you can never be completely immune to being sued. You can, however, reduce your exposure to lawsuits and other legal action through careful planning and preparation. In the following sections, we explore several strategies that can help you minimize the risk of owning and operating your own agent team.

Note: Defending yourself against a lawsuit can be time-consuming, stressful, and costly. It can also open you up to personal liability. Don't wait for a lawsuit to strike. Be proactive in building your business in such a way that lawsuits are less likely and you are better able to defend yourself when the unavoidable lawsuit comes your way.

Choosing a Qualified Attorney

Hiring an attorney is a major decision, so take some time finding an attorney who is specifically qualified to assist you in legal matters related to real estate. Following are some qualities to consider when searching for an attorney:

• **Years of experience:** All other things being equal, a veteran is usually better than a rookie. A veteran will know the ropes and be more familiar with all the issues that might arise. Veteran attorneys also have a network of people they know and can sometimes call in favors to help smooth out rough issues.

• **Time in court:** How often does this attorney appear in court? This is an important question especially if you are hiring a transactional attorney. This may seem odd, but you actually want an attorney who spends less time in court, meaning that the documents they draft are clearly worded and enforceable. A wise attorney once said that attorneys should draft their documents as if they're drafting evidence, because if any issues arise, those documents will be exhibit one, and a judge will have to interpret them. Clear and unambiguous language that binds the parties (or not) is the goal.

• **Experience in real estate-related law:** Most firms have "practice groups" or areas of focus for groups of their attorneys. An attorney who is in the criminal litigation practice group probably isn't the one you want to hire to help establish the C corp for your agent team. They might be able to find the paperwork needed to get the job done, but you want expert representation. Some firms specialize in business law. These "boutique" firms may cost more, but they often offer specialized legal advice that is worth the extra money.

• **Cost:** As with any service, you want value—high-quality, affordable service. Don't assume that just because an attorney charges $500/hour that the attorney is better than another one who charges $250/hour. Of course, you should never hire an attorney based on the fact that he or she is cheap—it could end up costing you more in the long run.

• **Positive referrals:** One of the best ways to find a good attorney is to obtain a referral from another agent or team in your area. Talk to them, find out why they were pleased, and if they were not pleased, why not? Was the attorney attentive, responsive, available? Did the attorney solve the problem? Contact the state or local bar association for a referral or to perform a rudimentary background check. Was the attorney ever sanctioned? If so, for what? Try to get as much information on the attorney as you can.

• **First impressions and interviews:** The attorney isn't going to automatically agree to represent you without an interview; likewise, you shouldn't necessarily pick the first lawyer you meet. You are going to be working intimately with this person, and you need to know and make sure that you can work together. Ask questions that will give you insight into their attitude and approach.

• **Positive references:** Ask the attorney for references. Of course, the attorney is probably going to steer you in the direction of satisfied clients, but it is still a good check. If the attorney isn't willing to give references, why not? Is his or her reason valid, or is it a smokescreen for something you need to be concerned about?

• **Web site and biography:** If the attorney has a Web site or blog, check it out and read the person's biography. You may also want to Google the person's name to see if anyone else has something to say about him or her.

Establishing Your Team as an Official Business Entity

Although your team can function as a loosely organized group of individuals, incorporating the business can often help establish the team as a business entity. It gives the business an official name, assists in handling some of the issues surrounding compensation, provides your team with important legal protections, and can even save the team money on income taxes.

If your team is considering forming a business entity, then you should sit down with an attorney and discuss all the pros and cons. You need to make some fairly significant considerations, including organizational structure, profit sharing, membership interests, and tax considerations.

The legal structure you choose for your business can be your best protection in the event that a client or team member files a lawsuit against you. Which type of business entity is best for you, we really cannot say, but we can offer some general recommendations. In the following sections, we describe the most common business entities for agent teams and point out the pros and cons of each. In most cases, a limited liability corporation (LLC) is the way to go, but because it offers the combined advantages of other structures, we discuss it last in this section.

Warning: Some people foolishly believe that a business entity gives the proprietor of the business carte blanche to do whatever they want with no liability. How wrong they are! Certain business entities may prevent business-related lawsuits from affecting your personal finances, but they do not provide full protection for the business entity itself. You still must abide by the laws. Another common misconception is that setting up separate business entities for separate departments or divisions in your business fully protects each entity from the liabilities of other entities. While that may hold true in some cases, it isn't guaranteed. If the entities act in a certain way, or fail to follow the rules required to keep the entities separate, they may be viewed as mere alter egos or a "shell company," and a plaintiff might be able to "pierce the corporate veil." When that happens, it exposes all of the company's assets and may even result in making the owners personally liable.

Overall, establishing your team as a separate business entity is a great way to minimize personal risk and to limit liability. Working with an attorney who has expertise in this area can create even more protection. Don't try to set it up all by yourself. An attorney who specializes in this will be well aware of various strategies that can help insulate your personal assets from your business risks.

Sole Proprietorship

A sole proprietorship is not much of a business entity at all. The business owner and the business are one in the same. When sole proprietors file their personal tax returns, for example, the return contains all the tax information for the business. The major benefit of structuring a business as a sole proprietorship is that it is simple. As long as you are the sole "owner" of your team, you make all the management decisions, and you enjoy all the profits or suffer all the losses, you can set up your team as a sole proprietorship. You can even hire employees.

A sole proprietorship that has employees operates under the principals of common law *agency*—an *agent* (employee) acting on behalf of a *principal* (business owner). In a sole proprietorship, the principal becomes liable for the actions of his or her agent.

To establish an agency relationship, you need to satisfy three conditions:

• **The agent and the principal must have a fiduciary relationship.** A fiduciary relationship essentially means that the agent is required to act in the best interest of the principal. You can compare it to a case of a stock broker investing money on behalf of a client.

• **The principal must consent to the agent that the agent shall act on the principal's behalf and be subject to the principal's control.** In other words, the principal has to consent to allow the agent to act on his or her behalf, and the principal must exercise control over the agent.

  - As principal, you can become liable for an agent's action by either giving the agent *actual authority* (detailed instructions to carry out a specific task) or giving the agent power to act without spelling out the details.

  - Another type of authority is *apparent authority*, in which the principal has not actually given the agent any authority to act on his or her behalf. Apparent authority involves a third party who is led to believe that the agent is acting on the principal's behalf. For example, the principal may tell a car dealer that she will be sending her employee (agent) to pick up the car. When the employee shows up, the car dealer reasonably concludes that the employee is acting as the agent of the principal.

· • The agent must consent to act under the control of the principal and solely in the best interests of the principal. This reinforces what the previous two items already establish.

Warning: Unfortunately, the simplicity of sole proprietorships carry significant risks. The first risk is created by the very nature of the structure—you're liable for the actions (even negligent actions) of anyone who is working for you (employees) or representing you (agents). In other words, if someone on your team is accused of fraud or negligence, you could be held legally responsible. You could lose everything. And because a sole proprietorship provides no separation between your business and personal assets, your personal assets would also be at risk. Because this risk is so great, we strongly recommend that you structure your team as a business entity that provides you with greater legal protection.

Partnership

A partnership is an association of two or more persons who act as co-owners to run a business for profit. One advantage of a partnership is that for tax purposes, the IRS does not recognize the partnership as a separate entity; thus, the profits and losses flow through to the individual partners, and the entity itself does not have to pay taxes (although the partnership must still file a return).

Partnerships are primarily used for business ventures that involve the joint holding of assets that appreciate, such as real estate or businesses. If you are the sole "owner" of your team, then a partnership is not an option.

Forming a partnership requires no formal steps, but having a partnership agreement in place (although not required) is essential. Without an agreement in writing, any conflict will be decided based not on the planning of the partners but rather on the guidelines in the UPA (Uniform Partnership Act) and RUPA (Revised Uniform Partnership Act). Ask your attorney whether your state has adopted either of these acts, because it could affect the way the partnership is handled upon dissolution. Generally speaking, all partners are jointly and severally liable for all obligations of the partnership, meaning that any or all of them can be sued for claims against the partnership. This general rule varies somewhat between UPA and RUPA, so ask your attorney for specifics.

Your partnership agreement should include the following:

• **Nature and purpose:** State the type of business, the purpose of your relationship, and the roles that each of you will play in the partnership.

• **Capital contributions:** State how much start-up capital each partner is contributing to the business and how they will be reimbursed once the business becomes profitable. If more capital is required later, what percentage of the needed capital is each partner responsible for contributing? What happens if that partner cannot contribute his or her portion?

• **Profit & loss sharing:** Specify how the partners will share any profits or losses, including how the accounting will be done and how profits and losses will be reported to all partners.

• **Authority:** How much authority does each partner have in running the team and making decisions? Spell it out.

• **Signature authority:** Who has to sign checks, documents, and agreements with vendors? Are two or more signatures required or does one person hold sole authority?

• **Addition of new partners:** If you add new partners later, how will the profits be divided? Make sure this is addressed well in advance of taking on any new partners.

• **Dissolution of the partnership:** This is one of the most important areas of any partnership agreement. If the partnership dissolves for whatever reason, this provides you with an exit strategy. Your partnership agreement should cover the following:

  - **Death of a partner:** If a partner dies, how will that partner's shares be distributed? Will they be given to the deceased's family or distributed among other partners?

  - **Buyout:** Under what conditions can partners buy out the interest of another partner—death, divorce, bankruptcy, illegal activity? Specify the circumstances and how the buyout amount will be calculated.

  - **Division of clients:** Who gets to keep existing clients? Which clients does a partner who's leaving get to take?

  - **Division of property:** If the partners jointly own property, how will that property be divided when the partnership dissolves?

  - **Ongoing transactions:** If a partner who is leaving has outstanding transactions, what percentage of the commissions, if any, is the partner entitled to?

Your partnership agreement should also indicate whether this is a *general* or *limited partnership*. In a general partnership, all partners share in the management and liability of the team. Limited partners have little or no say in the management of the team and can limit their personal exposure to liability. Defining what it means to be a limited partner can be confusing and complex, so consult your attorney.

Remember: When forming a partnership agreement, you and your partner(s) should each be represented by your own attorneys to ensure that each partner's interests are protected.

Tip: Because of the lack of legal protection afforded by partnerships, they have fallen out of favor, but they are still a viable way to structure a business entity when two or more owners are involved. Drawing up a partnership agreement, however, can be a very complex operation, so consult an attorney with experience in this area.

C Corporation

A properly incorporated C corporation (C corp for short) is its own distinct entity. It is separate and apart from its shareholders and can thus sue and be sued. The main benefit to the shareholders is that they are not personally liable for what the corporation does or fails to do, unless the corporate veil is pierced. An attorney can pierce the corporate veil by proving that the corporation failed to observe corporate formalities or was acting merely as a façade for the operations of the dominant stockholder(s).

C corps offer a couple of additional benefits, including the ability to form mergers and offer employee benefits packages with favorable tax treatment. A C corp, for example, can offer an employee health plan and other such perks and claim the cost against earnings. This is one reason why most C corps exist—you generally can't claim the costs of healthcare plans and other benefits against earnings with a partnership or S corp.

The drawbacks of C corps generally revolve around the fact that they are relatively complex to set up and manage, and they tend to carry a heavier tax burden:

• Establishing a C corp requires state filings of articles of incorporation and the establishment of corporation bylaws.

• Banks and lenders may refuse to extend credit to corporations with limited assets unless the shareholders agree to make personal guarantees. When this occurs, the shareholders are personally liable for the loans.

• A corporation cannot make decisions on its own despite its separate legal status. A board of directors is elected and carries out the functions of the corporation. The board of directors can then select corporate officers to carry out the daily functions of the corporation. The directors are generally protected from liability by what is known as the business judgment rule (BJR). The BJR protects the individual director from liability unless it can be shown that the director somehow violated a duty or was somehow not making informed decisions. The board and/or officers are also further protected by indemnity clauses in the corporate charter or bylaws.

• C corps are subject to what is known as the double tax. The corporation is taxed as a separate entity, and the distribution is taxed at the time it is distributed to shareholders. One way a C corp could get around this is to not distribute earnings to shareholders, so Congress devised an accumulated earnings tax that is levied on all earnings that exceed $250,000 and are not distributed. All of this gets very complex, so consult your attorney and accountant for details. At this point, you should simply be aware that there are additional tax issues when forming a C corp.

Note: No universally adopted set of rules for setting up a C corp exist; however, many states have adopted the MBCA (Model Business Corporations Act) or have modeled their state statutes after it.

You would generally only see a C corp used when you have a very large organization, because they are complex and expensive to operate. They do provide some flexibilities over an S corp, but the double taxation is usually enough to scare people away from using them. Few teams are structured as C corps.

S Corporation

The S corporation (or S corp for short) is a bit like a hybrid of the partnership and a C corporation. An S corp is organized under subchapter S of the Internal Revenue Code and therefore allows for pass-through treatment of profits like that of a partnership, yet it still affords the full protections from liability to its owners as a regular C corp. In exchange for liability protection, an S corp requires filings and registration with the state similar to what's required for creating a C corp.

One of the main advantages that an S corp has over a C corp is that an S corp is free from the dreaded double taxation explained in the previous section. The S corp is not taxed at the corporate level. Only the distributions are taxed.

Another main difference is that an S corp is unable to have certain stock-holders as owners. A business cannot elect S corp status if it has a shareholder that is a corporation, a partnership, a nonresident alien, a bank, or an insurance company. A business wishing to have one of these as a shareholder is stuck with C corp status and cannot take advantage of the S corp benefits.

Another restriction and trade-off for pass-through distributions is that the corporation cannot have more than 100 shareholders, and those shares cannot be of more than one class of stock. That means you can't have both preferred and common stock inside an S corp. You are permitted, however, to have voting and nonvoting stock without violating the S corp restrictions.

Warning: A company may elect S corp status, but it must be careful not to violate the rules, or it will be automatically booted from S corp favor and forced to operate as a C corp, which can create potentially thousands or even millions of dollars worth of tax liability depending on the size of the company.

An S corp is a viable option for agent teams, but the restrictions on who can be an owner of S corp stock can often cause problems if not managed carefully. Also, an S corp is a tax election, so if you violate the rules of the S corp you'll get thrown into C corp status, which can result in big tax consequences. Make sure to comply with all the rules.

Limited Liability Company

The limited liability company (LLC) is often referred to as the "ultimate structure" or the "best of both worlds," because it combines the benefits of both corporations and partnerships without the disadvantages of either:

- Like a corporation, an LLC allows its members to fully participate in the management of the business without incurring personal liability, and it is organized as a creature of state law. It also allows for perks and benefits commonly reserved for C corps.

- Like a general partnership, an LLC allows for the favorable pass-through tax benefit, but it also avoids the restrictions of the S corp eligibility requirements. The LLC can have more than 100 members and it does not prevent partnerships, corporations, nonresident aliens, and trusts from being member owners.

Because an LLC is a business entity, it can carry on any lawful business purpose or activity. It can incur debt and is liable to creditors, but it does not create a liability for its members for these obligations. Piercing the corporate veil, as with a C corp, is still a possibility, but it does shield its members from personal liability for LLC obligations.

How do you make money in an LLC? A manager can receive a salary or an hourly wage per the operating agreement, but more typically members are paid their shares in profit distributions or by selling their interest in the LLC. The operating agreement will again govern when distributions are made, to whom, and in what ratio, and will also set the rules for selling (if allowed) membership interest.

Although the LLC is a type of business entity unto itself, it has several subtypes, including the following three major subtypes:

- **Member managed:** Member owners manage the LLC's daily business affairs and decisions, as they do in a general partnership.

- **Manager managed:** A select group of manager(s), who may be, but don't have to be, the member owners, manage the LLC's daily business affairs and decisions, similar to the way a board of directors manages a C corp.

- **Professional:** Reserved for professional service providers, including doctors and lawyers, a professional LLC provides personal liability protection for the errors, omissions, and negligence of other professionals under his/her supervision and control. The PLLC doesn't remove liability for the member's own actions, but can limit liability for contracts not personally guaranteed by the individual.

Your choice pretty much boils down to member managed or manager managed, and when making your choice, you should consider one point very carefully: A member in a manager-managed LLC does not owe the company a fiduciary duty. This means that a member owner in a manager-managed LLC is free to compete with the LLC for contracts. In a member-managed LLC, all member owners owe a fiduciary duty to the LLC and cannot compete with it for business. This is only one consideration to make, however. If you need to be the head honcho, then a manager-managed LLC is probably the best choice, regardless of whether other member owners can compete with the LLC.

The "existence" of an LLC begins when the articles of organization are filed with the state. A member may acquire membership upon making a contribution to the LLC. LLCs operate primarily under contract law, because they function based on the articles of organization and an operating agreement (which doesn't have to be in writing, but should be). Your operating agreement should account for important issues, including voting, decision making and daily management, and transfer of membership interests. Draw up your operating agreement with a competent attorney in the field.

Tip: In general, an LLC is a great business entity that incorporates many of the benefits of multiple entities and may be just the business structure you're looking for when establishing your team. Establishing a team in which each team member is given an LLC membership interest in return for an initial capital contribution can provide a very effective structure allowing the profits to flow freely through the hard work of the managers or members. Seek out a competent attorney who can more fully evaluate your individual situation and make the best business recommendation to fit your needs.

Being an Equal Opportunity Employer

If your team consists of you and your spouse, you probably do not need to worry about your employer-employee relationship. You are functioning as business partners who have an equal stake in the business. As soon as you hire an assistant or someone else to work in the office, however, you officially become an employer, complete with legal obligations.

Most labor laws are intended to prevent discriminatory hiring practices, ensure safety, and make sure everyone is paid minimum wage or better. Penalties are in place to punish employers who violate state or federal antidiscrimination laws in the workplace. In a real estate office, as long as you are hiring the best person for the job, regardless of race, color, gender, or creed, and are compensating your staff equitably for the work they perform, you really should have no worries in this area.

To make sure your team is adhering to the current laws in your area, consult an attorney who is well versed in labor laws. In the following sections, we provide a brief overview of federal and state guidelines.

Remember: Labor laws apply to more than only hiring practices. They apply to all aspects of employment, including compensation. Anyone on your team who functions in a leadership capacity should be well aware of the applicable rules and regulations.

Federal guidelines

Federal employment guidelines are similar to state guidelines and are applicable to the states via the 14th amendment to the U.S. Constitution and the Civil Rights Act of 1964. The 14th amendment provides equal protection under the law to all citizens of the United States, regardless of race, color, or creed. The federal government also protects uniformed servicemen and women under the Uniformed Services Employment and Reemployment Rights Act, and certain "qualified" employees under the Family and Medical Leave Act. These two acts have specific requirements and you should check into the details, but essentially they require an employer to keep an employee's job available to them if they leave for uniformed (military) service, or for the purposes of caring for a newborn child or a spouse, child or parent who has a serious medical condition.

The Equal Employment Opportunity Commission (EEOC) has established equal employment guidelines for the federal government. The laws apply to state and federal employers, private employers, and educational institutions. The employee or applicant for employment cannot be discriminated against based on race, color, religion, sex, or national origin. It also prevents discrimination and requires affirmative action to employ and advance certain individuals such as those with disabilities and veterans of The Vietnam War.

An employer is also prohibited from age discrimination and from discriminating in the payment of wages based on gender (paying men more than women, for instance). Under both state and federal law, it is unlawful to punish or fire someone who files an equal opportunity complaint against an employer. This is done so that the employees are not bullied into just tolerating the discrimination against them or another employee.

These rules are not difficult to comply with, but they are important, and again it comes down to you hiring the best person for the job and compensating employees fairly for the work and responsibility they take on.

State guidelines

State guidelines are obviously state specific, but they primarily take their direction from federal guidelines and adhere to civil rights requirements. As an employer, you may be required by law to post antidiscrimination laws in your office or in a conspicuous place in your building. Discriminating against anyone based on religion, race, color, national origin, gender, disability, age, marital status, or family status is illegal and is subject to penalty.

Each state may add its own definition of what it considers to be a protected class, but they cannot choose to ignore a federally protected class. States may add sexual orientation, height, weight, arrest record, genetic information, medical history, and other qualities to the list of characteristics that cannot be discriminated against.

Other ways to ensure you're protected

Although adhering to federal, state, and local employment laws is your best protection, you have a couple other options that can help insulate you from labor lawsuits:

- Hiring through employment agencies: Few team leaders we talked with like to hire through employment agencies, but this is certainly an option—an option that can provide you with some additional legal protection. The employment agency assumes much of the liability, making it easier for you to fire someone who's not working out, avoid discrimination lawsuits, and "rent" employees for only the time you need them.

• Hiring virtual assistants (VAs): In Chapter 4, we discuss some of the benefits of hiring virtual assistants (freelancers who typically work out of their homes and conduct most of their business over the Internet). One of the main benefits to hiring virtual assistants is that they make you immune to many of the liabilities of hiring people to work at your place of business. Hiring virtual assistants is more like dealing with contractors than with employees. You simply contract for a specific project or hire the VA when needed, and if the person doesn't work out, you never use that person again.

Drawing Up a Businessperson's Prenup

When a partnership or a team dissolves, the separation can be almost as messy as a divorce. This is why it is a good idea to have the equivalent of a prenuptial agreement in place whenever you establish your team. In the following sections, we lead you through the process of identifying your team's assets and then establishing a policy upfront, describing how you will liquidate those assets in the event the relationship ends.

Tip: Keep impeccable records concerning your assets and the way those assets are to be divided. If your team does dissolve, you should have a clear system in place that leaves nothing open to question.

Enabling your team members to sign off

When you establish your team as a separate business entity, you create a valuable asset that can continue to exist long after you have any interest in it. You can then pass the team down to family members, just like any other inheritance, sell your interest in the team to someone else, or retain ownership and still collect dividends during your retirement.

When you are building a team, you really need to give some thought to how you and other team members can ultimately dispose of their interest in the team. Can a team member, for example, sell his or her interest in the team to another party? Does the team have to approve of the person purchasing that interest? Can a team member pass ownership along to a family member?

Consult a qualified corporate attorney in your area to assist you and your team in answering these questions and others. This helps everyone sleep a little better at night, trust one another, and function more effectively without having to worry so much about the future.

Managing your team's collective assets

When you build a team as a business entity, you create a salable asset complete with assets (plural). In the course of your day-to-day business, you may overlook the importance and value of certain assets, such as the phone number that clients call to get in touch with your team or the Web site you created to promote the team. Who owns those assets, and how do you liquidate them if team members decide to part company?

When you draw up your partnership or corporate papers, make sure they include language instructing how the assets are to be divided in the event that the team is dissolved:

- For assets collectively owned by the team, the language should state that each team member is given his or her fair share of the asset's value.

- If a team member owns a particular asset, documentation should show that the asset is the sole property of that team member. (In some cases, the team member is better off leasing the asset to the team to avoid any disagreement later.)

A team's assets can be as obvious as the fleet of cars used to drive clients around or as obscure as a toll-free phone number or Internet domain name. However, all of these assets have value, and you should identify and account for them all. The following list of assets can help you begin to identify your team's assets:

- **Physical assets:** Physical assets consist of the obvious assets that your team owns, including computers, phones, file cabinets, vehicles, and real estate. Are these assets owned by the team, or the business entity? The answer to that question may not seem so obvious, especially when emotions are running high in the event that team members are heading off in separate directions.

- **Phone number:** Your team should have a single phone number that clients and prospective clients can call to obtain assistance. Individual team members may have their own phone numbers, as well, which are completely separate. The team's phone number should be owned by the business entity, not by any individual team member. If the business is sold, this phone number is included with the business.

- **Internet addresses:** Domain names, e-mail addresses, Web site addresses and blog addresses are all very important and valuable assets. After your team establishes a presence on the Internet, clients and prospective clients immediately learn these addresses and use them to gather information about and communicate with the team. These assets should also be owned by the business entity rather than any individual team member.

- **Database:** Perhaps the most valuable asset your team will develop is its database of clients and their contact information. The person who has control of the leads is the person who has control of the business.

Make sure you have policies in place to determine which clients belong to whom and who keeps the database if the team dissolves.

Tip: Consider putting a system in place that keeps a record of which team member acquired each new client. When it comes time to distribute client information to team members, each team member can receive his or her portion of the database.

• Property management accounts: Some companies manage real estate for landlords and owners in return for a servicing fee. If your team is involved in managing properties, then this is as much an asset as any listing you might have. These are like accounts payable.

Tip: Your team should have a life insurance policy for each key member of the team. If you would need $200,000 to replace your team leader with someone who could fill the position, then make sure you have $200,000 in key member life insurance. Planning for unfortunate occurrences can keep a difficult time from becoming a devastating one.

Handling Contracts

The relationships you have with your broker and your team members are likely to be long term and hopefully very profitable for all involved, but they're nonetheless business relationships and need to be approached as such. Although business is often said to have no emotions, business transactions often become very emotional and personal. Don't let emotions get in the way of making good business decisions; an attorney can help in this area. Throughout negotiations, strive to establish good working relationships with all your team members and with your broker. The agreement/contract should insure and preserve those relationships. In this section, we help you achieve that goal.

With your broker

Many real estate brokers are more accustomed to working with independent agents than with teams. A few may even consider agent teams to be in competition with them. The fact is that brokers and agent teams can form symbiotic and synergistic relationships that benefit everyone involved. An agent team can generate more revenue for the broker, and a trusted broker can give an agent team instant credibility along with the office space and support required to run a business.

One of the issues that often arises between agent teams and brokers is related to commissions. Agent teams cost more to run but tend to generate more revenue, so team leaders often feel as though they deserve a bigger slice of the pie. After all, by building and maintaining a team, they are taking on a bigger risk. Brokers who are unaccustomed to working with teams, however, may not want to budge on the commissions. As a team, you need to clearly communicate the additional expenses of running your team, the risks involved, and the increased revenue your team will bring in. In other words, you have to sell your broker on your agent team model, as discussed in Chapter 9.

When contracting with your broker, enlist a team spokesperson to ensure that the entire team is speaking with one voice. This benefits both the team and the broker. Prior to the meeting between the broker and the team spokesperson, the entire team should sit down and discuss all of the issues they want addressed. Work toward establishing a consensus and then highlight areas that are negotiable and those that are not. This shouldn't be like the United Auto Workers/Ford Motor Company negotiating standoff, but the team should be on the same page concerning what is and isn't negotiable. Following are some of the contract terms that you should consider:

- Team responsibilities (performance related):
    - Additional team expenses
    - Ability to hire clerical staff
    - Errors and omissions insurance and liability insurance
    - Minimum performance numbers
- Broker responsibilities (compensation related):
    - Overhead expenses (general)
    - Split percentages
    - Advertising incentives
- Remedies for nonpayment and for nonperformance
- Termination provisions
- Confidentiality provisions
- Noncompete provision (radius, time)
- Training programs
- Ability to market the team as well as the broker
- Renewal provisions

Remember: Before signing a broker contract, review it carefully and have your team's attorney review it as well. Be wary of signing any boilerplate or standard contract. Remember, as a team, you are bringing more to the table than an individual, independent agent, so you deserve some special treatment and compensation. Do your best to convince the broker that your team is worth this special consideration, but if your broker will not make concessions, then you may have no other choice but to present your offer to another broker. This would be a permanent, end-of-discussion decision, so don't make it lightly—sometimes, however, it's necessary.

Warning: Some states may require that one of the team members be an associate broker because of compensation restrictions. If the team is not under an associate broker, you may encounter an issue with paying commissions to a non-regulated company.

With your team members

Consider drawing up a contract that lays out the terms of your agreement with each new team member you bring on board. Contracts with team members should address the following points:

- **Team name:** What the team will be called and who owns the name.

- **Duration:** Whether the team is being set up for a long-term (perpetual) venture or for a fixed period of time or a specific project or transaction.

- **Capital contributions:** What capital contribution each member must make for their membership interest.

- **Additional capital contributions:** Whether members will need to make additional contributions and what, if anything, will trigger that capital call.

- **Distributions:** What ratio or percentage interest each team member will receive and how and when distributions will be paid. If a capital contribution was called for and not paid, is that member still entitled to full distribution? Offset distribution? No distribution?

- **Other compensation:** Will anyone receive compensation other than distributions? If so, what will they do for that money?

- **Scope:** What will be the business of the team? Will it be limited to real estate or open to any legally profitable ventures?

- **Business address:** What is the address of the team/company?

- **Job responsibility:** Specify the person's job title and duties. What must the person do to remain a member of the team in good standing and earn the specified compensation?

Your contract with team members can be structured very much like a partnership agreement, as described in the section on partnerships earlier in this chapter.

Caution: We often hear stories of agent teams gone bad. Driven by greed, team members choose to increase revenue through fraudulent means and drag the entire team into a real estate or mortgage fraud conspiracy that can destroy the business. All agents and other members of your team should be required to take real estate and mortgage fraud training, so they can spot the signs of fraud, stop it in its tracks, and report it to the team leader and other authorities. For more information, pick up a copy of *Protect Yourself from Real Estate and Mortgage Fraud: Preserving the American Dream of Homeownership* by Ralph R. Roberts and Rachel Dollar (Kaplan Publishing). Let your team know that a failure to report a suspected incident of fraud makes the person guilty of conspiracy.

The following provisions from an LLC demonstrate some of the issues that team members should consider when structuring their team. Assuming the team starts an LLC, these issues should be addressed in the LLC's Operating Agreement.

Purpose. The Company has been formed for the purpose or purposes enumerated in the Articles. The purpose of the Company is to engage in any activity for which limited liability companies may be formed under the Act, including, the building, marketing and selling of.... The Company shall have all the powers necessary or convenient to affect any purpose for which it is formed, including all powers granted by the Act.

Duration. The Company shall commence on the date of filing of the Articles with the Bureau and shall continue in perpetuity until the Company dissolves and its affairs are wound up in accordance with the Act or this Operating Agreement.

Title to Property. All company property shall be owned by the company as an entity and no member shall have any ownership interest in such property in the member's individual name or right, and each member's interest in the company shall be personal property for all purposes. Except as otherwise provided in this agreement, the company shall hold all company property in the name of the company and not in the name or names of any member or members.

Admission of New Members. The Members may, by UNANIMOUS vote, pursuant to and in accordance with the terms of this Operating Agreement, admit as an Admitted Member any Person determined by the Members to satisfy the criteria established by the Members, in their sole and absolute discretion, for membership in the Company. The Person shall, before being admitted as a Member of the Company and as a condition to admission, execute any documents required by the Company, agreeing to be and become a Member of the Company, subject to all of the terms and conditions of this Operating Agreement. The

Company may issue additional Shares in the Company to new Members on whatever terms and conditions and for whatever consideration, if any, the Members determine.

No Right of Withdrawal. The Members shall not have any right of withdrawal or any right to receive any payment or distribution from the Company on any actual or purported withdrawal. The Members agree not to withdraw, and they waive any right of withdrawal and any right to receive any payment or distribution on withdrawal provided for or under the Act.

Death or Incapacity.

• The death, incompetence, withdrawal, expulsion, bankruptcy or dissolution of a Member, or the occurrence of any event which terminates the continued membership of a Member in the company, SHALL NOT cause a dissolution of the company unless such member is the manager of the company.

• Any event which terminates the continued membership of the Manager-Member in the company, SHALL cause a dissolution of the company unless all other members UNANIMOUSLY consent and vote to continue the company.

Prohibition on Transfers of Shares. The Members each agree that they will not voluntarily, involuntarily, or by operation of law sell, transfer, assign, encumber, pledge, convey, or otherwise dispose of (Transfer) part or all of the Shares they now own or may acquire at a later time except pursuant to the terms and conditions of this article.... Any Transfer or attempted Transfer in violation of this article shall be null and void and of no effect.

Mandatory Offer to Sell in Case of a Bona Fide Offer. If any Member desires for any reason to Transfer any of the Shares then owned by the Member pursuant to an offer to purchase the Shares received from another person (a Bona Fide Offer), the selling Member shall immediately provide the Company and all other Members with written notice together with a copy of the Bona Fide Offer and all related agreements and documents. For 60 days following the receipt of the written notice and documents or for 30 days following the determination of the Purchase Price (as defined in section 9.11) under the terms and provisions of this article IX, whichever period is longer, the Company shall have the exclusive right and option (First Option), but not the obligation, to elect to purchase all (but not merely part) of the Shares subject to the Bona Fide Offer either (a) at the same price and terms as in the Bona Fide Offer or (b) at the price and terms in this Operating Agreement.

Death and Permanent Disability. Each Member who is a natural person agrees for himself or herself and his or her representatives or successors that, on his or her death or Permanent Disability, the Member shall be deemed to have made an offer to sell all of his or her Shares.

Setoff. Each Member agrees and acknowledges that if any amount is or becomes payable by the Member to the Company, the Company shall have the option to elect to reduce, on a dollar-for-dollar basis, any amount due or payable to the debtor Member under this Operating Agreement or otherwise by any amount due or payable by the debtor Member to the Company. This elective right of setoff shall be cumulative and in addition to any other remedies to which the Company may be entitled at law or equity.

Act Causing Dissolution.

• (a) the time, if any, specified in the Articles;

• (b) the happening of the event, if any, specified in the Articles;

• (c) the affirmative unanimous vote of the Members to dissolve the Company;

• (d) the sale or other disposition of all or substantially all of the assets of the Company;

• (e) the entry of a decree of judicial dissolution

Tip: Team members may also want to draw up contracts with one another that fuel success and allow each team member to focus on his or her area of expertise. If you have a member who is dynamite at getting listings, for example, but simply doesn't like to show homes, and another who loves working with buyers, you might just have a match made in heaven. The two agents could contract with each other to deliver the piece that the other lacks. They could simply agree that the one agent would refer all the listings she comes across to the listing expert, and the listing expert would likewise push all the buyers to the buyer's expert. Or, they could negotiate a contract to refer each other business for a referral fee.

Remember: Contracts between agents should serve to enhance the team, not to exclude other team members. Make sure all contracts are above board and have everyone's approval. If they get in the way of the team's success, you may want to put a policy in place stating that such agreements aren't allowed.

Chapter 8

Managing the Money

Assuming your team is even moderately successful, a lot of money is flowing through your office. You have to make sure that money is handled with extreme care and that everyone in the office is well aware of the cash flow. Any misappropriation of funds or confusion among team members about how the money is handled could potentially undermine the team and perhaps even lead to legal problems.

In this chapter, we team up with Ashley Leigh of The Ashley Leigh Team (www.ashleyleighteam.com) of Linton Hall, Realtors in Gainesville, Virginia, and Jerry VanGoethem, a specialist in small-business accounting, to provide you with strategies and tips for managing your team's money, choosing a qualified accountant, building a system of checks and balances, and making sure your team stays on track with weekly, quarterly and annual financial statements. By the end of this chapter, you will have the knowledge and expertise to act as your team's CFO or at least put someone in charge who is qualified to handle the financial operations for your team.

Throughout this chapter, we offer guidance and tips on how to handle the finances for your real estate team and deal with tax issues related to your business. To brush up on small-business tax basics, check out the IRS Small Business and Self-Employed One-Stop Resource at www.irs.gov/businesses/small/index.html.

Hiring an Accountant with Experience in Real Estate

Independent agents who are first starting out rarely see the need for an accountant, let alone one who specializes in real estate. Experienced agents who have plenty of income rolling in and perhaps even some of their own investment properties on the side, however, soon realize that good accountants are worth their weight in gold. Qualified accountants more than pay for themselves in the amount they can save you at tax time.

When you start a team, having an accountant on call is even more important. You now have more money coming into your business, more people sharing that revenue, and some payroll issues to deal with. Trying to take on this burden yourself or share it with other team members is often a costly mistake.

Warning: If you fail to set up your accounting the right way from the get-go, you are at risk of losing out in the long run by paying higher taxes and penalty fees, and having to hire a team of accountants to come in and clean up the mess. Prior to launching your team, meet with an accountant, so you have everything in place before more people and financial complexities enter the picture.

Learn from My Mistakes

When I first started Ralph Roberts Realty, I didn't have the benefit of the advice we offer in this chapter. I started my team and simply added personnel on the fly. When the person in charge of receivables couldn't keep up, I hired another person to pick up the slack. When the person managing payables fell behind, I hired another assistant.

Finally, I met with a CPA who came in, revamped my system, and hired a full-time bookkeeper. I now had one person handling all my finances in house and a CPA in charge of overseeing operations and handling the macro-accounting tasks. My CPA set up the systems, checks, and balances that are still in place today.

You don't have to have a full-time bookkeeper as part of your staff. You can hire a firm that will come in once a month and take care of your accounting. You can also hire a payroll service for a very reasonable price. *–Ralph R. Roberts*

Recognizing the value of a specialized CPA

As a real estate professional, you know the value of specialization, so you advise buyers to use a buyer's agent when purchasing a home and a seller's agent when placing their home on the market. Specialization is important in other fields as well, including accounting. A CPA (certified public accountant) who has experience in bookkeeping for real estate teams offers the following benefits:

• **Assists in making decisions regarding the best type of business entity to create for your team.** Can you save more on taxes by running your team as an S corp or an LLC? A CPA may be able to guide you in answering this question. For more about incorporating your business, refer to Chapter 7.

• **Recommends accounting systems that work well with agent teams.** Your CPA should be able to help you put systems in place that streamline the operations of your internal accounting department and result in better record keeping. If the CPA has other agent teams as clients, he or she already knows how they manage their books.

• **Manages your payroll and ensures that you provide all necessary tax forms to team members, employees, and independent contractors.** Your CPA or payroll service can even help you set up your accounting system to automate the process of keeping records.

Remember: Determining which team members are commissioned salespeople, which are employees, and which are independent contractors is very important, because you need to be fully informed of your payroll obligations as they relate to each group. (We explain that process in Chapter 6.) For example, you can pay an independent contractor a flat fee and issue the person Form 1099 at the end of the year, reporting exactly how much you paid him or her. With in-house employees, on the other hand, you need to withhold payroll taxes and keep detailed records of how much you withheld for federal, state, and local taxes, as well as Social Security and Medicare.

• **Advises you on compensation packages for different team members.** If you have no idea what is considered fair compensation, the CPA can offer advice based on experience with other agent teams.

• **Monitors your business growth and offers relevant and creative strategies to make the necessary adjustments.**

• **Advises you on how to maximize retirement plans for you and your fellow team members and other staff.**

• **Assists you with setting up health plans, employee compensation packages, college funds, and medical funds.**

• **Increases your after-tax earnings.** The CPA knows about any tax laws that apply specifically to real estate agents and can help use those laws in your favor.

The right CPA can serve as a key member of your team. My (Ralph's) CPA has enabled me to set up trust agreements for my children, my wife, and myself; put together a profit-sharing plan for employees; and put a money-saving tax strategy in place. Another CPA, a client of mine who became a friend, suggested that I put together an advisory board consisting of a CPA, attorney, and a public relations advisor. I meet with them twice a year and call them several times throughout the year to bounce my ideas off of them and ask for advice. My CPA goes on appointments along with my attorney; they are part of the negotiating team I use when I need to expand my bank facilities, or if I'm doing a subdivision, mobile home park, or acquisition of a large number of foreclosures.

Warning: If you are considering trimming expenses by hiring a more afford-able accountant, reconsider. A CPA with plenty of experience in real estate, specifically in relation to agent teams, and with a great reputation can save you much more money than the person will take in payments and fees. Hire the best.

Finding a qualified CPA

When you're in the market for a CPA with experience in real estate, the best way to begin your search is to ask your colleagues who they use. Contact your area's top five REALTORS® and ask who they use as their accountant. If you have several agent teams in your area, find out who the top agent teams use as their accountant. At least one or two of these top agents has a great real estate accountant that they will gladly refer to you.

Find two or three accountants who have stellar reputations serving the real estate industry and then schedule meetings to interview them. During the interviews, ask the following questions:

• **How long have you been in the business?** (An accountant with plenty of experience is usually better than someone who's just starting out.)

• **Which agents and agent teams are your clients?** (If possible, choose an accountant who works with the more successful agents and teams in your area.)

• **What kind of experience do you have assisting real estate businesses?** (Don't settle for an accountant who has no experience in real estate.)

• **What do you know about various tax strategies for real estate businesses?** (An accountant who is schooled in tax-saving strategies for real estate businesses may be able to save you more money than you'll spend on the accountant.)

• **What do you offer agent teams that other CPAs can't or don't offer?** (Let the accountant tell you why he or she is better than others in your area.)

• **How often should we meet?** (You should meet with your CPA at least once per quarter.) According to Ralph, "When I first started I met with my CPA once a year, then quarterly. As my business grew, he began coming in two half-days a week. He would give direction to the accounting department and he would review financial statements monthly and offer advice on larger transactions."

• **Can you supply me with references?**

Tip: After you find out who a particular CPA has worked for in the past, check the CPA's references just to make sure that more than just one agent or agent team highly recommends the person and has had no issues.

How Not to Handle Your Accounting

When Ashley Leigh tells you to hire an experienced accountant, he speaks from experience—the experience of not having hired a qualified CPA from the very start. We encourage you to learn from his mistakes so you don't have to learn from your own:

"In 2001, my team and I sold nearly 125 houses. By 2004, we were selling over 400 homes per year. In just a couple of years we were literally selling more than a house a day. I was receiving a commission check at least once a day, which was great. What wasn't so great is that we had virtually no accounting system in place to keep track of the money.

"Up until this point, I had never sat down with an experienced real estate accountant to put together a plan for the internal accounting of our business. I sort of treated this portion of my business as the three-headed stepchild and did almost everything imaginable to ignore it.

"At the time, our team was generating in excess of $4 million in gross commissions. In addition to all my other roles and duties on the team, I found myself working 10 to 15 hours a week just paying bills, recording commissions, cross-checking commissions, paying out commissions, and working with commission errors that were made by the settlement company and myself. This contributed highly to my near-burnout lifestyle and pace.

"To top it off, I had no working knowledge of electronic accounting software tools such as QuickBooks® software or electronic spreadsheets such as Microsoft® Excel® spreadsheet software. I was doing half of our accounting by hand in a large paper accounting ledger and the other half on a makeshift Microsoft® Word® document that I had created. I needed help and I needed it in a big way—fast!

"Instead of going out and seeking my accountant's advice, I quickly hired the first available body that claimed she knew QuickBooks®. I thought I was in the clear and that my internal accounting worries would soon pass. To make a long story short, she did have some working knowledge of QuickBooks®, but she did not account for all the details and was soon making a bigger mess than the one she had started with in the first place.

"I replaced her and brought on another gal that had more experience. This time, I got a bit wiser and went to a good accountant for assistance with organizing our internal accounting system. Shortly thereafter, we had a well-oiled system in place.

"Among other things, our tracking and reporting system reports to us how many contracts we produced in a given month, the total amount anticipated in commissions, and the projected date that we will receive those commissions. In my opinion, the tracking and reporting system is one of the most overlooked areas in managing the finances of a real estate team. Most team leaders talk about how many houses they have sold—note the use of the past tense. With regards to our team, I am concerned not only about this, but also with the existing deals that we have in escrow that have not yet settled. This information allows me to easily recognize any pending cash flow issues that might arise within the next four months. I am able to anticipate and plan well in advance for any dips as well as spikes in our business. I can then budget our team's marketing and expenses accordingly. It is this information that allows me to sleep at night without worrying about the $140,000 monthly expenses!"

Setting Up Your Internal Accounting System

Although your accountant can handle the quarterly and annual accounting tasks for you, you need an internal (back-end) accounting system to handle daily and weekly transactions. Consult your accountant when setting up an internal system. Your accountant should be able to recommend a software package and provide additional guidance to expedite the transfer of data between your system and your accountant's.

In the following sections, we lay out the goals for your accounting system and then suggest a way to structure it for maximum efficiency and to prevent mistakes and minimize opportunities for employees to exploit the system.

Tip: One of the first things your business should do is obtain a Federal Employer Identification Number (EIN), also referred to as a Tax Identification Number (TIN), from the IRS. All you need to do is file a form SS-4, which you can obtain from the IRS at www.irs.gov/pub/irs-pdf/fss4.pdf. Check with your accountant to determine whether you need to file additional forms with your state.

Identifying what you want your system to accomplish

Prior to setting up your internal accounting system, you should have a clear idea of what your system needs to accomplish on a daily basis. However you choose to structure your system, it should be able to do the following:

- Pay invoices and commissions promptly.

- Provide adequate security measures.

- Maintain an adequate account balance.

- Provide reporting and tracking features. The types of data you want the system to be able to track and report on include the following:

  - The source of business of a particular transaction

  - The date a contract was written

  - The date a contract was settled

  - The volume of the transaction

  - The agent involved who represented your team in the transaction

Among other uses, this tracking information is crucial in determining where your business is coming from, who is doing the business on your team, and where to spend your marketing dollars to generate the next transaction.

- Format data in a way that is compatible with your accountant's system.

- Enable you to sleep at night without worrying (about your books' security and accuracy, anyway!).

Putting three roles in place

Never set up an accounting system in which one person is solely responsible for managing the money. This makes the system highly vulnerable to errors and fraud. You should have at least two people involved, preferably three:

- **Check writer:** This person is in charge of paying the bills, writing commission checks, and entering transactions into whatever accounting software you use.

- **Account manager:** The account manager is in charge of cross-checking all checks against the account registry and cross-checking commission checks against the case sheets—sheets used to record the commission splits payable to agents when they sell a property or the property goes under agreement or contract. The account manager is also in charge of reconciling the accounts, making sure your team has an adequate account balance, and generating any financial reports that the team needs.

• **Financial officer:** The financial officer (typically the owner and team leader) spends a few minutes every week reviewing commission reports and the account registry to make sure nothing looks out of place.

None of these people who manage your internal accounting system needs to be a CPA. They simply need to follow the system you have in place. Your accountant may want to assist you in providing these team members with any necessary training.

Tip: One more person is involved outside of your internal accounting system—your accountant. Your accountant can function as the quality control person for your accounting system, auditing the accounts on a regular basis to check for any errors or suspicious activity.

Case Study on Building an Internal Accounting System: The Ashley Leigh Team

Every agent team has a somewhat different accounting system, so we don't have any hard-and-fast rules to offer you when doing so. The best way to go about designing your own system is to look at effective accounting systems that other teams use. We asked Ashley Leigh to share with us the system that his team has in place:

"Our accounting system consists of two part-time assistants. One assistant is responsible for all our accounting entries into QuickBooks, paying the bills, and writing commission checks to me and my team members. The other part-time accounting assistant cross-checks my personal commission checks and enters data into our financial reporting tool, Microsoft® Access®. She also matches the actual commissions paid to me and our agents with the commissions that were originally recorded and signed by me on our case sheets. Once I approve it, these numbers are set in stone unless I amend it with my signature at a later date.

"Each and every transaction that our team participates in is treated this way. One assistant writes the commission checks, and the other reviews them after they've been paid. I spend about two to three minutes, once a week, glancing down at the commission reports and looking for anything that seems to be amiss. This arrangement saves me many hours reviewing my own commission checks and gives me the security that nothing is slipping between the cracks. In addition, having several people check one another's work is helpful in deterring embezzlement."

Implementing a good tracking system for cash flow

A major concern with all business and even personal accounting is cash flow. In order to survive for any length of time, you must have at least as much cash flowing in as flowing out. Preferably, you want much more flowing in.

Once you have a system for tracking all revenue and expenses, the system pretty much runs itself. As long as your accounting assistants write the checks for the correct amounts and make no mistakes in their data entry, you should have an impeccable record of where all the money is coming from and where it's going.

To ensure a positive cash flow, you may consider the approach that The Ashley Leigh Team uses:

"I know, on average, that the monthly expenses for our business are $140,000. Therefore, each month, I write a check payable to our business in the amount of $140,000. Our accounting department deposits the money directly into our 'operating' account. This will cover the next 30 days' worth of expenses. In addition, she deposits the commission checks we receive from the settlement companies directly into the 'operating' account. This gives us a short-term overage in the account balance and assists with maintaining the necessary account balance to ensure the bills are paid.

"The great thing about this system is that it provides a simple method of providing checks and balances. If, in a given month, our accounting department comes to me and states that our account balance is too low to make invoice payments, an obvious yellow flag rises high, flapping me in the face. At this point, I can take a look at the numbers more closely to determine whether a mistake has been made or whether we might have had an unusual monthly expense such as the purchase of new computers or something that might account for a higher than normal monthly expense total.

"Commission checks are a piece of cake with this system as well. Once a week, our accounting department issues a check payable to our 'commission' account in an amount equal to the total commissions due to me and our agents for that given week. She will then issue commission payments to me and our agents directly from the 'commission' account. This further assists with maintaining adequate cash flow. In addition, it keeps our commission payments in a separate account altogether and makes it easy to track.

"Since we are an 'independent brokerage' company, we have a third account called our 'escrow' account. In Virginia, traditionally, the buyer's brokerage company usually holds the 'earnest money deposit' in the company's escrow account. Once a case closes, the escrow money is usually transferred to the 'commission' account and made available for commission disbursement along with any other remainder of the commission that is received by the settlement company."

Establishing policies for receipts and reimbursements

In most real estate offices, salespeople and other staff members may need to purchase equipment and supplies and cover other expenses out of pocket that really should be paid by the business. To handle these situations, your internal accounting system should have a policy in place for receipts and reimbursements. (Of course, you'll want to include this policy in your employee handbook, as we explain in Chapter 5.)

At Ralph Roberts Realty, team members must fill out the form in Figure 8-1 and attach any applicable receipts in order to be reimbursed for expenses they paid. After a manager receives the form, checks it for accuracy and signs off on it, the in-house accountant cuts the check. The process typically takes about 48 hours.

Accounting 24-Hour Check Request

Request Date: _____

Check Needed by: _____

Requested by: _____

Property Address: _____

Check Payable To: _____

Address Payable To: _____

Send Out Check? Yes No If no, give to: _____

Amount of Check: _____

Reason for Check: _____

Approval Initials: _____

Company Check to be Cut from: _____

Checks will be issued 24 hours after accounting receives check request. No checks will be issued without approval initials. Request must be attached to original invoice. Second installment requests must be attached to copy of invoice.

Date Received: _____

Date Issued: _____

Check #: _____

Figure 8-1: A sample reimbursement form.

Managing the Internal Accounting System

As we discuss in Chapter 12, your team should meet on a weekly basis, and at least one person from your accounting department should attend the meeting to determine how any changes in direction or procedures could affect accounting and to answer other team members' questions about the team's finances. In addition, no matter how smoothly your accounting system works, you should meet with your accounting department on a weekly basis for at least 10–15 minutes to review the previous week's financial statements, current cash balance, and any commission payment issues. Although money should never be the sole focus of your team, it is the blood that flows through its veins and keeps the team running. Keep your eye on the cashbox.

Take it from Ashley Leigh; the measure of security gained through the weekly meeting is well worth the investment of time: "Each week I review the financial status of our business. I compare the existing week to the previous week and look for any changes that seem abnormal or out of character. If I notice anything out of the ordinary, I bring it up with our accounting department. It takes me less than 10 minutes a week to review these statements, and I strongly recommend that you take the time to do this. Otherwise, your business will be vulnerable to such things as inadequate funds to cover expenses, high expenses, low profit, embezzlement, and so on. What used to take me 15 hours a week now takes me less than 10 minutes! That's what an efficient accounting system with the right technology and good people can do for you and your team."

At least once a year (more frequently if your accountant recommends it), your accountant should also do a thorough audit of your books to ensure that your team is keeping adequate records and that nothing appears to be out of the ordinary. If your team is successful and is pulling in tens of millions of dollars per year, as many teams do, a hundred thousand dollars can easily slip through the cracks or into someone's pocket much easier than you might think.

Tracking your progress with financial statements

Financial statements function as a barometer for your agent team, showing your progress (or regress) from week to week or month to month and enabling you to quickly observe problems in time to do something about them. All accounting programs can generate the required financial statements for you with a click of a button...assuming all the data has been entered properly. In other words, creating these reports is a snap if you or a team member is vigilant about entering the right data.

In the following sections, we discuss the two types of financial statements your internal accounting team should produce and how they can assist you in monitoring your business.

Creating a balance sheet to show your team's worth

A balance sheet, like the one shown in Figure 8-2, is a statement of your team's net worth. It simply lists all your team's assets and liabilities and then subtracts the total liabilities from the total assets to show what your team is worth in terms of dollars and cents.

The balance sheet enables you to quickly determine whether your team is operating in the red or the black and monitor your progress...or lack thereof. Generally speaking, if your team's net worth is increasing, you are doing a good job of managing the business overall.

Balance Sheet

ASSETS	
Current Assets	
Checking/Savings	
1002 · Checking	$436,500.00
1006 · Savings	$1,000,000.00
Total Checking/Savings	$1,436,500.00
Total Current Assets	$1,436,500.00
Fixed Assets	
1700 · Equipment	
1710 · Furniture & Fixtures	$100,000.00
Total 1700 · Equipment	$100,000.00
1800 · Depreciation	
1810 · Accum. Deprec. - Furniture & Fixtures	-$20,000.00
Total 1800 · Depreciation	-$20,000.00
Total Fixed Assets	$80,000.00
TOTAL ASSETS	**$1,516,500.00**

LIABILITIES & EQUITY

    Liabilities

        Current Liabilities

            Other Current Liabilities

2100 · Payroll Taxes Payable	
2110 · Federal Taxes Payable	$2,750.00
2160 · Michigan Withholding Taxes	$1,250.00
Total 2100 · Payroll Taxes Payable	$4,000.00
Total Other Current Liabilities	$4,000.00
Total Current Liabilities	$4,000.00
Total Liabilities	$4,000.00
Equity	
3000 · Capital Stock	$1,000.00
3900 · Retained Earnings	$0.00
Net Income	$1,511,500.00
Total Equity	$1,512,500.00
TOTAL LIABILITIES & EQUITY	**$1,516,500.00**

Figure 8-2: A sample balance sheet.

Creating a Profit & Loss statement to show cash flow over time

A Profit & Loss statement, like the one shown in Figure 8-3, shows income and expenses for a given period along with a statement of how much money is currently in the team's accounts. Income typically comes in the form of sales commissions. Expenses usually include the following:

- Commissions paid
- Salaries
- Office rent
- Office supplies
- Advertising
- Bank charges
- Dues and subscriptions
- Insurance

- Travel
- Meals and entertainment
- Education and training

Profit & Loss Sheet

	Dec, 2010
Ordinary Income/Expense	
Income	
4010 · Commission Income	$250,000.00
Total Income	$250,000.00
Expense	
6035 · Advertising	$12,500.00
6115 · Automobile Expense	$4,625.00
6125 · Bank Service Charges	$80.00
6140 · Commissions	$42,666.67
6165 · Dues and Subscriptions	$404.17
6185 · Insurance	$0.00
6190 · Health Insurance	$4,000.00
6410 · Liability Insurance	$2,916.67
6420 · Workmen's Compensation	$229.17
Total 6185 · Insurance	$7,145.83
6235 · Licenses and Permits	$13.33
6250 · Miscellaneous	$2,333.33
6275 · Professional Fees	$6,250.00
6345 · Telephone	$0.00
6346 · Telephones - Mobile Phones	$2,708.33
6345 · Telephone - Office	$2,050.00
Total 6345 · Telephone	$4,758.33
6550 · Office Supplies	$833.33
6560 · Travel & Entertainment	$4,041.67
6570 · Wages	$35,416.67
6820 · Taxes	$0.00
6830 · Federal	$2,708.33

6860 · Michigan Unemployment	$265.00
Total 6820 · Taxes	$2,973.33
Total Expense	$124,041.67
Net Income	**$125,958.33**

Figure 8-3: A sample Profit & Loss statement.

The Profit & Loss statement is a useful tool for spotting any inaccuracies and any suspicious activity. If you see your expenses suddenly jump $10,000 in a given period, you know that you need to contact accounting and find out the reason behind the increase. Likewise, if your income suddenly rises or dips, you may want to investigate to determine whether you have a problem (in the case of a decrease in income) or can identify new opportunities (if your team's income has suddenly jumped).

Keeping all team members involved and informed

Although you, your accountant, and your accounting personnel are in charge of setting and managing your internal accounting system, you need to keep other team members informed, especially team members who receive commissions. Distributing case sheets along with commission checks provides the agents with the information they need to ensure that they are receiving their fair share of commissions. You should share your team's balance sheet and Profit & Loss statement with the team as well, in order to keep them informed of the team's overall financial health.

Chapter 9

Teaming Up with Your Broker for Your Mutual Benefit

I f you work for a broker, especially one who has no experience with agent teams, you may face even greater challenges than those you have to deal with in forming a team. As you begin to grow, for example, your broker may suspect that you are trying to compete against him or her or looking for an excuse to demand a higher commission.

Communication is the key to overcoming such challenges. By pitching your agent team concept and business plan to your broker and listing the many benefits of agent teams, you can convince most brokers that agent teams offer clients superior service and a revenue boost for the brokerage.

In this chapter, we show you how to team up with your broker to maximize the benefits for your team and your broker. We also discuss the option of operating as your own, independent brokerage.

Convincing Your Broker to Buy into Your Team-Based Approach
By Domenic Manchisi

Many brokers become uneasy when agents begin talking about creating teams. They imagine a team leader stealing their best agents and other staff members, stealing clients, and essentially unionizing the agents to demand bigger splits. These concerns are very valid; a broker runs his or her own business and must protect that business from anyone who threatens it. Understanding your broker's concerns, therefore, and addressing them sufficiently is essential if you want to convince your broker to support your team.

Starting a team when you have an adversarial relationship with your broker is like having a baby to fix your marriage—it doesn't work. It simply adds more stress, and then if you eventually split up, you face a nasty custody battle deciding who gets to keep the various clients and team members. Establish a solid relationship with your broker prior to building your team.

Warning: Don't create a team simply to squeeze more money and benefits out of your broker; this is exactly what brokers fear most, and it could damage your relationship right out of the gate. Brokers shoulder a great deal of responsibility and take on the major burden of risk. They provide you with the brand presence and the credibility you need to successfully run your business. Most brokers also offer marketing and advertising, office space, mentoring, and perhaps even some support staff. Don't take these benefits for granted.

Before you begin assembling your team, meet with your broker to discuss your ideas. Share your business plan. (For more about creating a business plan, see Chapter 4.) Explain to your broker that your plans are to generate more business, which will result in higher revenue and profits. In addition, you will be bringing in additional, top-notch personnel who appreciate the role of the broker and will be committed to the agency's success.

Tip: Think of a turtle. A turtle makes no progress until it sticks its neck out. In the same way, your broker cannot hope to achieve greater levels of success until he or she takes a risk and gives your agent-team concept an opportunity to prove itself. Make sure your broker knows that your intention is to do better and to help the agency do better. Don't be a troublemaker, and don't try to cultivate your team members from the broker's barn.

To convince your broker to buy into your team-based approach, you have to achieve the following three goals:

> • **Prove that it will work.** Making a convincing argument that your team is going to generate more revenue for the brokerage than you can generate on your own requires an impeccable business plan that lays out exactly how you will accomplish your financial goals. This is only the first step in convincing your broker. You also need to demonstrate your value as a team player and rainmaker, which can be even more difficult.

> • **Demonstrate that you are a team player.** Prior to launching your team, team up with your broker and show an interest in the brokerage. Attend the office meetings, keep your broker involved in your business, share your business plan, and ask your broker's advice on important issues. When you meet outstanding agents in the field, pass along their contact information for recruiting purposes. By doing these things, you make your broker an integral part of your team, and he or she will get more excited when you share new ideas.

> • **Prove that you are a rainmaker.** You need to have an excellent track record for generating business. If your broker is currently providing you with all of your leads, you need to ramp up your own marketing campaign to build your own client base.

When you have established a solid relationship with your broker, pitching the team concept or any new ideas is less threatening. Because your broker already feels a part of the team, he or she is more willing to collaborate with you on your new venture.

Note: Just as your broker has value that far exceeds the commissions you receive, an excellent team has value that exceeds the revenue it generates. If your team is acting like the Energizer Bunny®, refreshing everyone's attitude and motivating them to do better, then everyone wins, including your broker.

Care as much about your broker's success as you do your own. ☐

Negotiating Commissions and Other Terms with Your Broker

Building a top-producing agent team requires a substantial investment on your part, in terms of time, money, and expertise. You also take on some added risk. You are doing more for your broker, so you should be receiving more in return.

We cannot give you a concrete definition of what "more" means in this context. It can mean bigger splits, training for team members, additional office space and equipment, a bigger advertising budget, or your broker paying a portion of your operating expenses. Anything and everything is open for negotiation. Of course, whenever you sit down at the negotiating table, you need to bring something to that table. You need to show your broker what your team promises to deliver.

In the following sections, we address the key topics you should discuss during negotiations, so you know what to offer and what is reasonable to request.

Step 1: Explaining the benefits your team will deliver

As a real estate agent, you are probably in the top ten percent of all negotiators in the country. You have the basic skills required to negotiate effectively. However, here are a few tips to help you negotiate specifically with your broker:

- Openly acknowledge that you understand what the broker is already contributing to your success—wisdom, experience and resources. Show your broker that you understand the risks and expenses of running the agency, and express your appreciation.

- Provide a spreadsheet demonstrating your level of production and the level of production you expect to accomplish when you have your team in place. In other words, know what you and your team are bringing to the table. Here are some of the benefits your broker can expect from your team:

   - Increased productivity

   - Higher sales volumes, which gives the agency a higher profile

   - Increased revenue

   - Improved customer satisfaction, resulting in a better reputation for the agency

   - Increased marketing and advertising

- Bring your business plan (see Chapter 4). This document is particularly important if you are going to be the first team in the brokerage. If your broker is already working with other teams, he or she can assist you in revising your plan, if necessary, to meet the broker's requirements. Having a detailed plan in place also demonstrates to your broker that you are well organized.

• Let your broker know that part of your agreement will state that you will not recruit agents from within. You may also consider including your broker in the interview process for all new recruits and giving your broker some say in who is allowed to join the team.

• Assure your broker that your commitment to your team will not interfere with your relationship with your broker and will probably improve it.

• Listen to what your broker has to say. Take time to process what he or she has to say and make sure that you understand fully. If you don't completely understand, ask.

• Begin your negotiating session by showing your broker what you bring to the table.

The equation for your broker's success is simple: higher production, more signs in the marketplace, more ambassadors of goodwill, and better branding all equal more volume. Show up with a plan and ask your broker for input.

Step 2: Requesting more support from your broker

After you have presented the benefits of your agent team, you can begin to request additional support and resources from your broker, including:

• **A higher commission percentage:** Although you should do your best to negotiate a fair split with your broker, don't focus solely on commissions. The level of support that your broker provides is equally if not more important. Focus on the bottom line—how successful you and your broker will be and how much money you get to keep in your pocket. A broker who pays a slightly lower percentage but provides plenty of training, marketing, support, and other resources may be offering a better deal than a broker who offers a higher commission.

• **Training for team members:** Brokers are generally well-trained individuals on the cutting edge of the industry. They often provide excellent training and coaching for your team members, particularly new agents who have little experience. Make training a priority and ask your broker to make a commitment to training new team members. In exchange, consider volunteering your services to assist with training new recruits.

You can expect your broker to act as the resident recruiter and trainer for your team as well as for the agency overall. The team leader should share these responsibilities, providing additional training for new recruits, making shadowing opportunities available, and accompanying novice agents on sales calls. The team leader functions as a broker within the brokerage, and the team functions as a company within a company.

- **Educational opportunities:** To keep you and your fellow team members on the cutting edge, your broker may be willing to pay for or share the cost of additional educational opportunities, such as seminars and workshops.

- **Additional office space:** As a team, you need more office space than an individual agent. Is your broker willing to provide this office space in exchange for increased productivity?

- **Additional equipment and supplies:** In addition to consuming more space, as a team, you consume more supplies and require more equipment. Your broker may be willing to cover some of the additional expense.

- **A bigger advertising budget:** With a team, you can serve more clients and process more transactions. To help attract additional clients, your broker may be willing to invest more in marketing your team.

You're essentially teaming up with your broker, so the two of you, as partners, need to contribute resources to your new venture. These resources may include advertising dollars, office equipment and supplies and E&O insurance. Be sure to discuss these resources and others with your broker to ensure that someone is covering them. In the case of E&O insurance, your broker is likely to maintain his or her own insurance, but check with your insurance carrier just in case you have additional liability.

Deciding Where to Set Up Shop: Stay Put, or Move on Out?

Many teams choose to stay put and run their business out of the brokerage. After all, the broker's building usually has an established brand presence, and investing in new office space could be a waste of money. However, if the office is too small to accommodate your team or you want your team to establish a presence of its own (and your broker agrees), you may decide to relocate, creating a satellite office. If you are thinking about relocating, consider the following:

- **What's your goal?** Do you want to cut expenses by relying on your broker's accommodations? Do you want to leverage the brand presence that your broker has already established? Are you looking to work with your broker to branch out to another geographical location via a satellite office? Where you choose to set up shop should support your and your broker's overall strategy for success.

• **Is the atmosphere at the brokerage counterproductive for your team?** You want your team to operate out of a positive workplace. If the brokerage is home to people with negative attitudes, relocating may be necessary.

• **Will relocating help you meet your financial goals and serve the best interests of everyone involved?** Don't forget to consider the financial aspects of relocating.

• **Does your broker support your relocation plans?** If your broker is confident and is encouraging your team's growth and success, he or she is very likely to support the move, but don't expect your broker to be financially responsible for the relocation costs—this falls on the team leader.

• **Do you have the resources to move?** You should have sufficient funds to cover your operating costs for at least one year before making a move. You should also have a solid business plan in place approved by your broker.

Managing Conflicts with Your Broker

Some brokers refuse to accept the agent team approach, usually because they are so ingrained in the old ways of doing business. We have heard stories of brokers who have refused to allow team leaders to give their team members any credit or to market the team rather than an individual agent. If your broker is not exactly agent-team-friendly, then you may want to give the person a copy of this book to read (and kindly direct him or her to the appendix, at the back of the book, which we include just for brokers).

When the broker understands the many benefits of agent teams, he or she may be a little more open-minded. Remember, people are often reluctant to change not because they are opposed to a new idea, but because they don't know enough about it. Open the lines of communication and explain your position.

If your broker still refuses to come around, you may want to consider moving to a different company. Which broker you work for is relatively unimportant compared to the health and welfare of your team. If you have been marketing your team properly, your clients will know you by your team brand first and only secondarily by the broker you work for.

A Case Study in Broker Conflict: The Vanderblue Team

The Vanderblue Team was not always with The Higgins Group. When the team started, it was working for another broker who refused to accept the agent team concept, according to Julie Vanderblue:

"Our broker did not see things the way I did. I could not give credit to my team but had to take all the credit myself. There were other issues as well. I spoke to the manager at least five times explaining my reasons, but the broker refused to make any adjustments.

"We ultimately had to make the decision to leave and go to The Higgins Group. It was not an easy decision (we had $17 million in pending sales when we left), but communication is everything. If your broker won't listen, you must move on. The market has plenty of good companies that support the agent team concept, so you should never feel handcuffed to one company. So many people are afraid of change, but without change, you are not really moving forward."

Recognizing the Value of Staying Put

High turnover can kill any business, from fast-food joints to the biggest corporations. I believe it's especially damaging to sales organizations. Believe me, I've tried it both ways—jumping from job to job and staying put for a decade with one firm—and I know that staying put is usually the best option.

Many salespeople jump from company to company hoping for a better commission split or a nicer boss or better hours. I did that myself when I was younger. I changed real estate firms seven or eight times, always hoping for a better arrangement, before I finally opened my own company.

It's clear to me that there is no perfect company or ideal marketplace. You can usually make more money by digging deep where you are right now and making it happen here and now. Switching from firm to firm often just wastes your time and resources.

Every time I switched real estate firms, I had to buy new business cards and let my client base know where I was. I had to create new stationery. I had to develop new marketing materials. Each time, I lost a lot of momentum. And, of course, I had to learn a whole new system with each new company.

Sometimes, you need to jump ship in order to break away from a broker who's limiting your opportunities in the marketplace and holding you down, but before you move on, take an honest look at your current situation. Is your broker really to blame or are you holding yourself back by not being more aggressive? *—Ralph R. Roberts*

Knowing when to part company

Although we recommend that you choose a real estate firm and stick with it, some situations can become unproductive, intolerable, and unfixable. In such cases, moving on is probably best. If you aren't getting what you expected or were promised and you have respectfully requested a meeting to no avail, then you need to weigh your options and prepare to leave.

Before you settle on your final decision, however, make sure you have done the following:

- Tried every possible solution you can think of.

- Weighed the consequences of leaving.

- Prepared in advance for your exit (see the next section for details).

Prior to leaving, schedule one last meeting with your broker. Tell your broker your intentions, making it clear that you will not be leaving with any hard feelings. Part as professionals, wish each other well and acknowledge the fact that you both benefited from your time together. By parting on good terms, you retain your reputation in the marketplace and leave open the possibility of doing business with the broker somewhere down the road. Don't burn your bridges.

Making a smooth transition

When you are ready to leave your current firm, avoid the temptation to simply storm out the door. A hasty exit can make it very difficult for both you and your clients. Plan well in advance, so you can make a smooth transition to your new firm. Planning should include the following:

- Save sufficient funds to cover one year's worth of operating costs.

- Give your broker sufficient notice and work out a payment schedule for deals pending and active listings.

• Prepare all your marketing materials, newsprint and notices, signage, letterhead, and so forth so they are ready to go several weeks before your departure. Make sure your new address and contact information is transferred to all your marketing materials.

• Let everyone know that you're going independent, including your clients, colleagues, and vendors. You don't need to go into great detail over why you've decided to leave your agency, particularly if you are leaving a bad situation. Send thank-you cards expressing your appreciation for being able to work with them and informing them of your new location.

Going Independent

Throughout this chapter, we recommend teaming up with your broker by creating a relationship that benefits both your broker and your team. Some team leaders who are more experienced, however, may decide that they prefer more independence. If you get to a point in your career when working for a broker does not appeal to you, you can go back to school to become a licensed broker and set up your own real estate firm. By owning your own firm, you no longer have to worry about commission splits, but you do take on the added responsibilities and expenses of a broker.

If you decide to go independent, here's what you need to do:

• Obtain your broker's license. Even if you plan on sticking with your broker but working out of your own satellite office, having your broker's license is a big plus.

• Hire an administrator. The first person you hire should be an assistant or administrator who can handle all of the day-to-day operations, so you can focus on hiring, training and marketing.

• Set up systems for everything, as explained in Chapter 4.

• Make sure you have sufficient cash on hand to cover expenses during the transition. Overestimate the amount you need; plan on spending up to 25 percent more than you think it will cost.

Involving Your State's Real Estate Commission When Setting Up Your Brokerage

By Wayne Turner

When you are in the process of setting up your brokerage, consider consulting with someone from your state's real estate commission. Tell the person that you are committed to complying with all rules and regulations and want to make sure that you are setting up your brokerage properly. A 30- to 60-minute meeting with someone from the state can help you make sure you are filing all the proper documents and following proper procedures.

Within three months of opening our office, the Tennessee Real Estate Commission visited, pulled files of closed transactions, and made sure we had processed escrow deposits properly, finalized contracts, and filed all the necessary paperwork. Their goal was to ensure that our transition was successful.

Fortunately, we had done our homework and passed with an A+. There wasn't so much as a dot out of place or an uncrossed *t*, and our entire team took great pride in that. That's what you want in a smooth transaction.

Chapter 10

Equipping Your Team with the Tools and Technologies to Succeed

Whether you like it or not, the real estate industry is going high-tech. Back in the 1980s, you could still compete in this business with a phone and a handheld calculator. Now, you need a notebook computer wired with broadband Internet and equipped with a host of software packages, including e-mail, contact management, word processing, presentation software, a spreadsheet program, and specialized real estate software, not to mention a BlackBerry® (or other personal digital assistant/cell phone device), one or more Web sites or blogs, and the training on how to use all this equipment effectively.

When you build a team, you can no longer worry about only yourself—you also have to make sure that everyone on the team has the proper equipment and training. In this chapter, we provide you with a list of recommended tools and technologies that your agents and support personnel need in order to maximize productivity.

Tip: If you are technologically challenged, make sure the next person you add to your team has the technical skills that you and your team are lacking. Ask this person to be in charge of providing in-service workshops to bring all other team members up to speed.

Uniformity can help you simplify training—consider having everyone in the office use identical cell phones, PDAs, and notebook computers.

Viewing Technology as Practical Tools

As a general rule, real estate agents don't hesitate to spend money to make money. We realize that any investment that has the real potential of at least paying for itself in the near future is an investment worth making. Take the myriad options that Web sites offer, for example—they're often a neglected opportunity for generating business. I believe that a Web site should offer clients much more than listings to keep them informed and to empower them to take control. If you're online, I invite you to stop by www.ralphroberts.com to take a look at what we're doing. We were the first to have a Web site, then the first to have an interactive Web site and then the first to use blogs as a marketing tool. I now use my blog www.flippingfrenzy.com as a national platform from which I can educate the industry and consumers about real estate and mortgage fraud.

If you are concerned about the cost of investing in new technologies, consider the potential benefits:

- Increased sales as the new technologies generate leads
- Enhanced productivity, giving you more time to deal directly with customers or pursue other interests
- Increased opportunities as you discover innovative uses for your new technology
- Improved visibility as technologies including Web pages and blogs draw the attention of customers online
- Increased ability to recommend new technologies to your clients as another way of providing value to your clients and demonstrating your genuine interest in their success
- Increased competitive advantage in your marketplace, as you differentiate your team as tech savvy

I don't see the Internet as something that's going to take over our industry (that was my view in 1995), but I do know that my company is getting more and more buyers and sellers through our Web site and because our use of technology has made us much better at selling homes and finding homes for buyers. You have to view the Web and any technology as a marketing tool that can make you money...or at least make your life easier. Probably both. *—Ralph R. Roberts*

Selecting the Right Computers

Everyone on your team should have a computer and either know how to use it or be in the process of learning how to use it. These computers should be tablet PCs (for agents on the go) and desktop or notebook PCs for the rest of the office. With today's technology, real estate businesses no longer require huge, brick-and-mortar offices. You can carry your entire office on an affordable tablet or notebook PC.

Rob Levy of The Rob Levy Team (www.roblevy.com), Prudential Northwest Properties in Portland, Oregon, is a trusted authority on practical technologies for the real estate industry. Levy highly recommends equipping all agents with tablet PCs and all office staff members with desktop PCs:

"A tablet PC is much like a notebook PC but the screen swivels and folds on itself and you can then pop out a hidden pen and sign, annotate, write or even doodle and draw on documents. The practicality of this is such that an agent can be out showing homes with a client, and if the client decides to buy, the agent can type up the offer, turn the screen into a tablet, have the client sign, and then either e-mail it or e-fax the document to the seller's agent—right from the house, the local coffee shop or from the front seat of her car. Using a tablet also means that you can be away from the office and when checking in you can also download and sign necessary documents rather than waiting until you get back to the office to do so.

*Figure 10-1: A tablet PC has a swivel monitor
and folds up neatly for easy transport.*

"Tablet PCs are made by several manufacturers, but popular computer magazines always seem to rate the Lenovo™ (from IBM®) products best. However, Toshiba®, HP and Gateway® make excellent machines. Windows Vista™ operating system, which is available on all new computers built since early 2007, was "made" for tablets, so if you had a tablet before, try it with Windows Vista—it's amazing.

"In regard to the desktops (and tablets when in the office, for that matter), another feature to look for is the ability to use two monitors (built into most tablets and notebooks but may require an extra card on a desktop). Two of your most popular programs can run at the same time on different monitors. For instance, I often have my Microsoft® Outlook messaging software open on one monitor and my contact manager or MLS software on the other."

If you're looking to cut costs, Alan Shafran of The Alan Shafran Group (www.alanshafran.com), Prudential California Realty in Carlsbad, California recommends buying Dell™-refurbished PCs: "Buy Dell™ OptiPlex™ machines (desktop models for the office), as they are considered business machines and will get better tech support. You can buy these on eBay, but I suggest you buy them from the Dell Outlet and/or www.dell.com. These machines typically come with a minimum one-year warranty, and you can add another couple of years on the site. The computers I buy are typically top-end machines, with minimum 1 gig of ram (2 gigs is ideal for today's software). I normally spend no more than $600. So think about that...you can furnish an office of five administrators and five buyer's agents for $6,000."

Remember: Before investing in any new technology, do a little research. Consult with a real estate peer you deem tech savvy. The last thing you want to do is arrive at a conference thinking you've adopted the latest, greatest technology only to discover that you invested money in the wrong product. Remember that the right tech solution differs from person to person depending upon your individual needs. Work with a trusted source or tech consultant to design a tech package that targets your needs.

Installing basic software

A computer is just a hunk of metal and silicon unless it has software that tells it how to operate. Whenever you are shopping for a computer for your own use or for other members of the team, consider the tasks you need to perform on the computer and then install the software that provides the computer with the capability to perform those tasks.

All computers should be equipped with the following software:

- Word processor, such as Microsoft® Word® word processing software.

- Spreadsheet, such as Microsoft® Excel® spreadsheet software. You can drag and drop data from MLS listings right into Excel® to create your own custom spreadsheets and graphs.

- Calendar program, such as Microsoft® Outlook® messaging software (for managing schedules). By using Outlook® as your calendar program and for managing contacts and e-mail, you can use the Appointment feature to e-mail any contact an invitation to join the meeting. When the contact accepts the meeting, the program books the appointment right in her calendar (and yours).

- Contact management program (for keeping track of clients). Consider adding ACTive Agent for Microsoft® Outlook® from www.sonomaenterprises.com on top of your current Microsoft® Outlook® installation. Active Agent for Microsoft® Outlook® adds all the custom fields, features, and functionality that agents need. Don't waste your time experimenting with different contact management programs—Microsoft® Outlook® is a powerful tool.

• Presentation program, such as Microsoft® PowerPoint® presentation software. With the most recent version of PowerPoint® presentation software, you can actually store presentations on a cell phone and play them back to clients or connect your phone to a projector and have a full size presentation.

• Desktop publishing program, such as Microsoft® Publisher® desktop publishing software. For marketing flyers and other publications, Rob Levy recommends Publisher® desktop publishing software. However, some programs such as Top Producer® (see the next section) include flyer creation tools, as do some of Pat Zaby's products (www.patzaby.com).

Tip: If you are looking to save some money, you can even download Word® templates on the Internet. Imprev™ (www.imprev.com) offers a unique blend of virtual tour software that now allows for photos to be exported into dozens of predesigned flyer templates.

• Specialized real estate and sales software, including transaction management software. Refer to the next section, "Maximizing potential with specialized software," for details.

• Antivirus software, such as Norton Internet Security™ software or McAfee® VirusScan®, (for protecting the computer and data from security threats).

• Online software, including lead-generation and blogging software. For real estate blogging tools, visit Kinetic Knowledge at http://kineticknowledge.com or Blogging Systems™ at www.bloggingsystems.com.

Tip: Although most people use Google™ to search for Web content, Google™ also offers a host of powerful tools for creating and sharing documents and spreadsheets, managing a notebook, sending and receiving e-mail, blogging, creating Web pages, and much more. Google™ even has a calendar that the entire team can share, which can make it much easier to coordinate activities. Visit Google™ at www.google.com and then click the "more" link at the top to view a menu of search features and other tools.

Maximizing potential with specialized software
By Rob Levy

I firmly believe that having the right computers and software and knowing how to use the technology is crucial to the success of any agent team. When asked what types of software should be installed on the team's computers, I recommend a word processor, spreadsheet, contact manager, presentation program, desktop publisher and a calendar program. In addition, every team should have a Web site, stealth sites and drip e-mail systems.

Real estate software suites

Several packages designed specifically for real estate encompass several of these essential software programs in one product. (These can either be installed locally on each PC or are Web based.)

For larger teams, Microsoft® Exchange® Server 2003 or 2007 is the best solution, although it does require a bit of an up-front investment. You need to install your own Internet server that's hooked up to the Internet with a broadband connection, such as a T1 line. This is no job for a weekend tech person—hire a professional.

The advantage of Microsoft® Exchange® Server is that each team member (with appropriate permissions set) can see each other's calendars, contacts and e-mails. Also, you can do this on your Outlook® on the desktop, tablet/notebook or PDA and it's all live. If a lead comes in, the lead coordinator can look at each agent's calendar and see who has time to take on a new client. The lead coordinator can then put the appointment on the agent's calendar and add the client's contact information to Outlook®. When the agent makes contact or shows homes, the agent can make notes from wherever the agent may be and store those notes centrally in Outlook®. This is important for accountability.

Exchange® is also useful for scheduling meetings and keeping everyone posted on upcoming events. When you need to schedule a meeting, you simply send an invitation addressed to everyone whose attendance is required, and the same invitation pops up on everyone's screen. We also use Exchange® to schedule our moving truck so that each buyer's agent can glance at their PDA and instantly tell if the truck will be available on a specific day.

For a team that does not have Microsoft® Exchange® Server installed, Top Producer® (www.topproducer.com; see Figure 10-2) is a good option, because it is Web based—all team members can access it from wherever they are. It includes a contact manager, word processor and a somewhat limited desktop publishing program. You can also set it up so that your team members can or cannot delete or print out clients. Top Producer® also has products to sync your database with a Palm® Treo™ smartphone, a Windows® mobile-based device, or a BlackBerry® device. With a large team, Top Producer® can get pricey, but the benefit is it is set up and ready to go—it requires little or no configuration.

Active Agent (www.sonomaenterprises.com) and Respond (www.patzaby.com) are also worth looking into.

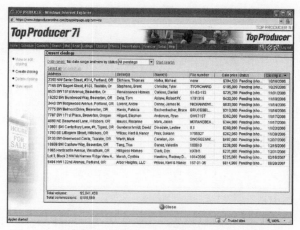

Figure 10-2: Top Producer is a Web-based suite of programs designed for agents.

Internet marketing and lead generation software

Many of the Web-based products are most useful in generating and managing leads. We use Real Pro Systems (www.realprosystems.com), which coordinates our Web site, stealth sites, blog, e-newsletter, and drip e-mail campaigns. (*Note:* Levy is one of the co-founders of Real Pro Systems). A stealth site is a Web site designed solely to attract traffic and send visitors to another site where they can actually do something. My main site is www.roblevy.com, but we have a stealth site (www.portlandmls.net) that is designed to attract buyers and sellers.

With the old way of doing business, we used the MLS book, so buyers had to come to us, because we had all the data. Nowadays, with IDX, www.REAL-TOR.com® and other sites, buyers can find the data themselves. In other words, in the old days, we sold the agent and then gave the buyers data; now, we give them the data and then sell the agent. The new way of doing business requires that you establish a Web presence to gather leads. However, a huge majority of the online leads you receive are garbage—I would estimate that 98 out of 100 are garbage. There is no way an agent can waste time on 98 bad leads to get the two good ones. With an automated drip e-mail campaign, you can literally work with several thousand buyers and sellers at one time, knowing that when the two real leads per hundred surface, you have a system in place that's following up with them. When a real lead comes in, the lead coordinator can then assign the lead to an agent. With this system in place, we can sell ourselves to thousands of prospective clients without lifting a finger.

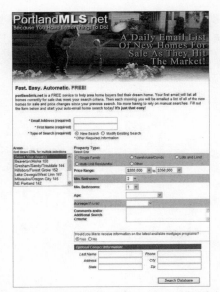

Figure 10-3: Rob Levy's www.portland-mls.net stealth site.

Feedback management software

A feedback management program is an absolute must for all listing agents. Although Real Pro Systems has a built-in feedback system, a great standalone product is HomeFeedback™ (www.homefeedback.com). I train my listing agents to input the showing agents' information on the protected Web site after they return to the property and find their card on the table. The system takes it from there and e-mails the showing agent, thanking them for showing the house and asking them for feedback in a survey format (in fact, it does this three times). When the showing agent fills out the form and submits it, the answers are e-mailed to the seller and to the listing agent.

Sellers have e-mailed me to ask me to reduce the price on a house based solely on feedback from this system. I use it as a listing tool, too. When I'm having trouble gaining consensus on an asking price, I may tell the sellers, "Mr. & Mrs. Seller, I know we are sitting here today trying to set a value on your house but at best we are making an educated guess. What I am going to do is survey each and every buyer's agent showing the home and see what his/her buyers thought of it. They are active buyers looking for a home like yours today and in this area and price range."

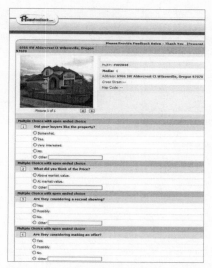

Figure 10-4: Managing feedback from showings can be a powerful tool for listing agents.

Transaction management software

The new, emerging transaction management software (TMS) is amazing, and if you don't have Microsoft® Exchange® Server, it is a must. Good TMS allows you to save all your documents on a server and truly have a paperless office. When an addendum comes in that needs to be signed by both buyers, one of whom is at home and can be e-mailed and one who is at the office and near a fax, you can send the document to each person in their preferred methods at the click of a button. Some programs also print out a cover sheet so that when the client sends it back via fax, the barcode tells the software where the document goes and to notify you immediately.

Some of the TMS products available include Sureclose® from Stewart Title®, TransactionPoint® from Fidelity National Real Estate Solutions® and Settlement Room™ by Settlement Room Systems, Inc. (www.settlementroom.com), shown on page 158, Figure 10-5, which charges as low as $7.50 per transaction. The best part is TMS puts the entire transaction into one PDF file that you can burn to a CD for the client and save to a separate drive for archiving. (We use a private-branded jump drive.)

Figure 10-5: Transaction management software can help you create a paperless office.

Comparative Market Analysis (CMA) software

Another new product type is the automated CMA (comparative market analysis). After performing a CMA for a client, save it on a server—then every 30 days, the software automatically e-mails a new and updated CMA to your client, complete with colored maps and with active, pending and recently sold homes placed on the map, as shown in Figures 10-6 and 10-7.

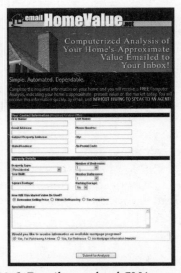

Figure 10-6: E-mail an updated CMA to your client.

Figure 10-7: Interactive online maps show additional market information.

I have found that doing this for all my clients, along with sending them a monthly e-newsletter, touches them 24 times a year for next to no cost and is very powerful. The CMA e-mail is about the one thing the client will not send to the junk file, so when not abused you always have their e-mail address. But the huge benefit comes when you are dealing with absentee owners. You see, when I mail postcards to absentee owners asking them to go not to my main site, but to www.emailhomevalue.net (my seller stealth site) to get "automated information on their home including active, pending and sold comparables," they go there with no hesitation. From there, I set them up to get the CMA and my e-newsletter, and I become their eyes and ears for their local property. ☐

Computer Connectivity

Even if you have a central office, you're likely to transact more and more of your business in a virtual office—on computers that are connected via the Internet and your office network. Because of this, connectivity is becoming as important as the computers themselves. In the following sections, we address your computer connectivity needs.

Providing broadband Internet access

With more and more home buyers and sellers researching and doing business on the Internet, having a fast Internet connection is essential. What's best for your team, however, depends on how it operates. Installing a turbocharged T3 line may not be the best investment if your team spends a great deal of time on the road. You may be better off looking into wireless connectivity provided by your phone company—something like Sprint® Mobile Broadband. When selecting an Internet service provider (ISP), take the following factors into consideration:

- **Speed:** The faster, the better, but you should plan on a 500Kbps connection or faster. That's the low end of satellite service. Wireless Internet through the phone company is a little faster, DSL service is faster than that, and cable is even faster. A T1, T2, or T3 line is the ultimate, because it essentially hardwires you into the Internet, but it's costly and won't do much good when you and other team members are on the road.

- **Reliability:** A reliable ISP has the infrastructure and security in place to remain up and running at all times. If you sign up with an ISP that commonly has to shut down nights and weekends for maintenance, you may find that your service to your clients is compromised. This is especially true if your office uses Voice over Internet Protocol (VoIP) phone service.

- **Privacy:** Whenever you share an Internet connection, you expose your computer to potential security risks. Make sure you have a system in place that prevents other agents (particularly any agents working in the same office who are not on your team) from gaining access to the files on your computer.

- **Mobility:** Real estate agents rarely set up shop in their office. They spend more time in the field, meeting with clients and prospective clients, delivering presentations and selling homes. Make sure you have an ISP that provides wireless coverage throughout your market area.

- **Sharing:** You can often save money by allowing all of the computers in your office to share a single broadband connection. You do this by connecting a router to the broadband modem and then connecting all of the computers, either using network cables or wireless connections, to the router. Ask your ISP if they recommend a specific router you should use.

Tip: Rob Levy recommends getting the aircard for notebook and tablet PCs: "The big change has come in the last six months or so with the aircards becoming true '3G' or third generation. With the so-called 'REV-A' enhancements to Sprint® and Verizon®'s networks, you can be on DSL-like connections almost anywhere and for certain in all the major cities. AT&T® offers a similar program that it has not yet rolled out (as of the writing of this book) but offers faster upload speeds."

Networking your office computers

You can often save money and add power to your computer system by installing a centralized server that all team member computers can connect to in order to share data and resources. We asked tech-savvy REALTOR® Alan Shafran to share his insights about building a computer network. According to Alan, his team uses three servers:

• **Main server:** The main server is a Microsoft® Exchange® Server, which stores all documents and pictures, administers e-mail via Outlook®, and runs all other centrally located software programs.

• **GoodLink server:** The second server is a basic server that delivers all of the Outlook® data to their phones. The difference with using GoodLink versus other server software for syncing with phones is that GoodLink allows you to sync public folders as well as your personal folders. This allows you to have a database of contacts that your whole team views and edits versus your personal contacts that you don't want anyone viewing. It syncs as many databases as you need and is very flexible. Also, it installs on your phones via a Web download right to the phone and delivers the data and e-mails to your phone faster than your computer will receive them on the local network.

• **Microsoft® Terminal® server:** This is a basic machine with server software that enables you to access your computer from a remote location over the Internet.

Installing centralized servers can cost anywhere from $4,000 to $10,000, but is generally worth the investment. By investing in servers, you can centralize the computing power and often share expensive equipment, such as high-end printers and broadband Internet service, saving money on those items.

Tip: According to Shafran, he prefers using GoodLink software for his wireless communications devices over the popular BlackBerry® platform: "One of the many benefits of this software versus the BlackBerry® is that it will work with almost any and all Palm® or Windows® phones. Currently, BlackBerry® software only works with the BlackBerry® phones. To receive the kind of features we get with GoodLink, one must purchase the BlackBerry® Enterprise server software, which can cost thousands of dollars. With GoodLink, you just need to set up your GoodLink server one time, and then for the most part your fee is included in the unlimited data fee that your cellular provider charges. This has changed from the past and may change again in the future, but for now it is the best system on the street."

Adding a power supply backup

To keep your network up and running in the event of power outages and to protect your computers against power surges, we recommend that you have your entire network running off of a conditioned power supply—a UPS or Uninterruptible Power Supply. A UPS consists of a battery that's plugged into the main power supply to charge. By plugging all of your computers and other equipment into one or more UPS devices, you allow those computers to run off of the conditioned power supplied by the battery, making them immune to any power surges, drops, or outages.

Backing up documents and other files

The most valuable part of any computer system is the documents and files stored on that system. All team members should be required to store copies of all documents on the centralized server and your server should be set up to do daily and weekly backups. This will help minimize the risk of data loss.

Warning: Don't simply back up files to another computer in the office. In the event of a fire or theft, it's likely that you will lose both the original files and the backups. Structure your system to store backups offsite. Several companies offer backup programs via the Internet, allowing you to store information at a remote location. Use your favorite Internet search tool and enter "online backup."

Gearing up for Reliable Communication

In this age of immediacy, today's clients expect to be able to reach you and other team members at a moment's notice—or at least have you return their call within one or two hours. In order to provide that level of customer service, you need cutting-edge communication technology:

• **Cell phone:** The latest generation of cell phones enables you to eliminate most of the other digital devices you need in the field. With a full-featured cell phone, you can take calls on the road, shoot photos and even short video clips of properties, receive text messages, check your e-mail, browse the Web, and even listen to podcasts!

• **Toll-free number:** If you market to clients from across the country or around the world, you really should have a toll-free number they can call. You want them to be able to get in touch with you without spending a dime of their own money. A toll-free number sends the message that you are ready to invest in your clients. The Alan Shafran Group uses Arch Telecom for its 800 number and lead capture system. Arch Telecom allows them to use a four-digit toll-free number, with the fourth digit representing the source of the advertisement. For example, someone who dials 8422 obtained the number from a newspaper ad, while someone calling 8424 saw the ad in a flyer. Arch Telecom allows for online reporting and stores data for three months. You can also obtain toll-free numbers from www.FreedomVoice.com, www.Freedom800.com, or www.Vanity800.com (to obtain a number that reflects your team's name).

• **Conference call center:** A conference call center allows you and your team to gather in virtual meetings wherever all of you may be and even record the session for later reference.

• **E-mail:** Although just about everyone has an e-mail program, few people take advantage of the advanced features of their e-mail programs. Most e-mail programs, for example, can automatically filter your e-mail into separate folders, so you can filter out many of the less important messages. You can also create groups of recipients that you often send the same messages to, so you don't have to address them individually to each recipient. Explore your e-mail program to discover its time-saving features.

• **Wireless communication device:** Wireless devices, such as the BlackBerry® and Treo® combine several technologies into a wireless, handheld device. These devices can often replace a phone, personal organizer, calendar, Web browser, and e-mail program. Perhaps best of all, they enable agents to send and receive messages in real time, wherever they may be, and are much more efficient than voice mail. You can even purchase specialized software that converts voice mail messages into text messages and have them forwarded to your wireless communication device.

Rob Levy recommends the Treo® with AT&T®, because "their broadband network allows you to talk on the phone and either surf the Web or e-mail at the same time. As of the writing of this book, other services don't allow this, so if you're browsing the Web or sending or receiving e-mail, any incoming calls will be sent to voicemail. The other advantage of using AT&T® is that it works worldwide with data, too. I have gotten e-mail on mine from a café in rural Morocco!

"One of the latest and long-awaited enhancements to popular cell phones is the Bluetooth® headset, and in particular the Jawbone® Bluetooth® headset (www.jawbone.com). This is a regular Bluetooth® headset but it picks up your voice from vibrations from your jaw, rather than from a microphone. It does have a microphone, but the microphone picks up all the ambient noise and then removes it from your listener's ear, meaning you can drive down the freeway with your sunroof open and your listener will think you are in the office!"

• **Teleconferencing:** With your computer, a high-speed Internet connection, and the right software, you can now teleconference with clients and colleagues from all around the world. One of the most exciting video teleconferencing companies we've seen lately is Extreme Video, which you can learn more about by visiting www.extremevideo.us. The Alan Shafran Group has a 42-inch plasma screen in their conference room and uses GoToMeeting®, a Web-based service, to manage video conference calls. The group also uses CoVideo systems to send video e-mail messages to clients. According to Alan Shafran, "It is a simple, easy way to separate yourself from your competition."

• **Internet-based fax program:** With an Internet-based fax program, such as Ufax, you can receive faxes via e-mail and read faxes via the Web regardless of your location. Imagine, reviewing an offer and forwarding it to your client with the click of a button. Another program called Zip-Form® enables you to print to a fax or e-mail it in PDF format.

Rob Levy recommends efax: "With eFax® (www.efax.com), all your faxes come into an e-mail account (or the e-mail accounts of everyone on your team). With a tablet PC, you can open up and sign or just forward the fax as a common Portable Document Format file (Adobe PDF is the de facto standard for e-mailing documents). Also, you can type out or write out a document or counter offer on your tablet PC and upload it to eFax, which sends to any fax machine or fax software in the world. Another side benefit, because you can forward the fax to the recipient without printing and rescanning it, the quality isn't downgraded at all."

• **Instant messaging software:** If your office tends to sound chaotic due to excess chatter, you may be able to reduce the chatter by encouraging team members to communicate via instant messaging (IM) software, such as AIM (America Online's Instant Messenger). IM enables people in the office to shoot each other quick messages without having to holler across rooms. Some of your clients may even prefer using IM to communicate with you. In addition, you can IM someone on your computer and have the message sent to their text-enabled cell phone or wireless communication device.

• **Interactive voice response system:** According to Levy, interactive voice response (IVR) is "a big income producer for my team. On your flyer, you include only the address, some pictures, and some bullet points, but not the asking price or local phone number. Instead, you include something like 'For the latest price, dial 800-555-1212 house number 1234.'" People will be more inclined to call this number, because they don't have to talk to a salesperson. Because they are calling an 800 line, they can't block their number. Good IVR systems capture the number, match it to the caller's name and phone number and then page you. For instance, I can get a page from my IVR system that tells me what house someone called on, how long the call was, and the name and phone of the person who called. I can then call them back and ask whether they want more information on the home they called on or if they would like to see it. The IVR I use is from Automatic Leads (www.automaticleads.com) and is very reasonable.

Investing in Office Accessories

Computers, software, connectivity services, and communications devices form the infrastructure on which you can run your business, but additional accessories can help you streamline operations and improve the quality of your marketing materials and presentations. In the following sections, we highlight some of the more important accessories you should consider for your office.

A high-quality digital camera

A digital camera is an essential tool for real estate agents and support personnel. Your office should have at least a couple of high-quality cameras agents can share, but equipping each agent with his or her own camera is best—you never know when a photo op will present itself.

Over the years, good digital cameras have become very affordable. For a couple hundred dollars, you can purchase a camera that takes excellent photos and even short video clips. Here are some of the features you should look for in a digital camera:

- 3.1 megapixels (for high-quality photos)
- 3X optical zoom lens
- LCD monitor (to preview photo before shooting and review it after the shot)
- 512MB or larger capacity memory cards
- Lithium batteries

Tip: According to Rob Levy, the perfect digital camera for REALTORS® may have finally arrived: "As of late, there have been few cameras that I would consider ideal for REALTORS®. The issue is that digital cameras now make up some 70% of all camera sales, and the public wants them for taking two types of shots—family photos and scenery (as in zoom) shots. As REALTORS®, we want to take a photo of a small 10-foot by 8-foot room and make it look huge. At the time of this writing, there's an ideal camera for both purposes. Kodak (www.kodak.com) makes a compact camera with both a zoom lens and a 23 mm ultra-wide-angle lens built-in for about $300 street. Plus it's a 7-megapixel camera that takes terrific shots. Its called the EasyShare V705 and it's terrific."

A global positioning system (GPS)

If agents are constantly getting lost on their way to their destinations, a GPS can provide them with directions that make getting lost nearly impossible. The cost of the device and the service may seem a little steep at first, but when you factor in the amount you save on mileage and efficiency, the investment is well worth it.

An all-in-one printer

Back at the office, you should have at least one all-in-one printer you can share. An all-in-one printer can print, copy, fax and scan documents. On some teams, each agent is equipped with his or her own printer, which is useful if the agents on the team primarily work out of their own homes. If you have a central office, consider purchasing a higher quality printer that everyone can share via the network. See the earlier section, "Networking your office computers," for details about networking options.

Tools & Technology Case Study: The Fairbanks Real Estate Group at Montecino & Associates

According to Brandon Fairbanks (www.brandonfairbanks.com) of Montecino & Associates in California, every sales executive on the Fairbanks Team receives the following resources:

- Transaction coordination with an online transaction program
- Full use of the client care coordinator
- The Fairbanks Real Estate Marketing Program
- Listing book and buyers book
- A comprehensive collection of STAR POWER® books and materials
- A library of real estate books and resources
- For Sale signs and lockboxes
- Fax, copy, and color printer
- DSL Internet access
- Phone service

- Use of the company's 2002 Jeep Grand Cherokee to show properties
- Conference room with computer and flat-panel television to preview properties with clients
- Business cards
- Continuous supply of buyer and seller leads
- AgentOffice® contact management program

All sales executives also receive the following training:
- Weekly training from Cheryl Montecino, the broker from whom Fairbanks bought the business
- Team coaching from a top-producing agent coach and trainer
- Tuition for the STAR POWER Universities
- Certified Residential Specialist (CRS) and Graduate Realtor Institute (GRI) classes
- Various conferences and classes throughout the year
- Individual training with Brandon Fairbanks
- Monday night conference calls with Ralph R. Roberts

In addition to supplying its sales executives with the technology they need to be successful, The Fairbanks Real Estate Group relies on several specialized software solutions, including the following:
- TransactionPoint® Software: Online software for transaction management, which allows the office to be virtually paperless
- WINForms Online®: A program that provides access to California real estate forms
- AgentOffice®: A contact management program and calendar
- SendOutCards®: An online marketing program for creating personal greeting cards to send to past clients
- Blogging Systems: This turnkey solution for real estate professionals enables the Fairbanks Real Estate Group to post news and information regularly and drive additional traffic to its Web sites.

Part III

Finally! Creating Your Team and Managing Them Well

Chapter 11

Handpicking Your Workforce

By the very nature of a team, relationships can become complex (and sometimes contentious). Because you and your team members voluntarily decide to work together, you often demand more from one another and expect to have more input on how things are done. You are essentially forming a partnership, a marriage of minds—you need to be as careful choosing someone to team up with as you are in choosing a mate.

In this chapter, we reveal strategies and techniques for identifying team members who are right for you, assessing a prospect's talents and personality, and managing the addition of a new member to the team.

Recognizing the Value of Diversity

Many of the top agent teams are also the most diverse. They contain a healthy mix of men, women and minorities; aggressive and laid-back personalities; different educational backgrounds; varying lifestyles; different family backgrounds; and so on. Diversity can benefit your team in several ways:

• Complementary personalities often can be instrumental in negotiations. One obvious manifestation of this is the good cop/bad cop routine. One agent plays the easygoing, cooperative, nurturing role, while the other is more aggressive, demanding, and willing to take risks. This approach often moves negotiations along, showing that the agent is not a welcome mat but is willing to be reasonable.

• Partnerships tend to fall into place naturally and can help both people achieve goals that each would find difficult to reach alone.

• Because some clients work better with men and others work better with women, having a mix of men and women enables your team to appeal to a broader clientele.

• Having people of different races and cultures in the office or people who speak other languages can also help your team become more accommodating.

When bringing new people on board, we all tend to hire people who are similar to us. Often, you have to fight against this urge and hire outside your comfort zone to add the right personnel for your team.

Identifying the Qualities of a Good Match for Your Team

Although you want some diversity on your team, avoid hiring anyone who is unlikely to embrace the same work ethic and overall goals you envision for the team. If you work 60 hours a week, you may become more than a little upset if you take on an agent who considers 30 hours a week full time. Ask yourself the following questions to identify the type of person you're looking for, and use your responses here to guide your assessments during the interview process (more on interviews later in this chapter):

• How do you address problems? Do you confront them immediately, finish what you are doing first, or take your time to analyze it and come up with a solution?

• Where do you see yourself in five years?

• Do you mind working evenings and weekends? What would you expect of your prospective teammates?

• Are you more of a people person or do you enjoy working on projects independently?

• Do you have any prior commitments or family commitments that could affect your work schedule? If so, how do you plan on dealing with scheduling conflicts?

Tip: When you take on a new team member, consider offering the position with a 30- to 60-day trial period. This gives you the chance to see whether the person is a good fit for the team and gives the new team member an opportunity to see whether he or she will be happy on your team. This approach also makes it much easier to part company

Be Careful Who You Hire!

Several years ago, I hired a general manager for my team. The person was vice president of a large financial company—somebody you might assume would be good at managing a real estate office.

I was speaking and traveling around the world and coaching clients, which took up a great deal of my time, so I hired the general manager to take care of the day-to-day operations. Everyone in the company embraced him—he was a fun guy! The caveat: He would come in late and, to make up for that, he would take an extra-long lunch. To make up for that, he would leave early. Needless to say, he wasn't exactly the golden boy of role models.

He complained about my 24/7 work ethic, and I complained about his—his 24/7 was 24 hours over the course of seven days! I figured that by bringing a general manager on board I would be better able to balance my workload, but I found myself having to work extra to pick up his slack. The moral of the story: When passing the baton, make sure the person you are passing it to has the same passion and drive as you do and is willing to do the work necessary to fulfill that passion. *–Ralph R. Roberts*

Finding and Attracting Talented Team Members

When you begin building a team, you soon realize that productive team members are revenue generators—bringing in revenue in excess of what it costs you to pay their commissions or salaries. As long as you can manage your team's growth, you always should be in the process of recruiting new members, who then can generate more revenue for the team.

Tip: Don't focus your recruiting efforts solely on people in the real estate industry. People in other industries, particularly those in customer service positions, often make top recruits. You can teach new team members the real estate business, but it is much tougher to teach them the people skills required to deal with clients.

Before approaching a prospective recruit, observe how the person interacts with others, including employees, colleagues and the general public. Also observe how the person takes direction—is the person able to accept input and guidance while still being assertive with his or her own ideas or solutions? All these "intangibles" are more important than experience in the real estate industry.

Consider the following ways to find and recruit potential team members:

• Networking for leads: When you start building your team and whenever you have an opening on your team from then on, tell everyone you know the position you need to fill and the qualifications you're looking for. Your most trusted friends and associates may have someone in mind who would be a good fit. Don't rule out any sources for good leads. You can find qualified candidates at your car dealer, in a restaurant or hotel, or anywhere you can see people in action doing their jobs.

Tip: Even when you don't have an opening on your team, you should be passively recruiting new members. Whenever you meet new people, ask them what they do and ask for their business card or contact information and then add them to your address book. When a need arises, you will have a complete database of individuals to contact to start your search.

• Advertising for qualified candidates and seeking them out online: After you determine what your team needs and draft a description of the duties you want new team members to perform (which we help you do in Chapter 4), create an ad describing the position and requesting qualified candidates to submit a cover letter and resume. You can post your want ad in the usual places, such as the local newspaper, but consider non-traditional placement as well:

- www.monster.com

- www.careerbuilder.com

- www.craigslist.org

- www.backpage.com

- base.google.com

- Local colleges and high schools that have co-op programs

Tip: The benefit of posting your want ad on Web sites like Craig's List and Backpage is that you can often find more tech-savvy team members at these sites.

Tip: Because virtual assistants conduct most of their operations online, you can find them on the Internet as well. Use one of your favorite search tools, such as Google™, to search for "real estate virtual assistant," or simply search for "virtual assistant," if you are looking for more general help.

You can also locate virtual assistants with experience in the real estate industry by visiting any of the following sites:

• International Virtual Assistants Association (IVAA) at www.ivaa.org

• Real Estate Virtual Assistants (REVA) Network at www.revanetwork.com

• Virtual Assistant Networking Association at www.virtualassistantnetworking.com

• Virtual Real Estate Assistant (VREA) at http://vrea.com

Scouting for Agents

As I learned through experience, team leaders should always be on the lookout for the right people no matter where that may be. This awareness enhanced my team's business at least twice:

I had been doing business for 20 years and kept running into a particular agent. She seemed to be everywhere, so I knew she was ambitious and diligent. She also was a natural salesperson, something that's hard to teach. She sold one of my listings, and I took the opportunity to sit down and talk with her about joining my team. She agreed.

I discovered another team member when I began losing out on prospective preforeclosure properties to another foreclosure investor. Time after time, this particular agent would contact a distressed homeowner with whom I was working and convince the homeowner to work with her rather than with me. She showed a lot of compassion, acted with integrity, and gave homeowners great advice. I knew I could never win against her, so I asked her to join our foreclosure team. Fortunately, she said yes. *—Ralph R. Roberts*

Getting Personal with Candidates (Within Reason!): Interviewing Successfully

After you have lined up a few promising candidates for a particular position, you have to assess their skills, personality and character through interviews and possibly even skills testing. This section shows you how to weed out the less-promising candidates and zero in on the best candidate for the team.

Warning: Don't hire someone simply based on one interview. Take your time and interview all the candidates to see what they all offer, then narrow it down again for a second interview. Involving other team members in the interview process is a good idea. Everyone will have a different perspective on the candidate that can give you greater insight. This process takes time— don't rush it just to fill an opening.

Before you start: Knowing what you're looking for

Before you begin searching for someone to fill a particular position on your team, you need to know what you're looking for. Hiring someone who is detail oriented and an expert at handling transactions may not be the best person to put in charge of handling the phones and dealing directly with clients. Likewise, making someone who loves working with people work independently crunching numbers may result in disaster.

Once you have identified a position you need to fill, jot down a detailed list of qualifications for that position. (This is especially important because if you reject a candidate who later files a discrimination complaint, you can point out exactly why the person you hired for the position was better qualified.) Does the position require typing, answering the phones, creating PowerPoint® presentations, crunching numbers, scheduling meetings, working directly with clients? What types of skills and training will the right candidate require? What sorts of tools and software should the person be experienced in using?

After you have a complete list of qualifications, review and prioritize the desired qualifications. Very rarely will you find a candidate who can fulfill all of the qualifications. By knowing which ones are most important, you can make a better choice.

Tip: Competency applies to more than just the knowledge and skills required to perform specific tasks. It also applies to attitude and ethics. Avoid the temptation to choose a candidate simply based on the fact that the person is attractive, well mannered, and knows what he or she is doing. The person also needs to have great values. A person who's just out for the easy money is not someone you want to add to your team. Here are some of the qualities you should be looking for:

- Does the person seem friendly and engaging? Does he smile while talking?

- Is the candidate a problem solver or a problem creator?

- Is the person's ultimate goal to take your position?

- Does the person have a strong work ethic?

- Does the person have strong family values, i.e., a good balance between her work and personal life?

- Does the person embody integrity? Integrity ensures that the money is handled properly and team members treat one another and their clients fairly. Without a sense of integrity, your team is at risk of losing its reputation and clients.

Warning: Many times team leaders can be guilty of trying to "help" someone by placing them on the team. They think that they can give them the opportunity to change or make their situation better. This is the wrong reason to add them to the team. It generally never works out and ends up hurting both parties. Don't waste time and resources on a candidate who is likely to drain your time, energy and resources.

Screening applicants

Some candidates will have a strong track record that indicates they are capable of fulfilling the position's requirements. In other cases, the person may have little or no related job experience—only what they claim they know and are capable of doing, which you should never completely trust. Some candidates will downplay their skills and talents while others exaggerate them.

To determine whether a candidate is truly qualified for a particular position, test the candidate's skills at performing actual tasks. Some teams create their own tests to assess skills such as typing, performing basic math, writing ad copy, and developing presentations. Candidates take the tests on-site, so the tests can be timed and to ensure that the candidate is the person who's actually completing the task. Figure 11-1 shows a math test that Marsha Waddelow gives to all applicants.

MATH TEST

Name_____ Date_____

1. 12,590.15 + 37,098.17 = _____   3. 5,750.25 − 2,060.17 = _____
2. 6,729.80 + 2,337.90 = _____   4. 12,590.50 − 37,098.25 = _____

Fill in the appropriate symbol : > , <, or =.

1. 0.297 _____ 1/3   4. 0.875 _____ 7/8

2. 1.50 _____ 2   5. 0.125 _____ 1/8

3. 0.750 _____ 7.5   6. 0.250 _____ 0.257

Answer the following.

1. 5% of 200,000 = _____   4. 100 = _____% of 100,000

2. 10% of 219,735 = _____   5. 50 = _____% of 100

3. 15% of 1,500 = _____   6. 15,000 = _____% of 150,000

Average the following numbers.

1. 2, 4, 6, 8 =_____   4. 0.5, 1 = _____

2. 3, 6, 9, 2 =_____   5. 0.75, 1.25 = _____

3. 10, 20, 33 = _____   6. 10%, 20% = _____

Bob Buyer purchases a home for $150,000. He decides on a 5% down payment. The mortgage is an 8%, 30-year, fixed-rate mortgage. Answer the following questions about Bob's situation:

---

1. What is the amount of the down payment? _____

2. What is the loan amount? _____

3. If Buyer earns 1.75% of the loan amount, what will Buyer's earnings be? _____

4. If Buyer decides on a down payment of 20% instead of 5%, how much more must he come up with? _____

Figure 11-1: A sample math assessment for prospective team members.

Administering a personality assessment
By Howard Brinton

Have you ever had the experience of meeting someone for the first time and feeling like you just hit it off? It was probably like you had known the person for years. You instantly felt comfortable with that person and the conversation flowed smoothly. You probably also have had first encounters that have gone less favorably. You probably met the person, exchanged a few words, and soon realized that you would probably never be able to communicate with this person or have a relationship at any level.

You've likely heard of the Golden Rule: "Do unto others as you would have done unto you." The premise of the Golden Rule has brought much good to the world, but as a professional in the customer service arena, you must graduate to the next level in order to be truly successful.

Tip: The Platinum Rule, simply put, is this: "Treat others as they want to be treated." This shift in thinking creates tremendous opportunity for you, not only in business, but also in your personal life. When you gain clarity of yourself and how you operate in relation to how people with different personality styles behave, you can begin to develop enhanced interactions with colleagues and clients. Moreover, selling becomes much more enjoyable and profitable.

Before you and your team members can apply your knowledge to working with others, you first need to understand yourselves. Many teams and even large companies rely on a professional personality assessment known as DISC® to screen applicants for a wide variety of positions in the real estate industry and in every other industry imaginable.

Breaking down the function of the DISC
DISC® is an acronym for the following, and its aim is to categorize people into one of four distinct personality styles:

D—Director: Characterized by control, power, and assertiveness.

I—Influencer: The ability to communicate effectively in social situations to influence an outcome.

S—Supporter: Patience, persistence, and thoughtfulness required to carry out a task that supports the work of others. (When William Moulton Marston created the DISC® assessment in the 1920s, this letter stood for "Submission.")

C—Critical Analyst: Structured and organized mind; tends to be very analytical and good at solving problems. (When Marston first devised the assessment, this letter stood for "caution" or "compliance.")

Generally speaking, the assessment boils down to two camps:

• People who fall into the D and I quadrants of the assessment scale tend to be better equipped for dealing with people. These are your frontline staff—your agents and customer service reps.

• People who fall into the S and C quadrants tend to be better at organizing and completing specific tasks and solving day-to-day problems. These are your behind-the-scenes people who make sure the office runs smoothly and transactions are processed correctly and efficiently.

Remember: It's critical that you realize that all people possess all four of these styles. For the vast majority of the population, one of the four is significantly more predominant than the others. You may find that when you're with clients, for example, you display more I personality traits, and when you're home with you children, you are more of an S. Approach each interaction with a person looking for cues; situations can arise that cause a person to be "out of character" at any given meeting. Exercise your common sense.

The DISC® in action, step-by-step

The following steps walk you through the DISC® so you can see how it works. First, you need to select where you fall on a supporting versus controlling continuum; then you choose where you fall on a direct versus indirect continuum. The combined result for these two categories defines which of the four personality styles you relate most closely to—D, I, S, or C.

Self-analysis: Supporting (open) versus controlling (guarded)

Do you consider yourself to be more supporting, or more controlling? The table below contains some indicators to help you distinguish between the two. After the table, mark a spot (a vertical line) on the continuum where you feel you fall.

Supporting (Open)	Controlling (Guarded)
relaxed and warm	formal and proper
opinion-oriented	fact-oriented
supportive	need to have control
flexible about time	time-disciplined
relationship-oriented	keep feelings to self
share feelings easily	task-disciplined
sensitive	

4	3	2	1
Very Supporting	**Somewhat Supporting**	**Somewhat Controlling**	**Very Controlling**

Self-analysis: Direct versus indirect

Do you consider yourself to be more direct, or more indirect? Here are some indicators to help you distinguish between the two. After the table, mark a spot (a vertical line) on the continuum where you feel you fall.

Indirect	Direct
Avoid risks	Take risks
Make decisions slowly	Make decisions quickly
Passive	Aggressive
Easygoing	Impatient
Listen well	Talkative
Reserved	Outgoing
Shy	Bold
Keep opinions to self	Express opinions readily

4	3	2	1
Very Indirect	**Somewhat Indirect**	**Somewhat Direct**	**Very Direct**

Self-analysis: Combining the continuums and evaluating

Transfer the spots you marked on the continuums to this grid to discover your result. For example, if you have a mark to the right of the 2 on the preceding continuum, draw a horizontal line about the same distance below the 2 in the center column that follows. If you have a mark to the left of the B in the continuum above, draw a vertical line the same distance to the left of the B in the center row below. Extend the two lines to the point at which they meet to determine the quadrant in which your personality falls—D, I, S, or C.

		4			
S		3		**I**	
A	**B**			**C**	**D**
C		2	**D**		
		1			

After you determine the quadrant in which your personality falls, use the following list to develop a clearer understanding of your personality type:

• **D—Director:** If you're both direct and controlling, you possess the D personality style. D's are bottom-line people. Common phrases you might hear from a D are, "Let's cut to the chase," or, "Just get it done." Others often perceive D's as impatient and insensitive. D's are often in sales or leadership positions because they are strong closers and are result oriented.

• **I—Influencer:** If you're both direct and supporting, you possess the I personality style. I's are the socializers—the people described as "the life of the party." Common phrases you might hear from an I are, "Ooh, here's an idea," or, "Are we having fun yet?" I's are perceived as emotional and energetic. They have great people skills and gravitate toward sales and other positions with high profiles and frequent recognition opportunities.

• **S—Supporter:** If you're both supporting and indirect, you possess the S personality style. S's are the nurturers and relaters; they live to serve and please others. They thrive on predictability, comfort and security. Common phrases you might hear from an S are, "Are you sure that's safe?" "Whatever makes you happy," or, "Whatever you think is best." S's are perceived as protective and supportive. S's gravitate toward positions with low risk or long-term stability that offer an opportunity to help others.

• **C—Critical Analyst:** If you're both indirect and controlling, you possess the C personality style. C's are perfectionists; they crave and thrive on order and process. Common phrases you might hear from a C are, "I need more information before I can make a decision," or, "Getting it 100 percent right is far more important than how quickly it gets done." C's are perceived as analytical, critical and inflexible. C's gravitate toward positions that require great attention to detail, thoroughness and accuracy.

Using DISC results to select team members

As a D-personality agent, you may be more inclined to select team members with D- or I-personalities, but that may not be the best choice. If you are taking on a new agent, a person with a D- or I-personality may be well suited for the position, but if you are looking for an assistant to handle phone calls, fill out paperwork, file documents, and manage your schedule and accounting, you are likely to be better off choosing someone with an S- or C-personality— someone who can act in a supporting role and who doesn't want *your* job.

Discussing the position and the candidate's qualifications: Q&A

Finding the right person or business relationship could be compared to finding the right spouse—it has a lot to do with chemistry. But don't forget that it has even more to do with business. The right business relationship should be based on a decisive assessment of the needs of both parties. To effectively achieve that end, you need to take four general steps, which encompass the whole of what your interview questions should cover:

1. Take a bit of time to get to know the candidate, starting out with general questions that don't pertain specifically to the job at hand. If you are unaccustomed to interviewing people, here are some questions that can help get the conversation going:

- Are you currently employed? Why are you looking to leave your current employer?
- What do you feel is your biggest accomplishment in life?
- What are your future goals?
- What was your worst customer service experience and how would you have handled it differently?
- Describe your best boss.
- Describe your worst boss.

2. Share your goals with each candidate and describe your team's philosophy and work ethic, so the person is well aware of your expectations. Write down everything you bring to the relationship and present it to each candidate during the interview. For example, let candidates know about the type of training you provide, the opportunities for earning bonuses or commissions, the resources at your disposal, your corporate culture, and opportunities for advancement. As you interview candidates, make sure they understand what you are looking for in terms of experience, skills and attitude. Present a detailed job description and explain what you expect. If you are willing to provide training, let the person know that although you expect her to ultimately be able to meet the job requirements, you will provide the training and resources she needs to perform these tasks.

3. Ask each candidate how he feels about your expectations; encourage him to be frank, and ask him what he can bring to the table. In other words, what can each candidate do to improve the team and take it to the next level? Remind him that if he accepts the position and cannot fulfill the requirements, he's unlikely to be happy working as part of your team.

4. Invite the interview candidate to ask any questions about the position, the company, the industry, and so on. Seeing what types of questions a candidate asks provides great insight into her capabilities and interest in the job. It also allows you to gauge her communication skills and professionalism. A good candidate should always have questions prepared ahead of time; think twice about considering someone who claims to have no questions at all.

Tip: Faye Rispoli recommends that you hire people who fit your business style: "When forming a team, keep your individual style in mind. If you are someone for whom training and motivating people comes naturally, then hiring the attitude and providing the training can work. If you are not much of a trainer and expect team members to hit the ground running, then be very thorough in the interview process—make sure you take on team members who have a proven track record in the industry and a solid client base to build on. Hiring team members who are not a fit for your business style can end up a drain on your time and resources."

Conducting a Behavioral Interview
The Waddelow Team, RE/MAX Associates of Arlington, Texas
(waddelowteam@hotmail.com)
By Marsha Waddelow

In a traditional job interview, a candidate can usually get away with telling you whatever you want to hear, even if he is fudg-

ing a bit on the truth. Even if you ask situational questions that start out "How would you handle XYZ situation?" the interviewee has minimal accountability. How do you know, after all, whether he would really react in a given situation the way he says he would?

In a behavioral interview, however, it's much more difficult for the interviewee to give responses that are untrue to her character. When she starts to tell a behavioral story, the behavioral interviewer typically will pick it apart to try to get at the specific behavior(s). The interviewer probes further for more depth or detail by asking follow-up questions, such as "What were you thinking at that point?" or "Tell me more about your meeting with that person," or "Lead me through your decision process." If the interviewee has told a story that's anything but totally honest, her response won't hold up through the barrage of probing questions.

Employers use the behavioral interview technique to evaluate a candidate's experiences and behaviors so they can determine the applicant's potential for success. The interviewer identifies job-related experiences, behaviors, knowledge, skills and abilities that the company has decided are desirable in a particular position. For example, some of the characteristics that companies look for include the following:

- Ability to think critically
- Self-motivation
- Willingness to learn
- Willingness to travel
- Self-confidence
- Cooperative as part of a team
- Professionalism

"Questions" typically start out with something like "Tell about a time..." or "Describe a situation..." Many employers use a rating system to evaluate selected criteria during the interview. Following are some questions we use to initiate our behavioral interviews:

- Give me a specific example of a time when you used good judgment and logic in solving a problem.
- Give me an example of a time when you set a goal and were able to meet or achieve it.

- Tell me about a time when you had to use your presentation skills to influence someone's opinion.
- Give me a specific example of a time when you had to conform to a policy with which you did not agree.
- Please discuss an important written document you were required to complete.
- Tell me about a time when you had to go above and beyond the call of duty in order to get a job done.
- Tell me about a time when you had too many things to do and you were required to prioritize your tasks.
- Give me an example of a time when you had to make a split-second decision.
- What is your typical way of dealing with conflict? Give me an example.
- Tell me about a time you were able to successfully deal with another person even when that individual may not have personally liked you (or vice versa).
- Tell me about a difficult decision you've made in the last year.
- Give me an example of a time when you tried to accomplish something and failed.
- Give me an example of when you showed initiative and took the lead.
- Tell me about a recent situation in which you had to deal with a very upset customer or coworker.
- Give me an example of a time when you motivated others.
- Tell me about a time when you delegated a project effectively.
- Give me an example of a time when you used your fact-finding skills to solve a problem.
- Tell me about a time when you missed an obvious solution to a problem.
- Describe a time when you anticipated potential problems and developed preventive measures.
- Tell me about a time when you were forced to make an unpopular decision.

Chapter 12

Establishing a Firm Foundation

When you serve in the military, the government provides everything you need to be the best soldier possible. They provide all your training, education, equipment and clothing, right down to your skivvies. They take care of your haircuts and provide you with everything you need to stay well groomed. They cover your healthcare and dental work. They help provide housing for your family and try to reassure you that while you are away, your family has the support it needs. As a result, when you are fighting on the front lines, your mind can focus on your job and on taking care of the others fighting alongside you rather than on your duties back home. How else could you fight?

The same is true when you are managing a team. You need to take care of the people who are taking care of business. You need to make sure that every team member is having his or her needs met both on the job and off the job. Keep in mind American psychologist Abraham Maslow's Hierarchy of Needs:

- **Self-actualization:** Creativity, morality, spontaneity, innovation

- **Esteem:** Self-esteem, confidence, achievement, respect

- **Love/belonging:** Friendship, family, and intimacy

- **Safety:** Shelter and security of body, employment, resources, health, and family

- **Physiological:** Breathing, eating, drinking, sleeping, reproducing

Generally speaking, needs lower down on the list must be satisfied first, so the person is free to pursue needs that are higher up on the list. Compensating team members with commissions, salary, or other monetary awards address only the two lowest needs brackets—physiological and safety. You also need to provide your team members with a sense of belonging, heightened self-esteem, and the opportunity to express themselves and play a creative role on the team.

In this chapter, we show you how to foster a positive working environment in which team members collaborate to achieve team-related goals. We present strategies for training and integrating new agents, providing the training team members need to use the technologies you provide them, managing without micromanaging, and fostering a positive work environment and a sense of community among you and your team members.

Raising Up New Agents

If you are bringing an experienced agent into the fold who already has a solid track record as a top producer, you may need to provide little if any training for that person. In fact, that person may be helpful in training the rest of your agents. Sometimes, however, you may be adding an agent to your team who has absolutely no experience in real estate. In such cases, serious training begins on day one.

Training should proceed according to a plan that's designed to ensure success. We recommend that new agents follow a plan that tracks these steps:

1. Obtain a real estate license. If your prospective agent isn't already licensed, send him to school to obtain his license, which provides him with the base level of education he needs to perform as an agent.

2. Shadow a top agent on the team for 30 days. Have your new agent shadow you or another top agent on your team for 30 days. The new agent should be with you at all times, observing how you work, accompanying you to meetings and appointments, and offering clerical assistance in return. This provides the person with a clear idea of how you operate and the level of commitment you expect. This is one of the best ways to train new agents.

3. Work as a buyer's agent for a year. Although you may ultimately want the new agent to work as a listing agent, it's often a mistake to start the person as a listing agent, because of the complexities involved. Your new agent should first obtain experience in an easier role—as a buyer's agent.

4. Work with a mentor for the first five listings. If you and your new agent decide to make the transition to being a listing agent, require your new agent to work under the supervision of your top listing agent for at least the first five transactions. In return, the supervising agent should receive a portion of the new agent's commissions.

5. Continue mentoring on an as-needed basis. After the new agent clears all the hurdles, let her know that she has the support of the entire team and can seek assistance whenever needed; be sure to point her in the right direction regarding whom to ask what.

6. Continue education and certification. Encourage new agents to become lifelong learners. Education should not end the day the agent begins listing homes. Your new agent should work toward becoming a full-fledged REALTOR® and receive the GRI (Graduate, Realtors Institute) and CRS (Certified Residential Specialist) certifications. If the person decides to focus on buyers, he or she should work toward obtaining the ABR (Accredited Buyer Representative) certification. These are all offered through the NATIONAL ASSOCIATION OF REALTORS®.

New Agent Training Case Study: The Ralph Roberts Team

Paul Corona, a restaurant manager whom I courted for several years before he finally decided to join our team, describes the intensive training that he obtained during his first year with Ralph Roberts Realty:

"As soon as I was hired, I went to school to get my real estate license. Ralph told me that once I received my license, I would shadow him for the next 30 days. I would go on every appointment he had, both professional and personal. The plan was that I would experience the entire industry in a crash course and hopefully get an idea of where I would best fit on the team—how to best utilize my skill set.

"Luckily for me, my first day was at the CRS (Certified Residential Specialists) convention in New Orleans. Ralph flew me to the convention and immediately put me to work in preparation for his speaking sessions through the weekend and working at our products booth. I was in awe of the industry and his standing in the industry and knew I had made the right decision.

"I think it was extremely important that I had confidence in what I was doing and that I was learning from the best. I cannot discount this because I think I was set up for success immediately.

"I proceeded to go on every appointment Ralph had for 30 days. The first thing I learned was the work ethic required to be a top broker in the industry. I think it is important for any new team member to get a taste of the pace required for success.

"I did a large portion of the preparation for Ralph's appointments, so I soon had a good working knowledge of everything we were doing. This is very important—understanding what the meetings were about and specific areas that Ralph focused on eased the learning curve. With the necessary framework in place, I was able to learn new skills quickly.

"I went on buyer appointments, listing appointments, home inspections, final walk-throughs and (most importantly) closings. I also went to bank meetings, board meetings and municipal meetings. I even was taught how to answer the phone system for the building.

"Ralph began by teaching me how to perform comparative market analyses for specific areas and types of homes. To be an effective REALTOR®, I needed to know values, market trends and area information. I had to learn about every area within our target market. I was taught the MLS system and how to utilize it by both the board and our company.

"I was taught the paperwork on every type of transaction. I had to write a practice offer on my own home and present it. I had to do a complete listing on my house including all the paperwork, pictures and so on. I was taught all of the costs associated with buying and selling a house including the mortgage and title costs.

"Ralph had manuals for all transactions readily available for reference. This may sound insignificant but it was invaluable to have these. You would be shocked at how many professionals in our industry do not know some of this basic material because they were not taught from the beginning.

"When the 30 days were up and I had learned all I could learn, it was time for trial and error. I had decided at the time that the buyer department was the most practical spot for me to start. I feel it is much easier and makes more sense to start a new agent with buyers. There is just too much knowledge required for listings that can only be learned with experience. Working with buyers is more about personality and helping someone find what they are looking for through the computer and constant showings. You're not exactly an order taker, because it takes more than that, but the buyer tells you what they want, and your job is to find it.

"Listings are a completely different animal. You need to have market knowledge and specific negotiating skills that can only be attained through practical experience. Except for the rarest of instances, any new team member should start with buyers for at least one year before any movement to listings is considered.

"I was then assigned to a veteran member of the team to continue my training. This person had to monitor my first five transactions. In exchange, they received a portion of my commissions. I was kind of irritated by this at first but as I went through the process, it made perfect sense. It was probably the best money I had ever spent!

"They were there every step of the way and after the five deals I was truly ready to be on my own. I still had a safety net of team members and Ralph to fall back on for questions and direction, but I clearly knew enough on my own and was showing the skill to close transactions. Finally, I was a REALTOR®!

"Not all recruitments went as smoothly and with as much success as mine did, but you cannot reasonably expect that they all will. I do know that how I was recruited, how I was trained, and how I was monitored from the outset was the single largest factor in my success. It helped form my character and develop insight into how I was going to fit into the team. I think it established rather quickly that I was going to be successful."

Although your approach to training may differ, you should have some system in place that's designed to make your new agents highly successful as quickly as possible. Simply throwing a new person into the mix without the proper training and resources is not fair to the new team member, existing team members or, most importantly, yourself and your business. *–Ralph R. Roberts*

Providing Technological Training

Equipping your team with the latest technology (as explained in Chapter 10) is only the first step toward getting your team up and running; you also need to teach team members the basics of using that technology and train them on how to use it most efficiently. You have two options for training, each of which suits different purposes:

• Whenever you introduce a new technology or new system, you may want to provide training for the entire team at once. You may even be able to use the opportunity as a bonding experience for team members. Traveling to a seminar or conference together and attending many of the same sessions can function as a nice break from the routine while at the same time making your entire team more tech savvy.

• When a particular type of training is expensive or only one or two team members require the training, consider providing the requisite training to individual team members. Those team members can then return and provide instruction for the other members of the team. This approach also lessens the amount of office downtime—while selected team members are getting trained, the others can be tending to clients.

Fostering a Team Mentality

When you have a team, everyone is in charge of making numerous decisions on a daily basis, but you want to make sure you have the right people making the most important decisions. A closing manager, for example, may not be qualified to make a decision that requires agent training and expertise. In addition, your team should have a system of checks and balances that prevents even the most powerful member of the team from making decisions without consulting the rest of the team members.

Think of your team as a governing body, but on a smaller scale, and try to structure it accordingly. In the following sections, we provide some direction to start your team out right.

Clarifying responsibilities of the team leader and other members

Every organization requires a go-to guy or gal who calls the shots. In large corporations, the CEO (chief executive officer) is in charge. On teams, the agent who initiated the team (so, you, in all likelihood) is probably the one in charge. This person is the one whom everyone consults when nobody else can answer their questions or when major decisions need to be made. The team leader is generally the person who takes on the most risk and "owns" the team, but it can be another key member of the team. The team leader is responsible for the following:

- **Goal setting:** Although each team member is responsible for setting and achieving his or her own goals, the team leader sets goals for the entire team.

- **Coaching/training:** Team members may train one another, but the team leader is responsible for making sure each member of the team has the training required to perform their job.

- **Making resources available:** Whatever team members need to perform their jobs effectively must be made readily available. This includes technology, human resources, office space, conference rooms, and so on.

- **Designing, implementing, and auditing systems:** The team leader should know best how to run the business and be able to break the entire business down into a set of procedures and tasks to run the office more efficiently. The team leader is constantly in the process of asking, "What are we doing and how can we do it better?"

- **Delegating sales responsibilities to agents:** To ensure that both work and opportunities are divided as fairly as possible, the team leader ultimately decides who's doing what, although the insights of other team members should be considered.

- **Delegating daily operational tasks to the director of operations:** If your team has a director of operations or office manager, that person should be in charge of running the office, ordering supplies and services, paying bills, and making sure everyone has the resources required to do their job. Think of the director of operations as the facilitator who reports directly to the team leader.

• **Facilitating communication:** Although the entire team should work toward establishing a system of open communications, the team leader must make sure that team members are actually communicating with one another as needed. The team leader may also need to step in during communication breakdowns and conflicts.

• **Monitoring progress:** The team leader checks the pulse of the team regularly to ensure that it is on track to meet its goals and is operating in accordance with the group's vision.

• **Maintaining quality:** The entire team should be committed to upholding the highest standards in the industry, but occasionally, certain items may fall through the cracks. The team leader is the unofficial quality control manager—an advocate for clients.

• **Spearheading career development:** All team members should be life-long learners, committed to staying on top of their game and constantly learning new ways to improve efficiency and productivity. The team leader should foster an atmosphere in which learning and career development are priorities.

• **Solving and avoiding problems:** Perhaps the most important role that the team leader plays is that of problem solver—identifying problems that arise and then developing and helping to implement solutions. A team leader has to be constantly on the lookout for problems, because some of them can be avoided, while others are opportunities for growth.

The team leader may call most of the shots, but to function effectively as a team, all members need to share power in the decision-making process. Teams are generally more effective and team members are generally more motivated when all team members have some level of input in the decision-making process. This gives team members a sense of ownership in the team and responsibility for the team's success. In this section, we lay out the types of decisions that team leaders can and cannot make without consulting the team.

Your team leader is capable of managing the daily office operations and is generally capable of making all but the most important decisions. Decisions that team leaders are qualified to make without consulting the team include the following:

• **No-brainers:** Decisions that require no verbal consent, because the team leader is confident regarding how the team feels about it. These are decisions that the group need not be bothered with.

• **Time-sensitive decisions:** Decisions that would negatively affect the team if the decision-making process were delayed.

• **Decisions that have no consensus:** When team members cannot come to agreement, the team leader has the power to make the ultimate decision.

In some cases, such as the following, input from team members is very important:

• Setting the team's vision and mission statement.

• Hiring new team members, particularly partners who will own a stake of the team.

• Firing team members who fail to perform up to well-defined standards.

• Major acquisitions or expenditures, such as investing in a new computer network or adding a new division.

Considering various team-building ideas

Although each player on the team is important, the team's needs take precedence over individual needs. When you have more than one agent on your team, you have more inventory and more people to market that inventory, so take full advantage of it. If the team is a healthy, thriving unit, then all individuals on the team will benefit accordingly. If only one team member is benefiting at the expense of all others, then the team and all its members will ultimately suffer.

Fortunately, most agents want to be team players. They have a natural desire to be a part of something that's bigger than themselves and they crave the support that an agent team provides. Even so, you can do a great deal as a team leader to encourage everyone to become more of a team player:

• Require attendance and participation at all team meetings.

• Encourage partnerships among team members. Team members can assist one another in rehearsing scripts and role playing and can shadow one another to acquire new strategies and techniques.

• Attend a conference or seminar as a team. Traveling together and attending the same presentations and seminars can function as a bonding experience for your team.

• Share listings at weekly meetings. Every agent on your team should do what he or she can to help the other agents with their listings:

-Offer bonuses to anyone on the team who sells a team member's listing.

-When an agent is having trouble moving a listing, brainstorm for ideas to help that agent.

• Celebrate one another's accomplishments.

• Conduct a brainstorming session when one of your agents is having trouble with a particular client or account.

• Assign team projects to improve marketing, office efficiency, customer service, or some other aspect of your business.

Tip: Consider banning cell phones and interruptions from weekly meetings. This is tough, but it sends a signal to the entire team that these meetings are of primary importance.

Hosting a No-Shoptalk Lunch

Wayne Turner (www.wayneturner.com) of the Wayne Turner Real Estate Company in Hendersonville, Tennessee, believes in having fun with his team, and one way he encourages his team to have fun and share other aspects of their lives is to have a No-Shoptalk lunch together:

"As a team, we go out to eat and put a bowl in the center of the table. If anyone mentions real estate, they have to toss a dollar in the bowl. Most of the team has gotten pretty good about not mentioning real estate, but if they do, they're penalized a dollar. That helps cover the cost of the lunch, but more importantly, it enables us to focus on topics that have nothing to do with real estate.

"We try to go out to lunch once a month as a team to take it easy and relax—just kick back and enjoy one another's company.

"I also treat my team as a family. I want to always be there for them and I expect them to always be there for me. I constantly remind my team that if they need anything or if they have any questions, not to hesitate to call me on the weekends, in the evenings or early in the morning, because this is what having a team is all about."

Motivating Team Members to Boost Profits

The biggest roadblock getting in the way of success is lack of motivation. People often have great ideas and even great plans for executing those ideas, but when it comes time to move forward, they lack the willpower and energy to do it.

To build a top-producing team, constantly motivate your agents to set and achieve higher goals. Following are suggestions for ways to motivate team members:

• **Set minimum production goals.** Team membership is not a right but a privilege that team members must earn. If they don't produce, they don't get to stay.

• **Provide motivational books, CDs, DVDs, and seminars.** As Charlie "Tremendous" Jones used to say, "You are only as good as the books you read, the tapes you listen to, and the people you know." Make sure your team is listening to positive messages on a regular basis, so they will think and act with a positive mindset.

• **Encourage goal setting.** Each team member should design and build their own goal board or collage, showing pictures that reflect their vision of what they want in their lives. You should also have team goals that the entire team can work together to achieve.

• **Recognize excellence.** By offering public recognition of outstanding performance and productivity, you reward the exceptional team member and spur other team members on to achieve even greater success. You can recognize excellence by offering monthly, quarterly, and annual awards; announcing events via press releases and newsletters; acknowledging performance during team meetings; and so on.

• **Reward excellence.** Although recognition is often enough, prizes in the form of bonus money, free trips, and gift certificates can also help motivate team members. When they see that you appreciate their efforts and are willing to invest in them, they will work harder for you.

Improving Employee Retention

At a recent Howard Brinton STAR POWER® Leadership University Retreat, the presenter revealed the results of a military study designed to improve retention rates. Although most of us think that we lose team members because of their desire to earn more money, this study showed that money was not the overriding reason why people keep or leave their jobs.

The results of the study revealed that the top reasons soldiers stayed in the military was not for money but because:

- They enjoyed their job
- They liked the people they worked with
- They were treated with kindness and respect
- They found value in their work
- They felt needed and appreciated

Money was way down near the bottom of the list. Keep this in mind when developing your incentive package. Relationships and work environment are far more important to most people than monetary compensation.

Building a Positive Working Environment

All too often, team leaders take a reactive approach to managing their teams, but the "if it ain't broke, don't fix it" approach can often lead to regular conflicts and a feeling that the team is constantly putting out fires.

Being proactive instead of reactive can place your team on a steady course, making it almost immune to counterproductive conflict and dissention among team members. In the following sections, we show you how to spot the differences between negative and positive teams, create a positive working environment, and shut down negative thoughts and language before they gain a foothold.

Recognizing characteristics of negative and positive workplaces

Before we get into the details of how to build a positive, forward-thinking team, let's define what we mean by negative and positive workplace. This can help you form your vision of the type of workplace you want for your team and the type of workplace you need to avoid.

The negative workplace

A negative workplace is one in which everyone involved dreads getting up in the morning and coming to work—a place where people can't wait to leave and go home. Here are some of the typical signs of a negative work environment:

- The boss is unfriendly.
- The boss is critical.
- Employee turnover is high.
- Employee morale is low.

- Everyone watches the clock.
- People receive very little performance feedback.

The negative workplace usually has one or more negative personalities driving it—the "sky is falling" Chicken Littles, for example, or the woe-is-me Eeyores from Winnie the Pooh fame. No matter how good these people have it, they will always look for (and find) the negative in everything. You may be able to turn around the attitudes of these Negative Nancys, or you may just need to purge the team of them.

The positive workplace
The positive workplace is one in which team members go to bed excited about waking up in the morning to new opportunities. It is a place where everyone feels like anything is possible—a place where people feel they can achieve whatever goal they set. Here are some signs of a positive workplace:

- The boss demonstrates interest in team members.
- The boss has an encouraging attitude.
- People enjoy their work.
- Team members exude company pride and loyalty.
- People know where they stand with their supervisors.
- Team members and other staff receive plenty of constructive feedback.
- The staff regularly works past office hours without ever realizing it.

The positive workplace is filled with people who are eternal optimists. Words like "can't" and "impossible" rarely cross their lips, because, as they see it, anything that the team puts its collective minds and resources into achieving is possible. The positive workplace is usually led by a positive team leader who understands the importance of living with the right attitude.

Creating a positive workplace
A positive workplace doesn't just happen. Workplaces can quickly become negative without any effort, but a positive workplace requires leadership and nurturing. Hundreds of books have been written on the subject of managing and motivating people, and just as many training seminars are conducted on the same subject around the world every day. Yet, too few businesses are committed enough to doing what's necessary to create a positive workplace.
In the following sections, we distill all the information on managing and motivating people into the following six skills:

- Be positive.

• Tell people what you expect of them.

• Show interest in your fellow team members.

• Create an encouraging environment.

• Recognize and reward good performance.

• Curb office gossip.

Skill #1: Remain positive at all times

A positive team begins with a positive leader. You can't expect your fellow team members and staff to exude a positive attitude and a strong work ethic unless you do so yourself. One of your main jobs as team leader is to model the type of behavior you expect:

• Be positive no matter what the situation. Being positive when times are good is easy, but remaining positive when things are bad is even more important.

• Expect bad things to happen. Keep Murphy's Law in mind: "If anything can go wrong, it will." Expect bad things to happen and make the best of the wrongs that roll your way.

• Laugh it off. Laughing with your team over mishaps can transform negative situations into positive bonding experiences. Creating a "Can you believe that!" moment can significantly lift team morale.

• Learn from it. Every mistake is an opportunity to learn and grow as a team. Make the most of your mistakes.

• Install a suggestion box. You can make a joke of it by ducttaping over the slot, but then encourage team members to take it more seriously. You may also consider distributing problem/solution forms that team members and staff can complete and submit.

Remember: The word "problem" has a nasty connotation for most people, but the fact is that inside every problem is an opportunity. Nearly every invention has been born of a problem that an innovative and industrious human being decided to solve.

According to Wayne Turner, one of the best things you can do for your team is to stop using the word "problem" altogether:

Without problems there is no profit, so I don't like to use the word "problem." My team, my staff, my family, and everyone else in my circle of influence has agreed to replace the word "problem" with "challenge," because in our society, there is nothing that we cannot do.

The moment that you say "problem," people are stricken with terror, "Oh no, what's happened?!" But if you say we have a little challenge that we are going to overcome, it instantly fills people with hope and motivates them to come up with their own ideas of how to overcome the challenge.

This little change in language has made a huge difference for me and my team. We know that whenever a challenge presents itself, we have an opportunity to profit, to learn, to develop. You may not profit monetarily, but each challenge has the potential to make you a better agent, a better human being, and a better team. Each challenge opens an opportunity to write a new article, write a book, or come up with a speaking topic at a seminar. Whatever your goals may be, those opportunities will come forward to you full circle.

Skill #2: Clearly state your expectations

Chances are pretty good that at least once in your life, you disappointed someone by failing to meet their expectations—expectations that you were completely unaware of, by the way. Maybe it was a parent, a teacher or a boss. This probably made you feel more than a little frustrated. After all, how can you be expected to achieve a goal you're unaware of?

Before you can expect team members to behave in a certain way, perform specific tasks or achieve milestones, you must let them know what is expected of them:

- Communicate expectations clearly.

- Present each person with a detailed job description.

- Identify specific performance standards and policies you have in place if the person fails to fulfill his or her responsibilities.

- Specify deadlines.

- Set goals.

Tip: Everyone has a different learning style, so state your expectations both verbally and in writing. Meet with the person in private and review your expectations. Ask questions to ensure that the person fully understands you. This can help you avoid hearing statements such as "Nobody ever told me that."

Improving E-mail Efficiency

Alan Shafran has taken e-mail efficiency to new levels and offered to share some of his tips:

- Contact your ISP to see if it offers any spam-filtering tools, and then learn how to use them. We use Virusguard® to assist in spam filtering.
- If you receive faxes via e-mail, create a rule in Outlook® or whatever e-mail program you use to have all incoming faxes moved to a separate folder.
- Create a rule to automatically file outgoing faxes in a separate folder.
- Create another rule to automatically file failed outgoing faxes in a separate folder. This allows agents to go to one place to make sure that the faxes they sent were actually delivered.
- To handle regular e-mail more efficiently, create a filing system under your Inbox. You can name it whatever you'd like but we use Listings, Escrows, Team Related Items, and Offers. I have folders for each person on the team so I can quickly reference an e-mail when needed. It saves time and keeps my inbox clear.
- Another time-saving tool is to create a task from your e-mail. If I get an e-mail from a seller, for example, stating that they are out of flyers, I can drag that e-mail into the task list in Outlook, make a due date for it, and assign it to my listing coordinator. It automatically sends her the task, she accepts it, and when she has sent out the flyers, she marks the task "complete," and it sends me an e-mail stating such. The same thing can be done for the calendar item. If I receive an e-mail regarding an appointment time, I drag it to my calendar and drop it into the appropriate date and time. That way I have all the information needed from the e-mail at my fingertips in the calendar item.

Skill #3: Show sincere interest in team members

A team is like a marriage. If you were married to someone who never greeted you, never looked you in the eye, never asked for your opinion, and never followed your advice, you probably would not want to stay married to that person for very long. The same is true with a team. Team members must feel accepted, respected and needed by the team leader and all other team members.

To show interest in team members, practice the following:

- Make eye contact.
- Address team members and other staff by name.

- Ask team members and other staff for opinions and suggestions—and implement the worthwhile ones.
- Greet people with a smile.
- Compliment team members and other staff on their performance.
- Listen when people talk.

Tip: Make a conscious effort to become more sensitive to teammates and staff. Are you giving preferential treatment to certain people? Do you listen to suggestions from certain members only after you hear them from someone else? Do you sense jealousy among staff members that is instigated by your behavior?

The way you treat your fellow team members and staff can have a huge effect on productivity. Failing to demonstrate a sincere interest in others can hinder productivity and make people feel angry, less confident and stripped of self-esteem.

Team Player Responsibility Case Study: The Vanderblue Team

At the Vanderblue Team (www.vanderblueteam.com) in Fairfield, Connecticut, only family takes precedence over team. We asked team leader Julie Vanderblue what she expected of her team, and this is what she had to say:

"Our rule is that we all have to be there for each other. I feel that this comes naturally for the agents on our team, because we truly do care about each other both in the business world and as people. Everyone has to be accountable and responsible for being there for each other. Obviously, some team members will have more time to commit to certain things than others, but every team member should give what they can.

"Team support must be a constant by all team members. On our team, every team member must see every listing, and team members are expected to attend and participate in team events as much as possible. We have many team events; we don't expect all team members to be able to attend every event, but they have to commit to a good percentage of them.

"Team meetings are mandatory, no cell phones in meetings,

and no interrupting in meetings (although that is a tough one). We also require attendance at brainstorming sessions for agents who are struggling with an account.

"When you feel that others are there to help you, it makes you want to help back. I find that most people truly enjoy helping others. We are all in this together and it creates many opportunities to help."

Skill #4: Create an encouraging environment

As a team, one of your goals should be to create a dynamic work environment—one in which team members feel as though they can achieve anything and have your support in achieving new heights.

An encouraging work environment is more fun and rewarding for everyone and delivers some very tangible benefits:

- Increased productivity

- New ideas

- Strengthened sense of commitment and loyalty

- Increased motivation

- Improved self-esteem

- Lower turnover

- Less sabotage

- Stronger reputation as a good employer, making it easier to recruit new talent

To foster such an environment, do your best to:

- Demonstrate how much you value innovation and new ideas.

- Promote creativity.

- Reward risk taking.

- Encourage fun and laughter.

- Show your appreciation of the team and individual members.

- Thank people for their contributions.

- Show others that you appreciate their flexibility.

- Make everyone feel like a part of the team.

Above all, avoid micromanaging. The best way to fuel resentment is to constantly look over the shoulders of your team and second-guess their decisions. If you micromanage your team, you essentially have a stranglehold on it that can choke the creativity and energy out of your staff. Anyone who begins to feel as though they are wasting their time and creative energy is going to be spending more energy looking for another position somewhere else. When assigning tasks to various team members, make sure that you are giving them real responsibility to make the decisions required to carry out those tasks.

Remember that whenever you start a team, you give up some control, but the tradeoff is generally beneficial. You no longer get to have everything your way. In return, you get people to take on some of the workload and perhaps even school you on better ways to do business. As team leader, one of your main jobs is to manage your human resources in such a way as to tap their full potential. You cannot accomplish this by dispensing orders—all people are not like you, and the way one person performs a certain task is not always the best way for others. When you are playing the role of human resource manager, you should:

- Involve all team members and other staff members in setting the direction and goals for the company and for themselves. They may come up with more challenging goals than you would have set for them. (We talk about goal setting in Chapter 13.)

- Let go—let them do their jobs.

- Get rid of any thoughts you may have that "nobody can do it better than me," "my way is best," and "it's my way or the highway."

- Don't question every decision that other team members make.

Julie Vanderblue sums it up best when she says, "Teach them to fly, but let them soar on their own."

Remember: Give your personnel the leeway to make mistakes. If a mistake is made, you can then step in, review the situation and use it as a learning experience. When team members see your faith in them and they begin to feel that faith, they will soar to new heights beyond what you could ever have expected—but you have to let go for this to happen.

Skill #5: Recognize and reward good performance
When you reward good performance, you send a message to the entire team that you:

- Noticed the job they performed

- Value performance

- Reward performance

Recognition and reward function as a reinforcer—anything that happens after a behavior that tends to increase the chances that the behavior will be

repeated. Reinforcers include the following:
- Compliments
- Smiles
- Thumbs-up gesture
- Saying "Thank you"
- Public announcement of achievement
- Positive letter in the personnel file
- Promotion
- Time off
- Special parking space
- First choice on schedule
- Dinner with the "boss"

Skill #6: Curb office gossip
Nothing can drag down an entire staff faster than negative chitchat. Even knocking the competition can be counterproductive. The key is to nip negative speak in the bud. As soon as someone on your team begins spewing negativity, shut it down:
- Lead by example—don't gossip and avoid saying anything bad about someone else, even if it happens to be true.
- Change the subject.
- Obtain accurate information to counter any false or misleading statements.
- Tell the gossiper that you don't feel comfortable discussing this topic.
- Walk out of the room when people begin talking negatively about others in the industry.

Tip: Gossip is like playing a kids game of telephone. Each time the gossip is repeated, it is embellished in some way with additional falsehoods. It takes a strong person to stand up and say, "Let's change the subject." Be that person. You will instantly gain trust and respect as someone who refuses to talk behind the backs of others.

Chapter 13

Taking on the Role of Mentor and Motivator

When you take the leap from agent to team leader, it is usually because you are already an excellent agent, and you can prove it— you have too much work to handle all by yourself. It also indicates that you are pretty effective at motivating yourself and acquiring whatever training and information you need to be successful.

Now, you need to transfer these skills to your new role as team leader. Instead of teaching and motivating yourself, your new job is to mentor and motivate the people you add to your team. Wayne Turner (www.wayneturner. com) of the Wayne Turner Real Estate Company in Hendersonville, Tennessee, offers two excellent suggestions on the topic:

• Praise in public.

• Scold in private.

The idea that people are primarily motivated by money is a myth. People need money to survive and to be able to drive to work every day, but they need something else to motivate them to do an outstanding job—and what most people need is recognition. By praising people in public, you give them the recognition they hunger for. By scolding them in private, you let them know that you are well aware of the fact that they are not living up to the agreed-upon standards. It's a highly effective carrot-and-stick approach.

Remember also that team members often lose their motivation when they begin to feel like second-class citizens. In most cases, this occurs when team members are not given a voice in the team's vision and mission and have not been given enough responsibility. They begin to feel that what they are doing is a job instead of a career, and they simply lose interest.

Helping Team Members Establish Professional Goals

Assuming every team member has the same goals as you can be very counterproductive; if your goal is to sell more homes, but another team member's goal is to sell fewer homes for more money, for example, you could be undermining one another's efforts. You may want to be the top-producing team in the state or in the nation, but some team members may value family time more than making a boatload of money or they may find greater rewards in helping distressed homeowners than in earning sales awards. As team leader, you need to develop a strong vision and goals for the team as a whole, but you also need to make sure that other team members have some freedom in developing their own individual goals.

As a team, you need to share your goals and make sure that everyone's goals fit with the overall team vision, but you cannot impose individual goals on others. As team leader, you should assist other members of the team with goal setting, but not to the point of setting goals for someone else or even setting sales quotas for agents on your team. Find out where each team member is in her career, where she wants to be, and how she plans to get there, and then assist her in setting milestones that put her on the path to success. As long as the goals are well defined and everyone is in agreement, the individual responsibilities can vary accordingly without causing tension on the team.

Remember: Allowing team members to be self-directed does not mean that you give them complete freedom to set their own goals and hold themselves accountable—unless, of course, they have a proven track record. Goals should be shared, so that team members have someone else to hold them accountable and provide the support they need to achieve their goals.

One of the best ways to motivate yourself and your teammates is to encourage everyone to set goals, develop plans for achieving those goals, and then work the plan. The process pretty much follows this six-step approach:

1. Describe a goal or vision.

2. Break the goal into milestones and create a timeline.

3. Devise a strategy.

4. Identify tasks.

5. Identify resources.

6. Work the plan.

In this section, we take you step-by-step through this process.

Describing a goal or vision

When drawing up a plan for success, it's usually a good idea to start at the end and then work backwards. Begin with what you hope to achieve—your objective—and then figure out how you are going to get there.

For most teams, setting a goal consists of specifying the number of houses the team will sell in a year or specifying the gross sales for the year in terms of millions of dollars. The team can then develop a strategy for meeting this goal together. Other teams may have a goal-setting meeting in which each agent commits to selling a certain number of homes and generating a specific portion of the team's revenue. However you choose to proceed, avoid the temptation of setting sales quotas for agents—work with them to set their own goals or quotas.

Several teams we talked with take a rewards approach. All the team members envision what they would use their commissions to purchase, and then they work back from rewards to setting sales goals that would secure those rewards. See the nearby sidebar, "Creating Reward Collages to Stir Motivation," for details.

Creating Reward Collages to Stir Motivation

At Ralph Roberts Realty, I passed out 6-foot tall sheets of paper and rallied all the team members to create massive collages of everything they envisioned would make them happy—a new car, a new home, more time with family, a vacation, a garden... whatever they dreamed of. When I realized that I was one of only a few team members who was actually creating a collage, I offered everyone who completed their collage a $1,000 bonus, to show them just how important I think goal setting really is.

Wayne Turner takes a similar approach. He goes around to every person on his 10-member team and asks them, "If you had a day to just relax on your back porch and read magazines, which two magazines would you read?" He then heads to the store and buys everyone their favorite magazines, a medium-sized corkboard and a box of thumbtacks. After giving the team a couple of days to thumb through the magazines, they all gather with their scissors, magazines and corkboards to create a collage of all the things they want in their lives—everything that brings them peace and happiness, whether it be a pool in the backyard, a new car or diamond ring, or time with family. It can even be a motivational phrase...anything that can keep you focused and on track. Everyone hangs his reward collage near his desk, where he can glance at it every day for motivation. *–Ralph R. Roberts*

Breaking the goal into milestones

Goals, especially ambitious goals, can seem overwhelming at first. If your team sold 300 homes last year and you set a goal to sell 400 homes this year, that goal may seem nearly impossible. One hundred more homes in a year?!

To make whatever goal you set seem more realistic, break it down. One hundred more homes per year translates into 8 or 9 more homes each month or only a couple of extra homes per week. You could also break it down by agent. If your team has five agents, selling 100 more homes per year means that each agent has to sell 20 more homes—fewer than two more homes per month per agent. After you set milestones in place for your team, work with individual team members to develop their goals for helping the team meet its overall goal.

Tip: Set a timeline to achieve your goals and then at least once a month, look at that timeline to determine whether you are on track. If you have wandered off course, you may need to make a few adjustments to get back on track.

Devising a strategy

When you need to travel from point A to point B on a map, you can do it in any number of ways—train, plane, car, bus, taxicab, boat, bicycle, on foot and so on. In the same way, when you are trying to get from point A to point B in business, you can usually accomplish your goal in any number of ways. To be effective, you probably want to narrow your focus and choose only one or two strategies. We cannot prescribe a specific strategy for your team, because it varies according to each situation and each market and with the makeup of your team and the resources you have at your disposal. We can, however, help you identify strategies that will work best for you.

As soon as you have a goal in mind, call a strategy meeting with the key players on your team—perhaps the office manager, listing manager, closing manager and your agents—and determine how you want to go about achieving your goal. You typically want to focus on the areas that are driving the most business your way or areas that you have neglected as a team. Many teams that discover they are receiving 80% of their business from referrals, for example, choose to ramp up their efforts on referrals when trying to boost sales. Other teams who are receiving only 40% of their business from referrals may decide that they are not doing enough to generate referral business and also decide to focus on this area.

For example, you may want to meet and discuss the following questions:

- What did you do this past year to achieve your sales goal?

- What is the primary source for your sales? How many were FSBOs, expired listings, repeat clients or referrals?

- How many leads did you receive from TV ads, radio spots, home magazines, or your Web sites?

Tip: If you have little or no presence on the Web, you may want to invest in building or redesigning your Web site, creating and maintaining a blog, launching a drip e-mail campaign, and exploring various Internet lead-generation services.

Team members can take the same approach to develop strategies for achieving their individual goals. Your transaction coordinator, for example, might consider developing a new system to process transactions 10%more efficiently. Agents may want to develop their own strategies for achieving their sales goals, as well.

Goal-Setting Case Study: Team Ralph

As team leader, I often set sales goals for my agents and share those goals with them. Unfortunately, this practice sent one of my best agents packing.

This particular real estate agent was one of the top salespeople I've ever trained. In one year, he sold 157 homes! Unbeknownst to me, he had set sales goals and developed his own business plan. His goal was to sell 125 homes. My goal was for him to sell 175 homes. Both of our plans were designed to increase revenue. My plan called for selling 20% more houses while his called for selling fewer houses at a 20% higher profit. His plan actually would have resulted in a bigger boost in revenue than my plan had called for, with the added bonus of giving him more quality time with his family and friends.

Unaware that my top agent had his own plan in place, I told him that I had expected him to sell 175 houses. Understandably, he felt as though I didn't appreciate his efforts. Before I could correct my mistake, my top agent was headed out the door to launch his own business. He's doing very well, and I learned an important lesson—encourage your agents and other team members to set their own goals. *—Ralph R. Roberts*

Identifying tasks

If you think of your goal as your ultimate destination, the tasks are the steps you take to reach that destination. Think of tasks as your to-do list. If you accomplish everything on your list, you can't help but achieve your goal or at least get pretty close.

Say you have a goal to increase sales by 20%. Your strategy is to increase the amount of business you obtain from referrals. The steps you take to achieve your goal may look something like the following:

1. Spend one hour every day calling past clients.

2. Send out cards to clients on birthdays and anniversaries.

3. Create a newsletter to send to all past clients once a month.

4. Host an annual party for past clients asking them to bring a guest.

5. Whenever someone thanks you, ask for referrals.

Identifying resources

Whenever you plan to do more than what you are already doing, you need to double-check the fuel gauge to make sure you have enough gas in the tank (and other supplies and resources) to get where you are going. You may need additional talent, supplies or personnel. Ask yourself the following questions:

• How many total hours are required to complete all tasks?

• How much time can I personally invest in the project?

• What talent is needed that I don't currently have?

• How much money is this going to cost?

• Do I need any special equipment?

• Are some resources already available?

Tip: If you are thinking that you cannot possibly afford to put your plan into action, think again, but this time, think more creatively. If you have plans to ramp up marketing, for example, but you don't have the money, consider partnering with a mortgage broker or other real estate business to share the expense in exchange for adding them to your marketing materials. Set your goal and then use your mind to figure out how to get there. There's usually a way.

Working the plan

When all the pieces are in place, working the plan is a simple matter of execution. Or as the marketing team at Nike recommends—Just Do It! This part sounds simple enough, but execution is where most teams (and independent agents) get hung up. They plan well, have the best of intentions, and then get so busy that the goal, strategy, and steps fall by the wayside.

On a team, it's a little harder to dodge the work. Communicate your plan with everyone on the team, so everyone on the team can hold one another accountable. If certain members are responsible for specific aspects of the plan, make sure they have a sheet to fill out every week or month reporting their progress. This will keep everyone on track.

The figure on page 214 illustrates a basic agent goal sheet that you can use to encourage agents to commit selling a certain number of properties each year and then track their progress on a monthly basis. Your goal sheets can contain additional details to enable you and your agents to keep track of exactly what each agent is doing to generate more business. For example, you may want to keep track of the following data:

• Total number of properties shown

• Number of company or team listings shown

• Number of phone calls made to past clients

• Number of thank-you notes sent

• Number of personal visits to client neighbors

• Number of contracts written

Accountability Case Study: The Wayne Turner Team

Wayne Turner takes a similar approach to keep his team on track. Every team member has an accountability sheet. According to Wayne, these are particularly useful for the agents in the sales department:

"I have a little plastic file holder hanging on my wall. Every Monday, my listing partner and buyers' agents drop their accountability forms into the plastic file folder for my review.

"I want to know how many properties they have shown, how many company or team listings they have shown, the number of thank-you notes they have sent, how many new buyers they've met, and how many contracts they've written. I also want to know their projected income from the past week based on the contracts they have written and finalized and also their monthly income goal.

"Every Monday, I receive the accountability sheets, review them, and meet individually with each agent. I can then say, 'You're ahead of last week. You're doing a great job! Keep it up.' Or, if the person has wandered off track, I can ask him if he's okay.

"The first thing the accountability form asks each agent is to rate their week on a scale of one to 10, with one being the least great week ever and 10 being fantastic.

"Remember that setting goals and holding people accountable

isn't just for the benefit of the team leader or team; it creates a map for monitoring your actions. When you start to wander off course (something everyone eventually does), your goals ground you, help you refocus, and get you back on track."

<u>Agent Goal Sheet</u>

YTD Summary

Agent: _____ Month: _____ Year: _____

Annual Goal: _____ YTD: _____ To Go: _____

Current Deals Pending: _____

Current Monthly Goal

Month: _____
Goal: _____

Steps to achieve goal:

1. _____
2. _____
3. _____

Closed Transactions

Total: _____

Property Address	Lead Source
_____	_____
_____	_____
_____	_____

Sign-off

Agent: _____ Date: _____

Team Leader: _____ Date: _____

Providing Growth Incentives

Despite what some people say about not needing to be rewarded for doing a job well, positive affirmation is still a wonderful way to celebrate success. Lots of teams decide together what the reward will be for goal achievement. They create the reward based on a sliding scale. For example, "If we hit our goals, we'll do X. If we beat our goals by 10%, we'll do Y. If we supercharge the goals and beat them by 20% or more, we're off to a tropical isle for a week!"

The leader who understands that small celebrations along the way are inspirational and fun and enhance team cohesiveness is a wise leader indeed. A just-because pizza party during a tough day will pay off in ways far greater than the cost of the six pies with extra cheese, pepperoni, and peppers! Never underestimate the element of surprise when rewarding the team.

Teams need to be coached, empowered, and developed. The goal is not to manage the members but rather to have them learn how to be independent of the leader rather than dependent upon him or her. When the leader is able to take a well-deserved vacation, be out of phone coverage for two weeks and the team is competent and confident that things will be just fine, that team has arrived at the highest level of functioning. That's a team leader who can be proud!

In the following sections, we show you how to further encourage team members to meet and even exceed their goals.

Asking team members what they want

Although some people are fairly good at sensing what others want and need, nobody is a mind reader, so ask individual team members what they want and expect. Otherwise, you may do more harm than good. Promoting your top salesperson to a sales manager position, for example, could hurt your team, especially if the person is not management material. The promotion could very well take the person away from his or her area of strength (selling) and force them into their area of weakness (management). This does a disservice not only to the person you promoted, but to all the people working under that person. It can destroy your bottom line.

Ask team members how they would like to be rewarded. You may be surprised by the variety of responses. The following list describes rewards that may not have crossed your mind:

- **Better tools to fulfill job responsibilities:** Having a new computer, printer, or wireless device can simplify a specific task and make a team member more productive.

- **Getaways:** Many team members value free time or family time over money. Instead of giving the person a bonus, you may want to offer them time off, instead, or give the person a choice—time or money.

• **Recognition:** Some people just want to be thanked for all their hard work. They want the boss to say "thank you." Say "thank you" often and in different ways—tell your teammates "thank you," give them hand-written thank-you cards, take them to lunch, give them tickets to a show, and so on.

• **Opportunities:** Discover the dreams of each and every team member, and do whatever you can to help them achieve those dreams. Perhaps a team member really wants to be a public speaker, a writer, or a marketing guru. Give each team member opportunities to acquire the necessary skills and education and practice those skills in the workplace. Be a dream facilitator.

• **Service:** When a team member suffers a setback, offer to help in any way possible. Treat team members like family members.

Promoting team members

Team members often feel as though they need to make a difference. They need to be able to have some input on the direction of the team and the decision-making process. If you treat these team members as employees rather than integral parts of the team, they are either going to seek positions where they have more input or begin acting as employees—simply doing what they are told rather than taking initiative. The key is to remain sensitive to each team member's needs for responsibility and power and ensure that the right people are in the right positions. These factors may seem unimportant to certain team members, but for others, they could have a tremendous impact on their job satisfaction.

If you've hired the right people, you probably have several members of the team who are ambitious. They are happy in their current position, but they want more. Hopefully, they don't want your job, but they probably want to feel as though they can climb the ladder of success instead of being stuck in a dead-end job.

As team members continue to achieve higher levels of success, consider creating positions or at least job titles that acknowledge those achievements. Simply calling your top-producing agents "Senior Salespeople" and giving them a higher commission may provide them with the recognition and reward they crave. Consider offering special assignments to team members who need more power and responsibility. They can train others, serve as an advisor, head up a new department, or manage an important project. By consulting with your top performers, you are telling them that you value them and hold them in high regard. You are also demonstrating to everyone on the team the type of conduct and performance that you reward, inspiring everyone on the team.

Tip: For some salespeople who have plenty of money, it's all about ego. They want a high-profile position on a high-profile team or they want to be well recognized in the industry. Nothing is wrong with that, as long as it does not minimize the contributions of other team members or lead to a major conflict with the team leader.

Raising salaries

Remember that the more success the team enjoys, the more benefits the team should receive. When they see that direct relationship between hard work and success, they will work harder and smarter for you. If all they see is that you are taking long vacations with your family and enjoying the fruits of their labor, they are likely to head out to greener pastures.

Most teams find that they need to adjust their compensation package as conditions change or when certain events indicate that the compensation package is not as effective as it could be. Here are some signs that your current compensation package is not working:

• Everyone on the team is earning more than you are.

• Team members appear unhappy.

• Team members are satisfied with taking orders rather than pursuing new clients.

• Team members are leaving to pursue better opportunities with your competition.

When you first notice that your compensation package is not working, call a team meeting to find out what is going on. Ask team members what they are looking for and what sorts of adjustments they would like to see. Listen carefully to what everyone has to say, but put off making any immediate, spur of the moment changes. Ultimately, the team leader has to decide on a compensation package that is best for the team and fits within the team's budget, but everyone should have the opportunity to provide their insight.

Remember: People usually do what is financially rewarding. They will sign on to your mission and work diligently under the expectation that you will eventually reward them accordingly. If the reward doesn't arrive, however, and they begin to feel taken advantage of, your relationship can sour very quickly. Nobody strives to be mediocre, but when they give all they have and fail to receive what they deserve, they usually scale back their productivity.

Motivating with bonuses

In Chapter 6, we discuss various methods of compensating team members in order to maximize productivity and morale, but we would like to mention one form of compensation that is often particularly effective at motivating agents—bonuses.

Consider offering a bonus to anyone on the team who sells a team listing. That is, if one of your seller's agents has a listing and one of your buyer's agents sells it, that buyer's agent gets an additional bonus on top of the standard commission. This encourages team play.

If your team sells new construction (it should), then offer an even bigger bonus for anyone who sells a new construction listing. The reason for this is that your team wants to keep builders happy so that they continue to send business your way. If the builder is happy, the builder sends you more listings, which draws more buyers. And the more buyers you have, the more potential you have for future sellers and increased referrals.

Tip: Wayne Turner says that sellers buy off image, while buyers buy off homes. In other words, it doesn't matter to the average buyer who calls or shows them the property. They want to see inside that home, because they think it may fit their needs. A seller chooses an agent based on the agent's image or reputation—sellers are looking for an agent who's approachable, trustworthy, knowledgeable, caring, compassionate, and valued as the absolute number one agent in the area. To draw buyers, you need inventory. To draw sellers, you need to market your team.

Opening doors to other opportunities

Team leaders generally are well-connected individuals. They know everyone in the community and a good number of high-profile people throughout the industry. If a team member has a lifelong dream to pursue some other area of interest, opening the doors for that person can be the biggest reward you can offer.

Of course, you probably do not want to open a door that will encourage a top-producing team member to exit, but by empowering the person to explore other areas of interest, you prove to the person and to other team members that you are committed to their success. This increases their commitment and loyalty to you and to the rest of the team.

Raises or Bonuses?

We asked Chip Neumann of Neumann Real Estate (www.chip-neumann.com) in Ridgefield, Connecticut, how he rewards team members for their performance. Here's what Chip had to say:

"I have not raised the salary of any of my team members in years nor do I plan to in the future. Rather, each year I increase the bonus dollar amount that they receive on closed units. This has always been a large incentive for my team members.

"In addition, each of my team members is licensed, and I encourage them strongly to bring in business from their sphere of influence. My team members receive 50% of what I earn on any buyer or seller of theirs we close with.

"Their sphere of influence has also been brought into all aspects of farming, marketing, and so on, under The Chip Neumann Team. Each team member is responsible at the beginning of each year to build their sphere by a certain percentage."

Managing Conflict

Whenever two or more people enter into a business arrangement, tensions can begin to rise, especially when everyone involved is highly creative and driven and has a strong personality—and just about every real estate agent we have met fits that description. Some creative conflict is unavoidable, and sometimes these conflicts can actually be productive, but negative conflict and dissension among team members can creep in like a cancer and literally destroy a team.

Although we talk a great deal about trusting the people on your team and letting go, you are ultimately responsible for making sure that everyone on the team is acting with integrity and working together to make the entire team successful. In other words, you have to know what's going on, so you can address issues as soon as they arise.

Establishing open communication

The best way to remain on top of things is to establish open communication with all team members and hold them accountable for informing you of any problems they observe. In far too many businesses, employees are reluctant to blow the whistle, either believing that the boss won't do anything about it or that they will suffer retribution from their fellow employees.

Tip: Julie Vanderblue of The Vanderblue Team recommends installing a troubleshooting basket in the office, in which team members can anonymously submit issues for her review. She can then address individual issues with the person who's causing the problem or bring up team-related issues in the weekly meeting. Julie also warns teams to be on the lookout for "pot stirrers"—team members who love to watch problems flourish and often function as instigators. If you identify a pot stirrer, you should deal with that person immediately and decisively, as discussed in the following section.

Confronting the team member

When a team member is not performing in accordance with the agreed-upon standards, you need to confront the person and express your concerns. Describe the situation as you see it—describe how it makes you feel and try to get at the root of what's going on. Avoid making any accusations. Give the person the benefit of the doubt. Ask questions, so you have a better understanding of the facts before making any statements that you can't take back.

If someone is constantly late for meetings, for example, instead of saying, "You are always late, and this has to stop," say something like, "Over the past few weeks, I've noticed that you've arrived late to almost every meeting. Is everything okay? Is there anything I or the rest of the team can do to help?"

If office gossip is a problem, talk to the person who is the main source of the gossip. If the entire office has a problem, you may want to bring it up during one of your weekly meetings. Perhaps you can share an article with the entire team on the negative effects of gossip. Give the people who are guilty of gossiping the opportunity to change themselves. This allows them to make a positive change without feeling compelled by the boss to do so. If an individual continues to gossip, then a one-on-one meeting may be required.

Consequences for issues may include one or more verbal warnings followed by one or more written warnings and finally termination of employment or the end of a partnership if the person is unwilling or unable to correct the problem. You may be able to resolve issues with poor performance by providing additional training or resources, changing the way certain tasks are performed or making other minor adjustments. Take a problem-solving approach—identify the problem and then brainstorm possible solutions with the person involved. If you make changes and the problem remains, then a reassignment may be the next step.

Tip: Stating consequences is only the first step. Be sure to enforce office rules consistently and fairly. If you fail to reprimand an employee who is underperforming, the entire team may turn against you.

Reassigning roles within your team

When a member of your team is ill suited for the position he's been assigned to but is still a valuable team member, you may need to reassign him to another position. Although this reassigning could be uncomfortable for you, chances are that if someone is better suited for another role, he'll probably be happier in that role as well.

After you've made the decision to reassign a team member, avoid overanalyzing it. Don't apologize for it or make excuses. Call the person into your office (in private) and have a heart-to-heart meeting with him to explain why you feel a change would be in everyone's best interest. Ask him how he feels about it, and then sit back and listen to what he has to say.

If tensions start to rise, it's often a good idea to sleep on it and resume the discussion the following day. This break gives you both some time to let the idea of the reassignment settle in and approach the subject more rationally (and less emotionally) the following day. Julie Vanderblue suggests saying something like, "Listen, I obviously value you as a partner and fellow team member. Let's take a day to think about what we've discussed and then talk again tomorrow." This puts the other person back in the driver's seat and gives him a sense that he has a voice in the outcome.

Warning: The longer you wait to make a reassignment, the more difficult it becomes to actually do it. As soon as your instincts tell you that a change is needed, take action.

Letting a team member go

When a team member just doesn't work out, you must encourage the person to leave if you want to keep the team on track. Real estate professionals who are new to the practice of hiring and firing people often have trouble deciding whether their reasons for termination are sufficient. They have trouble spotting the signs. Consider letting a team member go if the person:

- Goofs around in meetings and distracts team members from being productive
- Constantly complains or stirs the pot
- Lies
- Steals
- Commits fraud
- Talks negatively about others (on or off the team)
- Doesn't show up or is persistently late
- Gossips

- Always makes excuses for mistakes (fails to take responsibility)
- Fails to demonstrate support for other team members

Firing someone isn't easy, so try to cut the team member loose without going through the ugly process of firing the person. This allows them to walk away with their dignity and confidence intact and without resenting you and the other team members. Julie Vanderblue offers some tips for letting team members go:

- Make them believe that they are the ones choosing to leave.
- Describe why you feel the fit is not right.
- Focus on the person's strengths and discuss other positions or situations that might be a better fit for this person.
- If possible, don't burn bridges. This person may be able to help you somewhere down the road.
- Sometimes just saying, "You are an amazing person, and I wish this was a better fit, because I will miss you" can ease the pain and make the person feel better about leaving.

Part IV

Executing Outward to Capitalize on Success

Chapter 14

Marketing Your Team to Build a Strong Brand Presence

One of the biggest challenges to running a team is making sure you generate enough business to keep everyone busy—and that takes marketing. The type of marketing we are talking about consists of much more than marketing the properties you sell. This type of marketing goes beyond the typical things most agents do—handing out business cards, designing attractive mailers, and distributing marketing materials to prospective clients.

The type of marketing we discuss in this chapter is madman marketing: the full-court-press approach to marketing. It's a comprehensive and unrelenting campaign designed to transform your team into a brand name—a high-profile real estate icon. With the right marketing, your team's name becomes synonymous with "real estate." When people in your community (and even nationally, if you do it right) start thinking about buying or selling a home, they instantly think of your team.

When you succeed at establishing a brand presence for your team, you no longer have to target a market; your market targets you. Prospects come to you and opportunities arise with no additional effort on your part. News organizations that need insight and information for real estate-related stories begin to seek you out. Companies that service the real estate industry may even approach you with opportunities to become their spokesperson. Publishers may contact you to write articles or books, and organizations from around the world will want you to speak to their members.

After you achieve this status, you and your team can then cherry-pick the opportunities you want to pursue—those you find most rewarding, fulfilling and enjoyable. You'll wake up every morning knowing that you'll never be without an opportunity to capture your interest and generate enthusiasm. And all this will come to you as a result of your marketing efforts.

How do you do it? Where do you get started? The answers to those questions drive the content of this chapter. Here you learn how to orchestrate an effective marketing campaign of your very own.

Keeping Your Focus on the Greatest Goals

The first and perhaps most important point to keep in mind concerning marketing is that it is all about your team, not your broker (if you happen to operate within a brokerage). Your team is an entrepreneurial small business unto itself, a revenue generator, and perhaps even a corporation. Think of your team as Your Team, Inc. and never forget it.

You may be marketing your broker and the homes you are selling, but those entities are only peripheral interests. You include them because they are a part of what you sell, but by marketing yourself, you ensure long-term success. Even if you happen to move to a different broker, you retain all the benefits of the time, money, and energy you invested in your marketing efforts.

Remember that before clients will buy from you, they have to buy into you. They have to know your team and believe that your team is going to treat them right. The goal of your marketing campaign should always be to build a high, positive profile that constantly reinforces your image and the fact that your team is knowledgeable, trustworthy and can get the job done better than anyone else.

Selling Your Team-Based Approach to Clients

One of the major issues that most teams deal with up front is convincing clients that your team will provide them with a superior level of service. Most clients want to deal exclusively with the head honcho. They don't want to be passed off to an assistant. Be sure that your marketing stresses the high-quality service that you provide. Let your clients know that your team can provide an increased level of service compared to what any individual agent could possibly provide—and stress the point that they receive this superior service at no extra cost. Giving your "assistants" job titles that command more respect can also help.

Designing a Comprehensive and Unrelenting Marketing Campaign

Many real estate agents make the mistake of indulging in hit or miss marketing campaigns. They run a TV commercial and see how that does. The next week, they place an ad in the paper or run something on the radio to determine whether that will drive in more business. Perhaps they dabble on the Internet, creating a second-rate Web site that they later lose interest in.

Hit or miss marketing strategies are destined to fail, because they have no impact on clients and prospects whose minds are cluttered with a daily barrage of advertisements. One ad does not imprint an image on the minds of your audience.

To be effective, a marketing campaign must be comprehensive (as in multimedia) and unrelenting (as in "never let up"). Build a marketing blitz that never loses its intensity. Eventually, word will spread like a virus. Publicity generates publicity. Eventually, your marketing will develop a life of its own, delivering countless opportunities to your door.

Crossing all your t's and dotting your i's

An effective marketing campaign includes most (if not all) of the following components (described in greater detail later in this chapter):

- Brand focus
- Print marketing packet, including a business card and brochure
- Press releases
- At least one Web site
- At least one blog
- A presence on several social networking sites
- E-mail
- Drip e-mail campaigns
- Interviews with the press
- Paid advertising
- Articles for relevant publications
- Professional networking
- Networking with past clients
- Books or e-books
- Community service

A comprehensive campaign serves three main purposes, allowing you to:

- **Spread the word.** If people do not see your message in one media channel, they are likely to see it in another.

- **Reinforce your message.** When people see you on TV, hear you on the radio, read about you in the newspapers, and see your Web sites or blogs on the Internet, you begin to become a permanent resident in their minds.

- **Leverage your marketing muscle.** Every marketing media reinforces the effectiveness of the other media. Your Web site or blog may draw interest from the press, for instance, who will then mention your Web site or blog in their reports and draw even more traffic to you. A publisher may notice your popularity and offer you a book deal, which adds to your credibility and drives even more customers in your direction.

You may hand someone a business card with your Web site address on it, encouraging them to visit your site, where you sell them a book that convinces them they want to hire you to sell their house.

Warning: Before launching your marketing campaign, gear up for the increase in interest and business you're about to receive. If you're ill prepared, you could drive away the people you spent so much effort in attracting.

Maintaining your momentum

Madman marketing relies on energy, enthusiasm, and momentum. If you ease off the marketing accelerator for even one or two weeks, you begin to lose all of that. Memories of you begin to fade in the minds of your marketplace.

Before you decide to begin, make a commitment to your marketing campaign. To do it properly, we estimate that you'll spend at least 16 hours per week. Of that 16 hours, you should spend approximately six hours a week of your own time connecting with past clients, and that is only one part of your marketing campaign. You also need time to do the following tasks:

- Talk with reporters

- Come up with ideas for articles and perhaps even books

- Provide direction to other team members, employees, or freelancers who will perform the following tasks (and then some):

  - Design and build your Web site(s)

  - Print marketing materials

  - Write or edit articles

  - Post to your blogs

Discovering Your Team's Unique Brand Focus

Close your eyes and imagine the president of the United States or Madonna or Martin Luther King Jr. You can probably come up with a pretty clear image of what they look like, because these people have attained celebrity status. That's what you want, and proper branding can deliver it. First, however, you need a central brand focus—something unique, something that excites you and everyone around you. This can be a logo, a phrase that defines your team's vision, something unique about the way you dress, or just about anything else that will catch the attention of prospective clients.

You can discover or define your team's unique brand focus in any of the following ways:

- **Shine the light on one charismatic team member.** Many teams develop their brand presence around their fearless leader—typically the agent who decides to form a team in the first place. This person becomes the rainmaker and has the primary responsibility of generating business for the team.

In Montgomery, Alabama, Sandra Nickel has taken on the role of rain woman for her team. Known far and wide as "The Hat Lady," Sandra wears a distinctive hat wherever she goes. Her hat logo appears on her business card, on all of her correspondence, and even on her Web site Invest in Montgomery, Alabama (www.investinmontgomeryalabama.com).

Sandra has a solid team of real estate professionals who handle the daily business. She functions as the rainmaker, ensuring that the phones keep ringing and the Internet remains abuzz with the voices of interested buyers and sellers. She tells the story of Midtown Montgomery, Alabama and volunteers tirelessly to improve the community. In the process, the Hat Lady attracts a lot of attention...and lots of business for her team.

• **Market your team as a unit.** Some teams prefer to share the limelight or simply have no one team member who is willing or able to function as the face of the team. In a case such as this, you can powwow with your fellow team members to identify your team's unique character—the character that can fuel your marketing campaign.

To do this, review your mission statement to see if it contains anything you can use to market your team. What is your focus? How is your team going to distinguish itself from the other teams and agents in your market? What does your team want to be famous for? By fielding these questions as a team, you can usually arrive at a clear vision of how to market your team.

• **Pick a brand focus outside of yourself or your team.** Your brand focus need not be centered on yourself or your team. You can pick anything that's likely to draw attention and generate positive publicity. We know of one agent who wears mismatched shoes. Whenever someone asks him about his shoes, he says, "I have a pair just like them at home." The Hat Lady wears hats. The leader of one team billed himself as "The Real Estate Guy." Whenever people called the office wanting to talk with him, they simply asked to speak with The Real Estate Guy.

Remember: Spend some time identifying or defining your brand focus, because after you launch your marketing campaign, changing your brand focus later can be nearly impossible. If you do change it later, you lose a lot of what you gained. When you come up with an idea, your team should ask itself if 20 years from now, they will still be happy with the brand focus they chose.

Is your team okay with the idea of wearing hats for the next 20 years…or mismatched shoes?

Ralph's Big Nail

Several years ago, I decided to form a brand around an 11-foot tall, 500-pound nail. The nail already had some local appeal and a good story behind it. In 1998, to demonstrate how their NailGard® self-sealing passenger tire worked, the Uniroyal® tire company inserted the nail into the tread of The Giant Uniroyal Tire that towers alongside Interstate 94 outside of Detroit, Michigan. In the fall of 2003, as part of a $1,000,000 renovation to the 80-foot tire, Michelin, Uniroyal's parent company, donated the nail to the city of Allen Park, Michigan, which a short time later auctioned it off on eBay to raise funds for the Allen Park Historical Society's programs and facilities.

I purchased it on eBay for $3,000 (the seller donated the proceeds to a local charity), and then I proceeded to parade it around town and loan it out for charity events. Now, all my marketing materials have the Big Nail on them. I even have a Web site about it at (you've probably guessed) www.bignail.com, where you can read all about it. (BigNail.com is the site to go and get more information on branding. *Branding For Dummies*, by Bill Chiaravalle and Barbara Findlay Schenck, is another good resource.)

I'm not suggesting that you have your own 11-foot, 500-pound nail custom built for you, but you should have something that sets you apart from the competition and will appeal to your target market. Then, you should drive home that image in every piece of your marketing materials, including your Web sites and blogs. *—Ralph R. Roberts*

Designing an Attractive Marketing Packet
The first component of your marketing campaign is an attractive marketing packet that you can deliver to prospects before meeting with them. You should have two standard packets for prospective clients—buyers and sellers. You should then put together custom marketing packets to introduce yourself to reporters, potential partners, and other professionals you may want to team up with.

If someone on your team is artistic, you can design the marketing materials yourself and take them over to a local print shop to have them produced in mass quantity. Otherwise, hire a graphic artist to draw up some designs from which to choose. The proprietor of the print shop can recommend local artists, or a colleague may refer you to one. Try to find someone who can design everything for you, including your Web site or blog whenever you're ready to add those components to your marketing campaign.

Your marketing packet should include the following materials:

• **Folder:** A legal-size folder into which you can place all of your other marketing materials. Since the folder is the first item that prospects will see, make sure it has an impeccable design.

• **Business card:** Your business card is a key component of your marketing packet. You will hand it out to everyone you meet, even if they are not receiving the full packet. Don't go cheap. Use high-quality card stock with raised lettering. Your business card should include your team's logo, a photo of you, your job title or a brief mention of what you do, and your phone number, e-mail address, and main Web site address.

• **Information about your team, including a letter of introduction and a photo of the team.** A one- or two-page letter introducing your team and describing some of its major accomplishments and the team's commitment to clients can help prospects get to know you better. Every marketing packet should also include the names and specialties of all your team members and complete contact information, so people can get in touch with team members by phone, e-mail, or via your Web site or blog. You want everyone to be able to recognize all the members of the team.

• **Resume:** Your resume should highlight your team's knowledge, education, certifications, areas of expertise, experience, professional associations, community service, and other items that establish your credibility and skill.

• **Statement of benefits:** Why should this prospect hire your team rather than one of your competitors? What can you offer the client that others in the field can't? Put down in writing a list of key ways the person will benefit by choosing your team.

• **Testimonials:** Prospects generally place more trust in what other people say about you than what you say about yourself. Whenever a client thanks you for a job well done, you should ask for two things—referrals to friends and family and a testimonial that you can quote in your marketing materials. Use these testimonials in your marketing packet.

• **Press clippings:** When a newspaper or magazine prints a story about you, they can usually provide you with reprints of the article (you may need to ask for them) so you don't have to purchase stacks of the magazine or newspaper. Always order reprints and include them in your marketing packet. Positive press about your team or a member of your team reinforces the message that you are a credible authority who delivers on promises.

Tip: Consistency is critical in an effective marketing campaign. Everything should have a consistent appearance and color scheme, collectively known as your brand's look and feel. Creative people tend to want to add some variation because they're afraid of coming across as boringly consistent, but this is a common mistake. Consistency tattoos your team's image on the minds of your clients, prospects, competitors, and others in the industry. It gives your team a recognizable face.

Sending Out Regular Press Releases

People tend to believe what they read in the news, so to increase your credibility, make yourself newsworthy. RISMedia can deliver your press releases to thousands of subscribers almost instantaneously, distributing announcements of your team's newsworthy events to eager readers from around the world. First, however, you have to write the press release.

Writing your press release

When a newsworthy event occurs (or is about to occur), start writing. Announcing something that happened a week ago isn't news. As you write, follow these guidelines for composing your press release:

- **Read some sample press releases first.** Model your press release after others that you enjoy.

- **Start with an intriguing headline.** Nobody is going to read your press release if the headline is boring. The headline should draw people into the article.

- **Start the first paragraph with the city, state, and date.** Location and time set the stage for the rest of what you have to say.

- **Stick to a single page.** You have very little time to make your point. Remember, your goal is to convince people who read the release to call you—300 to 750 words is best.

- **Don't advertise.** A press release is an announcement worthy of the news, not an advertisement for products or services.

- **Edit carefully.** Your press release is a reflection of you and your team, so make sure it is well written and free of typos and grammatical errors.

• **Obtain permission for quoted material.** If you want to quote someone in a press release, obtain permission from the person or company you're quoting.

• **Include contact information.** You want the press to call or e-mail you or your assistant to set up interviews and perhaps appearances. Decide who on your team is going to handle the phone calls and e-mail messages and put that person's contact info in the piece.

Sending out your press release

After you write and carefully edit your press release, you have to find some way to get it into the media channels. Several companies offer such services, including PRWeb® at www.prwebdirect.com, 24-7 Press release at www.24-7pressrelease.com, and RISMedia at www.rismedia.com. RISMedia is unique in that its subscribers are primarily real estate professionals or reporters who specialize in real estate. You can also search the Web for "press release distribution" or other related words and phrases to find other companies that distribute press releases, or e-mail Ralph at RalphRoberts@RalphRoberts.com for a few more options.

Tip: Another option is to hire a publicist for your team or add a team member who's in charge of PR. Your publicist can handle the writing and distribution of the press release, so you won't have to do it yourself. Most publicists offer different levels of service, so you can usually find a package that meets your budget needs.

Establishing a Strong Presence on the Internet

If your team isn't marketing on the Internet, then you're missing out on a huge segment of the population. Just because most homeowners and buyers aren't carrying out transactions online doesn't mean that they aren't shopping online. More and more people are doing their preliminary research on the Web before they ever get serious about buying or selling a home. They go to Zillow.com®, HomeGain.com®, and other sites to get ballpark estimates of property values in their area. They search for tips and tricks on how to buy a house for less or sell it for more. And homeowners are constantly looking for ways to improve the value of their homes and protect their investments.

By establishing a presence on the Internet and building a reputation as the go-to team on real estate-related topics, you position yourselves to become the real estate team of choice when someone finally makes the decision to buy or sell a home or start investing in real estate. In this section, we discuss various ways to increase your presence on the Internet.

Building a personal, professional Web site

Your team should have at least one Web site it calls home. This Web site should provide an online version of your marketing packet, including a photo of your team (on the front page), your contact information, information about you and what you do, information about your broker (if applicable), and links to your online listings. For an example of what you should include on your Web site, visit www.ralphroberts.com.

Before creating your Web site, choose a domain name that people can remember easily and preferably one that reflects the team's identity. Most teams choose a domain name that reflects the team leader's name, such as www.roblevy.com, which we discuss later in this section. (You can have several domain names that all point to the same Web site.)

You can easily check domain name availability (for free) and register domain names online (for about $10 per domain name per year, assuming the domain name isn't already registered). A Web hosting service stores your Web site on a server that provides visitors with access to your site. Hosting costs vary, but last we checked, most services charge less than $100 for a full year of service that includes several e-mail accounts, Web site management tools, and a host of other tools to build and manage your Web sites and blogs. You can manage several domains through a single account, so the cost of adding a domain later is only $10 a year (or whatever the service charges for domain registration). You do not need to set up a separate account for each domain. Visit online Web hosting services such as GoDaddy.com®, BlueHost®, or Register.com® for more information about domain names and hosting services.

Tip: Most Web hosting services partner with professional Web site design companies and can recommend a professional designer. If you go with a pro, you can expect to pay about $5,000 for the initial Web site design and setup.

"Of course, the appearance and functionality of your main Web site (you can see my home page in Figure 14-1) are equally crucial," says Rob Levy. "It's important to not just have listings, but also the ability to make the site 'sticky.' This means giving buyers and sellers reasons to bookmark your site and frequently return. On my listings, for instance, I have a full multipage flyer the buyers can download on each home...if they tell me who they are. Also, I have well over 100 different Web sites attached to my 'Recommended Links' page, meaning people can go there to see everything from bus schedules to weather forecasts, which are always at my site, hence the word 'sticky.'"

Figure 14-1: The home page for www.roblevy.com.

Building communities through blogging

"Another important component of an Internet marketing program," says Rob Levy, "is a blog (short for Web log), which enables you attract information-hungry prospects, educate the public, and build credibility as a real estate expert in your market. My blog (see Figure 14-2) has information on everything from Portland's dog parks to leaking oil tanks. Both existing and prospective clients know they can visit my blog to find useful and timely information and also find out about me."

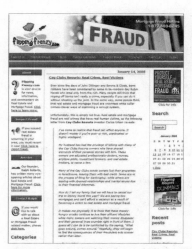

Figure 14-2: A blog can help you build credibility and generate leads.

Although you can set up free blogs on any of several services, including WordPress®, Blogger®, and Yahoo! 360°®, we encourage your team to set up its own blog with its own domain name to further reinforce your team's brand presence. You can find hundreds of Web hosting services that support blogs, but we recommend that you look for a company that specializes in blogging for real estate professionals, such as Blogging Systems™ at www.bloggingsystems.com or Kinetic Knowledge™ at http://kineticknowledge.com.

If you already have a Web site, you can create a separate folder on your server for your blog. In this folder, you install the blogging software required to post messages to the blog and manage it. (Your hosting company should be able to assist you with the setup.) After you get the blog up and running, you'll find that it's incredibly easy to manage and post messages. You can even set up most blogs in a way that you can post messages by e-mailing them to a certain address.

Don't forget about online communities. Establish a presence on ActiveRain (www.activerain.com)—a blogging community for real estate agents. Set up a page on MySpace® (www.myspace.com)—see the section "Tapping the sales power of social networking sites," later in this chapter, for more info. Work with other people in your area to create a community blog, reporting events and information of interest to homeowners in your market.

Tip: Although all members of the team should be contributing content to the blog, one team member should be responsible for monitoring the blog and posting fresh content, so that this particular job doesn't get moved to the backburner when your team is busy. All team members should know how to post messages and respond to visitor comments, so if something happens to the person in charge, another team member can take over.

"How do you find the time to blog?" asks Levy. "Well, that's one of the best parts of having a team—we all participate. Everyone on my team has to write a blog article once a week, and it grows fast; and the more it grows the more powerful it becomes!"

After setting up your blog, create a link on your team's home page that points to your blog. One of the major benefits of a blog is that search engines love blogs, so adding a blog to your Web site will actually heighten your team Web site's profile and raise its ranking with search engines.

Warning: Start out blogging slowly at first to get a feel for blogging and social networking. Anything you say that upsets the online community can and will be used against your team, so you have to be very careful. You should also avoid any heavy-handed sales tactics. Online marketing in social networks is strictly soft sell. Your team needs to establish itself as a resident expert first, and then you can gently nudge prospective customers toward the listings on your site.

Driving traffic to your Web sites and blogs

Spend some resources on promoting your Web sites and blogs, especially soon after you set them up. Once people begin to visit your site and talk about it, word of mouth advertising will drive traffic to your sites, but people have to know about your site first. Following are some suggestions on how to improve the visibility of your site and start drawing traffic to it:

• **Post valuable content.** Content is king. People won't return to your site if it doesn't offer something fresh and valuable.

• **Add a Google® sitemap.** A Google sitemap helps Google and other search engines catalog the content on your site. For details, visit www.google.com/webmasters/sitemaps.

• **Add Google Analytics.** Google Analytics is a nifty tool that enables you to track traffic coming into and moving through your site. You can see where visitors are coming from, which pages they're pulling up most frequently, the percentage of new and returning visitors, and much more. Google Analytics provides the data you need to figure out what works and what doesn't, which pages are popular and which are not, and what visitors are looking for. For additional details, visit www.google.com/analytics.

• **Register with niche directories.** Page rankings are often determined by the number of "important" Web sites in your Web site's category that link to your site. By registering your site with directories of real estate-related sites, you can boost your page rank, so that when people use Google and other search engines to search for real estate-related terms, your page is more likely to pop up higher on the list. For a great list of niche directories, visit Incoming Links at www.incominglinks.com.

• **Post messages in real estate discussion forums or blogs.** By contributing to community discussions, you automatically increase your credibility. If the forum (or blog) allows members to include their Web site or blog address in posts, this gives you another way of linking to your site from another site and increasing your search engine page rank.

• **Write articles and reviews for other Web sites.** Offer to write articles and reviews for real estate–related online publications. Most online publishers allow you to add a brief bio at the end of the article complete with a link back to your site.

• **Add your site's address to your business cards and other marketing materials.** Use your printed marketing materials to drive more traffic to your team's Web site or blog.

• **Add a signature file to your team's outgoing e-mail messages with**

a link to your Web site. Every e-mail program enables you to have a signature automatically added to the end of every outgoing e-mail message. Use your e-mail program's signature option (in Outlook Express, choose Tools, Options, Signatures) to add a signature file including your name, contact information, and live links to your Web sites and blogs. Every member on the team should be using signature files to reinforce the team's marketing message. You do not all have to be using identical signatures, but everyone's signature file should direct the recipient to the team's Web sites and blogs.

In addition to promoting your Web sites and blogs, your signature file provides the recipient with instant contact information, including your phone number. Keep in mind that many of the people you're e-mailing are going to be checking their messages while they are on the road using some sort of portable device, such as a BlackBerry®. By including your phone number in all outgoing e-mail messages, you make it easy for the recipients to get back in touch with you.

"Don't forget the power of an e-newsletter," reminds Rob Levy. "Our newsletter, which again is built into my Real Pro Systems site, is at www.roblevy.com/newsletter.asp. You can see while it covers useful information such as average sales prices, it also brands me to the client. Even if a recipient never read the newsletter and simply deleted it, the person would see me, the Prudential sign and logo, my team logo and more. Perhaps the best part of the e-newsletter is that with one click I can send out more than 23,000 e-mails simultaneously and for free, not to mention that I'm sending the information in the format most buyers and sellers want—by e-mail. The cost (not counting time) to do this same push manually and by snail mail would be huge."

Generating Free Publicity and Positive Press

Although you can certainly spend hundreds of thousands of dollars on professionally produced multimedia marketing campaigns, you can also generate a great deal of free publicity and positive press by investing only your team's time and expertise. In this section, we show you how by providing tips on making yourself and others on your team available to reporters and creating a high profile in your market through community service.

Making yourself available to reporters

Every single day (a little less on Sundays), reporters need to produce stories. They need ideas for stories, background information, facts and figures, and expert insight. They can gather much of this material through researching documents and actually witnessing newsworthy events, but they often rely on experts to provide leads with background information and insight. For any real estate stories, you can position yourself or others on your team as your community's real estate experts. You have to be ready and willing to give interviews at a moment's notice, but other than that minor drawback, giving interviews provides you with valuable free press!

Contact reporters and news producers in your area and let them know that you're available on short notice for interviews. Send over a marketing packet that includes your business card, a photo, your resume or curriculum vitae noting your expertise, and clippings from any articles you or your team have written or other interviews you've given.

To make yourself a more attractive interviewee for the press, keep the following important points in mind:

• **Be accessible.** Reporters can't afford to wait around for return phone calls. Many of them expect you to be available within minutes. (This is a good reason to always dress professionally or at least have a change of clothes available.)

• **Be a good interviewee.** Speak candidly and answer questions directly. When preparing for the interview, think in short sound bites—memorable phrases that capture the essence of what you have to say in as few words as possible.

• **Establish long-term relationships with the media.** If a reporter knows an excellent source who plays well on the news, going straight to that person is easier and safer than contacting an unknown source.

Investing time and energy in community service

One of the best ways to promote yourself and your team is to get in the habit of giving back to your community. People buy from those they trust, and they trust those who show a genuine interest in their community—people who give back. The best way to build trust as a team and generate positive PR is to become actively involved in your community. Encourage all team members to become more involved in the communities in which they work.

Following are some suggestions on what you and your fellow team members can do:

• **Join BNI (Business Networking International).** BNI is an international organization whose purpose is to generate referrals within their chapters. There is only one chair for each profession in each chapter, meaning all the real estate referrals to your chapter will be sent your way. This is an excellent way to generate additional revenue from quality referrals.

- **Join your local Chamber of Commerce.** Your local Chamber of Commerce provides networking and lead groups. These groups may include several agents, however, which will compete for the leads. According to Marsha Waddelow, her team listed and sold American Idol Star Kelly Clarkson's home in Mansfield, Texas, through a referral that one of the team members received from a member of her Chamber of Commerce leads group.

- **Take leadership roles in local philanthropic organizations.** Get involved in the Rotary®, Lions Club®, Kiwanis® or other philanthropic organizations. Taking on a leadership role is even better, because it increases your visibility and exposure and often results in free press.

- **Join Habitat for Humanity®.** What better way is there for you to use your expertise in the real estate industry than to help provide housing for underprivileged families? For more information, visit www.habitat.org.

When giving, however, don't make the mistake of giving to get. Give for the sheer privilege and pleasure of giving. Pay it forward. Art Fettig clearly points out the distinction between giving to get and giving to give in his book *Platinum Rule.* As Fettig points out, most people expect payback when they help somebody, which often transforms a good deed into bitterness when the payback never comes.

To avoid the ugliness that often results from giving and lending, Fettig recommends the Platinum Rule—giving without expectations. The next time you give somebody something and that person says he'll pay you back, say, "Here's how you can repay me—never try to repay me. Instead, help someone else someday." And then tell him, "Please don't ever bring this up again. Consider the matter closed. I'm not going to say anything about it, and I don't want you telling anyone about it." What happens is that the person you helped usually begins telling everyone what a great person you are, even though you specifically told him or her not to say anything!

Remember: You get more payback in positive word-of-mouth advertising than you could ever have hoped to receive if the person actually paid you back the debt. The people you help are going to say great things about you for the rest of your life. And now they're going to do something nice for another person in need. You will be pleasantly surprised by the positive PR this brings your way. Do what's right and the rewards will come.

Investing in Paid Advertising
When you're looking for a significant, almost instantaneous marketing boost, you may want to consider investing in paid advertising. Most high-quality

advertisers have already established vehicles for distributing their ads, such as magazines, newspapers, and Web sites, so they can quickly get the word out about you.

If potential clients watch TV, listen to the radio, or read the local newspaper, your team should establish a presence in these media channels. Following are some possible options to consider:

- **TV commercials:** In most areas, you can find video production companies that will guide you through the process of producing and broadcasting a 30-second commercial on local or even national stations. The expense of producing and airing a commercial can vary greatly depending on the video production company and the advertising rates that stations charge.

- **Radio advertisements:** Radio used to be a great way to get the word out, but it is becoming less attractive, because satellite and Internet radio are fragmenting the listening audience. Unfortunately, radio advertising rates have remained fairly steep considering the fact that fewer and fewer listeners are tuning in.

- **Newspaper advertisements:** Taking out an ad in print publications, including newspapers, magazines, and professional journals that your clients are likely to read, can give you a marketing boost. Just remember to create an attractive ad that promotes your brand and has a catchy headline.

- **Billboards:** Although billboards are old-school, they can still be a very effective marketing tool. Keep in mind, however, that drivers have very little time to read anything you place on the billboard. Use an attractive design, which includes your team's photo and contact information, and keep your message short and powerful.

- **Internet advertising:** Most of the big search engines offer pay-per-click (PPC) advertising, displaying ads on their own site and on partner sites for products and services. Rates vary depending on how much you're willing to pay to have a higher ad placement on the site. You pay only if someone clicks the ad. For more about PPC advertising, visit Google Adwords® at adwords.google.com and Yahoo! Search Marketing® at search-marketing.yahoo.com. You may also want to check out *Pay Per Click Search Engine Marketing For Dummies* and the latest edition of *Search Engine Optimization For Dummies*, both by Peter Kent.

Tip: When preparing an advertisement, focus on a problem your prospective clients may have that you can solve, and try to make them curious enough to pick up the phone and call you. Every ad should contain a call to action, such as "Call Ralph Roberts at 586-751-0000" or "Visit RalphRoberts.com!"

Building Credibility by Writing Articles and Books

To establish yourself and other team members as experts in your field, you should regularly write articles and post them on your blog or have others publish them online or in newspapers, magazines, and journals. Jot down a list of topics you feel qualified to write about and start writing. RISMedia (www.rismedia.com) contains a vast collection of articles you can pull up as examples and to obtain reference material. You may even want to publish your own articles on RISMedia.

Although articles are a great way to boost your credibility as a real estate expert, books give you additional credibility and a relatively inexpensive product that you can give to clients and prospects as a promotional piece. Some additional benefits of books include the following:

• Covers you can display prominently on your Web site or blog

• Additional income from sales of the book

• Something to sell if you set up a booth at a convention

You can self-publish a short book on a specialized topic or even have a major publisher discover you. Many companies, including iUniverse® at www.iuniverse.com, offer services to assist authors in publishing their own books.

Tip: Having a team can make writing much easier. You can meet to brainstorm ideas and collaborate on projects. If someone on the team is an exceptional writer and enjoys writing, managing the writing projects may be one of the team member's primary roles.

Marketing through Professional and Personal Networks

One of the oldest and most powerful marketing tools on the planet is networking—rubbing elbows with people who are likely to buy your products and services or can steer business in your direction. Real estate trainer and coach Terry Brock calls this R-Commerce (Relationship Commerce). According to Brock, R-Commerce drives all other commerce, including e-commerce, and when you give it a little thought, you quickly realize that he's right.

Effective networking is key to your success in real estate. It enables you to establish connections and discover a never-ending supply of leads simply by talking to people, letting them know what you do, and then kicking back and letting your network work for you.

Where do you start? A better question would be, "Where don't you start?" You and your team should network constantly, everywhere you go. Whether you're rubbing elbows with colleagues at a convention, eating out with your family, buying a car, or attending a ball game, you should be meeting people and building relationships. Eventually, a good portion of the relationships you establish pays handsome dividends.

Marketing through professional networks

A healthy industry generates business for everyone, so connect with other professionals in your area to create a healthy real estate market, and then work together to drive business to one another. You can refer clients to loan officers, real estate attorneys, title companies, appraisers, and other businesses in your area, and they can refer their clients to you when their clients need a great real estate agent team.

Identifying networking opportunities

Everybody knows at least 250 other people, so every encounter you have with someone is an opportunity to connect with 250 people. If you're not quite ready to network with everyone you meet, consider focusing on more formal networking opportunities:

- **Meet people on the job.** Get to know everyone you work with a little better—your teammates, employees, and any virtual assistants you may hire.

- **Get involved in professional organizations.** Everyone on the team should be working to expand the network. Connect with people in your industry and with other salespeople. Join your trade association and start making a difference. By taking a leadership role in the organization, you significantly increase your visibility—instead of having to seek out people to meet, they will seek you.

- **Join a community service organization.** Rotary, Kiwanis, Toastmasters®, and other national organizations may have chapters in your area. These are excellent places to meet the most ambitious and successful businesspeople while giving something back to your community.

- **Network online via professional social networking sites.** You can sign up on professional social networking sites, such as LinkedIn® (www.linkedin.com), to network across the Internet with people in real estate and related fields. This is an excellent way to expand your circle with very little effort.

Asking vendors for referrals

You'll be surprised at the number of competitors that rarely if ever market to the individuals and companies from which they buy products and services. That's good news for you, because if you market to these people, you could be the only one! Market to the people to whom you send business:

- Home inspectors
- Appraisers

- Mortgage brokers and loan officers
- Carpet cleaners
- Painters
- Pest inspectors
- Title companies
- Attorneys

These business professionals deal with agents every day, but rarely do agents ask for their business. Invite your vendors and service providers to any client functions or parties you are hosting. Or, you can host an appreciation party to thank them for the wonderful service they provide for you and your clients. These individuals are often overlooked and seldom recognized for the support they give your business. They're a great source for revenue generation. Their business is there—all you have to do is ask.

Giving referrals to get referrals
Most salespeople are well aware that they need to give referrals to get referrals, but many salespeople handle the referral process all wrong. They end up losing control and losing out on opportunities to maximize the actual number of referrals they receive. When giving referrals, be aware of the wrong way and the right way to do it:

• **Wrong way:** A customer comes in to buy a house and mentions that she gets her homeowner's insurance from XYZ Insurance, Inc. You ask how much she's paying and then mention that she may want to get a second opinion from ABC Insurance, Inc., a company you know of in town. This referral is not going to expand your business, because you don't have direct contact with the folks at ABC Insurance, Inc.

• **Right way, same scenario:** The customer mentions her insurance company. You realize that this company is certainly reputable. You ask your customer if she has the name and contact information of the person she deals with at the insurance company. You call the insurance agent, introduce yourself, tell the person you have met one of his clients, say that you would like to offer your services to him in the future, and tell him that you would appreciate it if he would send his clients your way, as well. You now have a new source for referrals.

Tapping the sales power of social networking sites
Teenagers may have made MySpace® and other social networking areas on the Internet hugely popular at first, but that popularity has quickly spread through

every generation. MySpace is now home to more than 200 million separate MySpace hangouts. When you consider the fact that the entire population of the United States just reached the 300 million mark, that's pretty impressive.

More and more people are gathering on these social networking sites to obtain information and seek advice from peers. For no cost, you can set up a page on MySpace, invite other MySpace users to become your "friends," and start mingling with people who may want to buy a house someday. You can then use your MySpace page to drive traffic to your team's other Web sites and blogs. One word of caution, however: No heavy-handed selling on MySpace. This is a place to establish relationships and build your team's credibility. If people want to buy from you, they can visit your Web site. (Check out Ralph Roberts' MySpace page in Figure 14-3.)

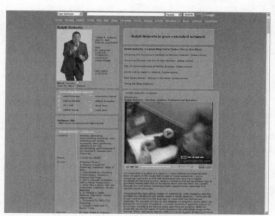

Figure 14-3: Ralph Roberts' MySpace site.

If you are a REALTOR® or a salesperson in some other industry, you may be wondering why you should care about these online hangouts. After all, people don't hang out on MySpace to buy houses, right? Well, not exactly. As people gather in these virtual communities, they start to talk about all sorts of things. They write about everything that happens to them, including when they buy a great product from a helpful salesperson and when they feel as though they have been ripped off. They talk about great sources of information where they can pick up free tips and tricks on an assortment of topics. They discuss the conversations they have online with celebrities and other famous people. And they listen to one another when someone recommends or pans a company or a product.

Through these social networking sites and other features, the Internet is transforming the world into a global open-air marketplace. Selling now is more like selling in small-town America in the 1950s, when your reputation in the community drove sales more than any fancy marketing campaign. These social networks are leveling the playing field, so anyone with knowledge, talent, and an Internet connection can log on and start competing with the big boys and girls.

Your team needs to be online, supporting the communities where your clients and prospective clients hang out. You need to publish articles and comments on a daily basis to establish your team as the real estate experts in these communities and in your market. And you need to listen to what these people need, what they're saying about the competition, and perhaps even what they're saying about your team!

Tip: Many salespeople go on MySpace and sign up with a nickname or handle. I strongly recommend that you use your real names. That's what MySpace is all about—getting people to know who you are, what you do, and what you sell. If you hide behind a fake name, you defeat the very purpose of relationship marketing on MySpace!

MySpace is not the only social networking site where you can set up shop. Check out these other social networking sites:

- RealTown® (specifically for real estate professionals) at www.realtown.com

- ActiveRain (specifically for real estate professionals) at www.activerain.com

- Facebook® at www.facebook.com

- Friendster® at www.friendster.com

- LiveJournal™ at www.livejournal.com

- Yahoo! 360° at 360.yahoo.com

- Squidoo™ at www.squidoo.com

Marketing through past clients

When you or one of your team members earns a customer's satisfaction, don't hesitate to ask the customer to refer you to others who may need your services. Supply your customer with a stack of business cards and ask her to hand them out freely and call you if she needs more.

Better yet, ask for the names and contact information of two or three people your customer knows who may be in need of your services. If your customer can't think of anyone right off the top of her head, ask whether you can call back in a couple of days. You may even offer the person some incentive to provide you with referrals, perhaps a discount or rebate of some sort.

The best time to ask a customer for a referral is when the person thanks you for going above and beyond the call of duty. The person says "thank you" probably because she has no better way of showing her appreciation. Give her that better way by asking for a referral.

Tip: Never let a productive relationship simply fade over time. Many of the most successful real estate teams we know of report that they receive as much as 80% of their business from referrals—that requires keeping in touch with past clients. Make sure you remain in contact with past and present clients and leverage their potential for driving new business your way. Here are some suggestions for increasing your referral business:

- Client phone calls
- Client lunches
- Greeting cards for birthdays, anniversaries and other occasions
- Thank-you notes
- Newsletters
- Client parties and visits
- Gifts

Tip: Host a customer appreciation day once a year to show how much you value your clients (both current and past). Most of your clients probably have children or grandchildren, so consider making it a family day at a local park, amusement park, or aquatic center.

Ralph's Hour of Power

Every weekday, I spend one hour making 100 phone calls. I call it my Hour of Power. I select a group of people I want to contact. The group may consist of the people I work with on the Macomb County Voice (a community blog we created). It may comprise the top selling real estate agents I know through STAR POWER®. It may be people I sold houses for or those I sold houses to. I tell everyone in the office that my Hour of Power is about to commence, and they know not to disturb me. Then, I shut myself in my office and start dialing.

If someone answers, I deliver my energetic greeting, ask him how he's doing, and perhaps mention one of the details I've recorded in my contact management program—maybe it's his anniversary or one of his children's birthdays. If nobody answers, I move on to my next call. If I get the answering machine, I leave a message. I may even sing "Happy Birthday," wish the person a happy St. Patrick's Day, or say something goofy right off the top of my head that I think will make them smile. *Remember:* What you say isn't all that important, but it can't be about selling—NO SELLING. The Hour of Power is about connecting on a personal level. It's about leveraging the power of the rule of 250—that each person knows at least 250 other people they can tell about you.

When you're doing your Hour of Power, you can't be interrupted. Make sure anyone who may be tempted to interrupt you knows not to. If you call someone and leave a message and that person calls back, someone in your office should answer the call and take a message. NO interruptions. You can call the person back later, after the hour is up. Your goal is to make it through your list of 100 people, and you have only 60 minutes to do it.

We strongly recommend that you implement the Hour of Power strategy. If you make 100 calls a day, five or six days a week, we can almost guarantee that you'll begin to see a dramatic boost in sales in a relatively short period of time. When you're ready to take the leap and implement your own Hour of Power, keep the following important points in mind:

- Keep a log sheet, so you have a record of the number of calls you actually placed.

- Strive to achieve the goal of 100 calls a day. Making the bare minimum of 25 calls a day delivers some benefit, but the truly successful salespeople are those who do closer to 100 calls a day.

- What you say when you call isn't all that important. What is important is that you make the call and establish contact. Leaving a voice message counts as contact.

- Do not sell. The Hour of Power is about building relationships.

- Don't get into a lengthy conversation. You have an average of 36 seconds per call.

- To avoid burnout, limit yourself to five or six days per week for making calls.

The single most important thing about the Hour of Power is that you do it. Keep a log and hold yourself accountable or make yourself accountable to the team. You get pearls called "referrals" when you make these calls. *—Ralph R. Roberts*

Categorizing your clients to maximize your cost-benefit ratio

Being a real estate agent often seems like being a migrant farm worker. You're busy during the planting season and when the crop is ready to harvest, but business is dead in between. To keep this from happening, you may be tempted to overcommit, taking on too many clients and being unable to provide them with quality customer service.

In the best of all possible worlds, you would have a steady stream of business, but that's a pipe dream—it's probably not going to happen. The next best thing you can do is to categorize your clients. List your top five customers, your top 25 customers, and your top 100 customers and then assign them to your slots as follows to decide whom to focus on:

A. The most dollar-productive clients: Paying clients receive your team's full attention when they demand it. These people are those who continue to drive business, leads, and opportunities in your direction. Keep them happy.

B. Top prospects: These may be existing clients who aren't exactly in the top bracket or prospects who you strongly believe could reach that upper bracket. These people are those you want to spend the most time nurturing.

C. Good prospects: These prospective clients are very promising candidates with whom you want to spend sufficient time and resources to nurture.

D. Prospects to let go: These clients are existing or prospective ones who drain you of time and resources and offer little if any return on your investment. You want to let these people go or refer them to some other salesperson down the road. Don't be rude about it, but find a way to get rid of them.

Tip: During your weekly team meeting, spend some time discussing your most challenging clients. If your style doesn't quite fit with what one of your clients needs, perhaps one of your teammates is a better fit. Swapping clients often delivers a win-win-win solution. You win because you no longer have to deal with a difficult client. Your client wins by obtaining better service. And your team wins because you don't have to send the client to an outside agent.

Finding Prospects through an Online Lead Generation Service

Another excellent way to get the word out about your team is to sign up with an online lead generation service, such as HomeGain.com®, RealEstate.com, HouseValues.com®, or HomePoint® (HomePoint.com). Making the most of an online lead generation service requires that you select a service that's right for you and then maximize the potential of the leads you receive by properly nurturing those leads. This section explores these two critical steps in greater detail.

Selecting an online lead generation service

All online lead generation services are not created equal. Some services pre-screen prospects to provide high-quality leads, and some simply provide you with a list of contacts. Some services distribute leads to every subscriber in their network, while others may provide exclusive leads to agents in certain geographical areas. And fees vary.

Don't sign up with just any online lead generation service. Use the following list of criteria to shop around and choose a service that's best for you and your team:

- **Cost per lead:** How much does each service charge per lead?

- **Prescreening:** Does the service screen leads before sending them on to your team? What process does the service use to screen out unpromising leads?

- **Lead distribution:** How many agents or agent teams in your area are receiving the same leads?

- **Notification:** How does the service notify your team of a lead—by phone, e-mail, or some other system?

- **Timeliness:** How fresh are the leads your team will be receiving? How much time does the service take to screen and process a lead before notifying your team?

Nurturing your leads

Far too many real estate agents buy leads and then completely drop the ball when it comes to nurturing those leads to turn them into clients. If your team is going to invest in a lead generation service, then make the most of that service by nurturing those leads.

Warning: The nurturing process commences as soon as you receive the lead. In most cases, you aren't the only agent team receiving the lead. In some cases, you may be the first agent team receiving the lead, but if you fail to follow up in a timely manner, the lead generation service may pass the lead on to the next agent or team on the list. Your team should set a goal of following up on an incoming lead within 15 minutes of receiving it.

You should have a system that enables you to check incoming leads wherever you may be. Even if you're out showing houses, you can check for incoming leads and contact the person immediately.

After that first contact, keep in touch with your lead. One of the best ways to do this is to add the person to a drip e-mail campaign. With drip e-mail, a series of messages are sent out automatically once every week or so, so the person doesn't have the opportunity to forget about you. When the prospect eventually decides to buy or sell, he or she can quickly open your e-mail message to obtain your contact information and call or e-mail you to obtain more information or hire your team. You can set up a drip e-mail campaign online at any of several drip e-mail management sites, including Rainmaker® E-Central™ at www.rainmakerecentral.com. At the same time, you should mail a marketing packet to your prospective client.

If you don't hear back from your lead within 24 hours, call the person and ask where he or she is in the decision-making process and whether you can do anything right now to assist him.

Remember: Whatever you do, don't let that lead off the hook. Remain persistent without nagging, and transform those leads into sales and those sales into commissions!

Real Estate Team Marketing Checklist

This chapter is packed with suggestions on how to properly market your team, so use the following checklist to make sure your team isn't missing out on any valuable marketing opportunities:

☐ We view and present our team as the product we're marketing.

☐ We have a separate budget for promotional materials and activities.

☐ We have a brand focus, complete with our own logo.

☐ All our marketing materials are branded with a consistent message and design.

☐ We have our own Web site, complete with a unique and catchy domain name.

☐ We have our own blog that we post messages on regularly.

☐ Our team has at least one page on ActiveRain and one other social networking site, such as MySpace.

☐ Everyone on the team has a signature file added to his or her e-mail program that includes contact information along with the team's Web site and blog addresses.

☐ All our marketing materials contain a team photograph, office address, phone number, e-mail address, and Web site and blog addresses.

☐ We regularly compose and send out press releases whenever a newsworthy event occurs.

☐ At least one member of the team spends at least one hour per day calling 100 past clients to keep in touch.

☐ We contact members of the news media on a regular basis.

☐ When we find articles written about our team or one of its members, we order reprints and mail them to our clients.

☐ We mail something to past clients on a regular basis.

☐ We routinely send out thank-you cards, birthday wishes, holiday greetings, and so on to our clients, both past and present.

☐ We hold a client appreciation day at least once a year and invite all our clients, past and present.

☐ We're active members of our communities, both online and off.

☐ All team members are active members of at least one real estate industry–related professional organization.

☐ We have an online lead generation service and a system in place for following up on leads quickly as well as nurturing the leads to convert them into clients.

☐ We regularly review our marketing campaign to build upon what works and to fix what doesn't.

Chapter 15

Identifying New Opportunities and Adding New Teams

Let's assume that you have found a way to clone yourself and delegate time- and labor-intensive tasks. You have a successful team churning out real estate deals. If you're their trainer as well as team leader, chances are good that they're practicing real estate similar to your style and serving the market you've chosen to focus on. You've assigned each person a specific position and delegated tasks to those who are best qualified to complete them. You have a designated buyer's agent, a couple of listing agents, closing administrators and so on.

Eventually, however, you begin to feel as though you've reached your plateau. Future growth seems impossible, but your ambition drives you to achieve higher levels of success. What do you do? Expand and diversify! Infinite opportunities are all around you. Your team simply has to identify which opportunities it's best suited to capitalize on and then pursue those opportunities with drive and determination.

In this chapter, we reveal some of the most lucrative growth opportunities for agent teams, and show you how to set up separate departments to diversify your team, grow your business and boost your team's revenue.

Expanding Your Team's Circle of Influence

Not so long ago, it felt as though the Great Wall of China separated the various divisions of real estate. Agents specialized. You'd be hard-pressed to find an agent who sold residential real estate also dabbling in commercial properties. Most traditional agents would not even consider selling new construction homes or REO properties. Agents simply had no time to explore these different areas. Specialization led to success.

Although this is still the case with most independent agents, agent teams can diversify to take advantage of a much wider range of opportunities. Agent teams have significantly more earning potential than any loosely connected group of real estate agents because they have an infrastructure in place to support their efforts, teammates who can help spread the word about one another's properties, and plenty of mentors to share techniques and provide motivation.

After you've established a successful team business and have some experience building and managing a team, you can begin to expand. You can create separate divisions or departments, each with its own manager and miniteam that can specialize in a particular area of real estate. This approach delivers the best of both worlds—you can diversify as a team while each department specializes in a given area. In this section, we consulted with Marsha Waddelow of The Waddelow Team, RE/MAX Associates of Arlington, Texas (Waddelowteam@hotmail.com), to explain how to use team-based selling to boost sales and profits. We introduce you to several opportunities you may not have considered when you were working alone.

Diversifying your real estate practice

Salespeople, including real estate agents, typically prefer to sell properties to people who are just like themselves and to focus on traditional markets. This focus leaves some segments of the marketplace underserved, providing your team with a golden opportunity to expand into new markets. Following are some new markets you may want to consider exploring:

• **Minority markets:** Identify minority markets in your area, including African-Americans, Hispanics, Asians, and so on, and work toward developing a better understanding of them all. You may even consider adding an agent to your team from one of these groups to help the entire team become more sensitive to the needs of a particular minority market.

• **Real estate investors:** Successful investors become returning customers. Cater to investors by providing them with leads on distressed homes, REO properties and foreclosures. Help them find a highly-skilled loan officer, reliable, affordable contractors, and other professionals who can help them achieve their goals. You can often profit from investors on both ends of the transaction—selling them properties and then selling their properties for them or helping them manage rental properties.

• **REO properties:** Banks and other lending institutions in your area that make mortgage loans are often stuck with properties that they've had to foreclose on. Look into the possibility of becoming the agent who sells these properties.

• **Foreclosures:** Some agent teams have their own foreclosure divisions in which they assist people who are facing foreclosure. This added focus can open several opportunities for generating revenue. If the homeowners find that it's best to sell their home, you can be the agent team to list it. If the homeowners need to sell in a hurry, your team can buy the property for cash, fix it up, and sell it as an investor. In addition, every distressed homeowner you help is a source of positive word-of-mouth advertising.

• **Builders:** New construction is a division of real estate that has a huge demand for talented and trained agents. And it isn't a field to be afraid of anymore. Many agents falsely assume that builders are their competition, but builders simply need to sell the homes they build. Contact builders and offer to list their homes. As you prove your value to builders in your area, they'll send you more and more business.

• **Upper-end properties:** Explore all housing markets in your area, including the upper-end market—farms, ranches, waterfront properties, second homes, and so on.

• **Condominiums:** More and more baby boomers are opting for low-maintenance condominiums over houses. By creating a separate division, you can focus on this growing market.

• **Urban properties:** Creating a division that specializes in housing for city dwellers can often help you expand from the suburbs into the city.

• **Cash Buys:** Setting up a cash-buy department enables you to generate additional revenue via investment properties. When a client needs to sell in a hurry, you can often purchase the property at a deep discount by having cash on hand.

• **Rental Properties:** Instead of buying, fixing, and selling properties, your team may prefer a long-term buy-and-hold strategy—leasing out the properties you own instead of selling them.

• **Commercial Properties:** Once you have cornered the residential real estate market in your area, the only way to expand may be to focus additional resources on commercial real estate.

• **Property Management Department:** If you already have rental properties of your own, you probably have a team in charge of managing those properties. Why not offer their services to your other clients who own rental properties?

• **Land Development and Acquisitions:** If you already have experience working with builders, a transition to land development and acquisitions may seem natural to you.

• **Staging:** Sellers are often reluctant to properly prepare their home prior to placing it on the market. Consider creating your own home staging division and offering the service to prospective clients for a reduced fee. You might even consider creating a stand-alone company that provides the service for other real estate agents and their clients, FSBO sellers, and builders.

• **Mortgages:** You can create your own mortgage company or team up with a mortgage broker to provide clients with a one-stop shop where they can secure the financing required to purchase the homes your team is selling.

• **Title Company:** Start your own title company or team up with a title company to provide clients with the title insurance they need when they purchase a home.

Ask for the Business
By Marsha Waddelow

Early in my career, while an agent with Coldwell Banker in an office with over 100 agents, I overheard the young receptionist talking about looking for her first home. When I asked her which agent she was working with, she replied, "No one." She was thrilled when I graciously offered to represent her.

She purchased her first home for only $85,000, but when her husband received a nice promotion, I listed and sold it for $100K. They then moved to the other side of town and purchased a $150,000 home.

She referred me three of her husband's coworkers who were moving to the area. This resulted in three more sales. When the company closed their local office, I was contacted to assist in the sale of the homes of the relocating employees. This all happened over the course of about five years...because *I asked for the business.*

Networking outside your geographical area
You can often boost sales by focusing on clients who are relocating to your area. One way to market to these clients is to establish a presence on the Web. Another way is to network with other agents from around the country by:

• Attending national conventions and conferences

• Exchanging business cards

• Following up with a handwritten note when you return home

According to Waddelow, "My team attaches small items to our cards at conventions—a highlighter with a note attached boasting, 'Your Referrals Are the Highlight of our Business.' Because we're from Texas, we try to give out items that remind agents of where we're from. At a national convention, we passed out small lighted star pins with a card saying, 'Your referrals will receive STAR treatment.' We had people coming up to us and begging for our stars. One of the speakers at the conference asked, 'Where do I get one of those star pins?' They really lit up the room...especially when the lights were off! To this day, people still recognize me as 'the REALTOR® with the star pins,' and all this positive PR cost me a grand total of $100."

Catering to people who are relocating

Businesses, especially large corporations, often need to relocate current or future employees, and that means that they need to find housing for these people. Your team should actively pursue this segment of the market:

• Associate yourself with large corporations to solicit their relocation business.

• Associate yourself with relocation companies for incoming referrals. (Just be sure to check their contracts, read the fine print, and find out how much they charge for referrals.)

• Market yourself on the Web as specializing in relocations.

Charging for outgoing referrals

One of the quickest and easiest ways to generate revenue is through outgoing referrals. If you know an agent in an area outside of your farm area, you can send referrals to that person and earn thousands of dollars with very little work. Anytime you hear of anyone moving, ask whether she has an agent working for her at her new destination. If she says "No," take down her contact information and call the agent you know who sells in that area or fax a referral form to the agent.

Waddelow tells the story of her travel agent who mentioned that she was going on vacation to Hawaii to look for a retirement home to purchase. The travel agent was thrilled when Marsha offered to put her in touch with a real estate agent in Hawaii. And Marsha was thrilled with the referral commission—25% of the agent's commission on the sale of a $400,000 condo. Not bad for making a phone call and sending a fax.

Tip: Encourage team members to add outgoing referrals to their list of goals. You can recognize outgoing referrals just as you do closed transactions.

Buying referrals from retiring agents

If you know any agents who are retiring, offer a referral fee in exchange for any business they send your way. To make this work, a retiring agent needs to maintain an active license, but the referral money can be a welcome addition to his monthly income. It can also generate revenue for you and help build your referral business.

<u>Real Estate Diversification Case Study: Jeannie Sample</u>

Jeannie Sample is the New Construction Specialist on the Ralph Roberts Team, but early in her career, she recognized the potential of agent teams and diversification and built her own successful team. We asked Jeannie to share her insights and experiences with team building, and this is what she had to say:

"I started new construction sales at the ripe old age of 15, working part time for a builder in the suburbs of Chicago as I was attending college. I didn't know anything about traditional real estate. I was hurled into the world of hammers, raw land, and clean new wood and watching piles of lumber, brick, and mortar grow into a home to forever stand on what used to be virgin soil. It was a real rush for me.

"My builder happened to be an English teacher before he became a builder and taught me everything about new construction and new home sales. I accompanied him to apply for permits and helped him decide on architectural designs. I watched and learned the different trades and the building process, experiencing everything firsthand. I found it all very exciting and couldn't imagine anyone being interested in traditional real estate.

"If a client showed up to buy a new home, we didn't even discuss selling her current home. She had to find her own listing agent. That was back in 1976, and it still works the same way around much of the nation. But for me, that was about to change.

"One day, I had an epiphany. I realized all the potential income I was missing by ignoring my buyers' other real estate needs. I immediately obtained my real estate license and started dealing in both new and used homes.

"I quickly became very successful and decided to document the system I used to sell homes of all kinds and train others. The builder saw my potential and added more subdivisions. I trained and added more associates to my team and voilà! I was a team leader. Through trial and error, I learned how to juggle team leading and diversification."

<u>Generating Business, from One Department to Another</u>

The most exciting aspect of having different departments under the same roof is that eventually, one department begins to generate business for another department. As more people join your team, their different personalities attract different types of buyers and sellers as well, fueling even more business. Here's an example:

You create a department for new construction sales and add a new construction agent to your team. Let's call this person Billie. Billie is quite busy selling homes for a builder of a new subdivision. While Billie is selling new construction homes, buyers often approach asking Billie for help selling the homes they currently own. Billie refers the buyers to the listing department and earns a referral fee.

Time marches on, and the builder is so happy with Billie that he asks for help selling new homes in a second subdivision. Billie is thrilled but is overloaded with work, so Billie takes on and trains another new construction salesperson to work at the second subdivision. As happened with Billie, buyers are often approaching the new salesperson asking for help selling the homes they currently own, and the second salesperson is referring even more business to the listing department (and earning referral fees for doing so).

Now Mr. Builder is a happy camper and wants to plan for the future with your team in mind. He needs to locate land to build more subdivisions, so he calls your team for assistance. You take on a land acquisitions specialist, who charges some big bucks. Now you have to pay this person, and working with only one builder doesn't generate sufficient revenue. However, now that you have a land acquisitions department, you can approach other builders and offer this new service. This generates additional business for your new construction department, which generates additional business for your listing department.

Soon your team machine is getting the word out to commercial and real estate builders, and you can build one success after another.

This is exactly how Jeannie Sample built her real estate business.

She started with one builder, which quickly became five, then hurled into 23 subdivisions at one time. Her used-home division was taking on new team members and listing the trade-in homes like crazy. In turn, those listings drove floor calls to her buyer's agents, who earned commissions from new buyers that she would never have caught before. The buyer's agents flipped leads to the used listing department as well, as they met new people from the floor calls.

Creating Departments within Your Team

In Chapter 3, we encourage you to develop systems and subsystems to break everything down into manageable steps. This same approach is useful for creating departments. Divide your business into specialized departments, provide each department with detailed expectations and procedures, and then hire skilled and talented personnel to perform the required tasks. By following this blueprint, you can, in essence, set up teams of experts required to manage each and every aspect of your real estate business.

This systematic approach offers several benefits, including the following:

• You can focus on the most dollar-productive activities in your organization.

• Your staff can specialize in separate areas, so they can better serve your clients.

• You can more easily replace key personnel when they leave because you have a system and procedures in place.

• You avoid the problem of having prospective clients who refuse to deal with anyone except you, because as soon as you meet the client, you can introduce him or her to your specialist: "Hi, Mr. and Mrs. Buyer, my name is Ralph Roberts. This is Jane Doe—she's our Buyer Specialist. Jane has helped hundreds of buyers find the homes of their dreams and I know she will do the same for you. Jane and I will be working very closely to put your transaction together, but Jane will be your primary contact here because she will have the most up-to-date information about you and your home search."

Most agent teams quickly discover that organizing their business through a systems approach results in a phenomenal increase in sales and enables them to free up their time and energy to pursue other professional and personal dreams. We highly recommend that you take the same approach.

Obviously it would be difficult, if not impossible, to set up all your systems at once, so we recommend that you tackle one at a time. Get one up and running smoothly and then move on to the next one. In this section, we introduce some of the top revenue-generating departments, explain how each department can be used to expand your business, and introduce the main considerations you need to make when setting up each department.

Cash-buy department

One way to get rich in real estate is through acquiring undervalued properties and either flipping them for profit or leasing them out and then selling them after they appreciate in value. As a real estate team, you are in a unique position to identify and act on these properties when the opportunities arise. By creating a cash-buy department, you can create an entirely new revenue stream for your real estate business.

Getting started

To succeed at buying and selling (or leasing out) investment properties, you need three things:
- Financing to purchase the properties
- Cash-buy specialists to identify and purchase undervalued properties
- Undervalued properties

You can't buy properties for cash if you don't have available cash to spend. Your first task is to gain access to money. Consider the following sources for financing:
- Your own financial resources, including the equity you have in properties you own, personal savings, and retirement savings
- Hard money loans that enable you to put up the investment property as collateral for the loan
- Lines of credit from banks
- Partnerships with private investors

Tip: You may have to begin by finding properties first and then getting them funded on an individual basis. In this case, you'd gather all the details of each deal—such as purchase price, estimated cost to rehab the property, and estimated market value after repairs and renovations—and present those details to a bank or investor. The financier may require you to put up some of your own money at first, but after you establish a track record, the cash you need will be easier to find.

The second component you need to have in place is someone who is devoted to buying, repairing, and preparing cash-buy properties to either lease them out or place them back on the market. This person must be:

- Well connected, so people know whom to come to when they need to sell their property in a hurry

- Knowledgeable concerning housing values in the area, so she can tell a good deal when she sees one

- A talented researcher who can find the best deals available

- A great negotiator who can convince homeowners to accept a price significantly below market value

After you have access to money and you have someone on staff to devote all her efforts to cash-buy opportunities, you'll need to find some deals. Knowing the property values in your area can help you spot the best deals, but you need to know where to look. Here are some places to start:

- **The MLS (Multiple Listing Service):** Check out the new listings as well as those that have been languishing on the market for months more than your area's average market time.

- **FSBO (For Sale by Owner) ads and signs:** Check the classified ads in the newspaper, FSBO sites on the Web, and FSBO signs in the neighborhood.

- **Contact banks for REO (Real Estate Owned) properties:** Banks are often highly motivated to cut their losses on properties they had to repossess in foreclosure.

- **Run-down properties:** You may notice properties in your area that are vacant and run-down but are not on the market. These may be abandoned properties or be owned by people who no longer care much about them and aren't even motivated enough to place their properties on the market.

For additional details on finding bargain properties, fixing them, and selling them for a profit, visit www.getflipping.com and check out *Flipping Houses For Dummies*, by Ralph R. Roberts, with Joe Kraynak.

Tip: People who are forced to relocate because of their jobs often want some assurance that their home will sell quickly. You can offer them a guaranteed listing, which means that you come up with the amount you'd be willing to pay to cash them out. You list the house for them and try to sell it at market value, but they have the option of accepting your cash offer if they feel the house is taking too long to sell. Ralph Roberts Realty always has an ad in the local paper offering cash for homes. Get your name out there and start developing relationships with people and organizations that can feed you business.

Optimizing success

The key to a successful cash buy is the size of the spread between what it costs you to purchase, rehab, and sell the house and the proceeds you receive from that sale. Obviously, the bigger the spread, the better the deal for you. But be careful—your spread can quickly shrink away to nothing if you don't do your homework.

Tip: Always shoot for earning at least a 20% profit on your total investment. In a slower market, you may need to shoot a little higher to hit your mark. On www.getflipping.com, you can find a Purchase Price Estimator that can perform the calculations for you. This site also offers a 31-day e-mail course on flipping properties along with some tips and cautions on how to minimize your risks and maximize your profits.

Following are some additional tips on how to maximize your success with cash buys:

- **Overestimate costs and underestimate profits.** Develop relationships with contractors and appraisers who can help you get more accurate numbers for value and rehab costs.

- **Be sure to figure in the cost of your money when looking at the numbers.** If you buy a property and it takes twice as long to fix up as you expected, the interest you pay to the bank or investor during the rehab could kill your profit margin.

- **Don't overlook holding costs.** These costs include property taxes, insurance payments, and utility bills for the duration of the project.

- **Resist the urge to over-improve the property.** The value of similar homes in the same neighborhood pretty much sets the upper limit on how much you can expect someone to pay for the property. Adding $100,000 worth of improvements to a home in an area where the most expensive home is worth $150,000 doesn't make a lot of sense.

Tip: When you sit down with someone interested in cashing out of his home, how quickly you can put the transaction together will usually make or break the deal. If you know it's a good deal, sign the deal right way. If you're uncomfortable, sign the deal but make it contingent upon the appraiser of your choice appraising the home at a minimum value. The point is, if this person is so motivated to get cash that he's willing to sell his home at a deep discount, you can be sure that he will, if he hasn't already, contact three other people to try to sell the property. One of those people will steal the transaction from you if you don't lock it up as quickly as possible.

Property management department

As your cash-buy department begins accumulating properties, you need someone to oversee rehab and make sure that properties are either being sold or rented in a timely manner.

Later, you can use the property management department as a profit center by managing rental properties owned by investors in your marketplace. Not only will this generate income through the management services you provide, but it also will give you the inside track to securing investors' listings and purchases, which will generate business for your other departments.

Getting started

It's usually best to hire someone who has prior property management experience to head up that department. Your property manager should be responsible for the following:

- Hiring contractors to perform repairs and renovations
- Securing insurance
- Making sure all taxes are up-to-date
- Leasing out rental properties
- Handling collections and evictions of past-due tenants
- Working with your listing department to get rehabbed houses on the market as quickly as possible

Warning: Because each of these areas is so important to your success, someone who's learning on the job could potentially cost you quite a bit of money. A situation where a single house without insurance burns down is all it takes to set the development of your whole organization back months or even years.

Your property manager must also be highly organized and focused on prioritizing, performing the most dollar-productive activities before attacking other projects. For example, immediately securing insurance for a new acquisition (an activity that will potentially save you multiple thousands of dollars) is much more important than making a collection call to a tenant who's a month behind on his rent (an activity that will bring in a few hundred or a thousand dollars in revenue). Although both tasks are important, you clearly must handle one before the other. This may sound rather obvious, but you'd be amazed at the number of people who don't have this ability to analyze and prioritize. You have to go out of your way to make sure your property manager possesses this skill.

Optimizing success

After you get both your cash-buy and property management departments in place, you may be able to take your property management department to the next level by offering seller financing in the form of land contracts or lease option deals. Seller financing opens the door to a whole new group of potential customers—people who may have difficulty financing the purchase with a conventional loan. This group includes first-time home buyers, self-employed people, buyers with bruised credit, and landlords looking for more rental properties. The beauty of this setup is that by putting off the realization of your total profit on a cash buy for two or three years, you can generate more buyers and listings while still earning a small spread between your monthly loan payment to the bank and what the buyer is paying you each month.

Obviously, if you don't have any experience with providing seller financing, you should consult a knowledgeable attorney before putting anything in place. But, if you already have a property management division in place, your property manager can service the loan—collecting payments, starting land contract forfeiture proceedings against those who don't pay, and so on.

Note: Remember that even though you have collected cash from the buyer, the buyer is still likely to pay a higher interest rate on a greater amount than the interest rate and principal you're paying to the bank.

Foreclosure department

Setting up a foreclosure department can be one of the best investments your team will ever make. It has the potential of delivering a host of benefits, including the following:

- It generates an incredible amount of business for your organization, including listings, buyers, cash acquisitions, land contract sales, and renters for company-owned properties.

- You gain the opportunity to help people who are in foreclosure—people who probably don't know what options they have available to them. You could be the one who offers them one last chance to get their lives back in order.

- You can offer one option that most foreclosure investors can't offer—the option to place the house on the market and sell it for the distressed homeowners. In other words, if the owners choose not to sell the property to you as an investor, they may hire you to list it, in which case you profit from the commission. Either way, you win.

- Your entire organization gets recession insurance—meaning that your foreclosure division could actually benefit from an economic downturn. Even when the U.S. economy is booming, a minimum of 4–5% of all homes in America are in foreclosure or facing foreclosure (the owners are 30 days or more behind in their mortgage payments). Take the total number of homes in your marketplace and multiply by 4%—that's the minimum number or prospects available to your foreclosure department. If the economy takes a downturn, the number will only go up.

Getting started

Getting started in the foreclosure arena requires some attention to detail. You can lose a lot of money if you're ill prepared and fail to do sufficient research. Your preparation must involve:

• **Securing financing (most foreclosures are cash buys):** Because most foreclosure opportunities are cash buys, you clear one of the major hurdles as a foreclosure investor by setting up a cash-buy department, as explained earlier in this section.

• **Brushing up on foreclosure laws and regulations in your area:** Every state has different laws and regulations and even some countries within a state may have different statutes. Find a knowledgeable foreclosure attorney and pick his brain. Read the law yourself and discuss the procedures with the person who handles the mortgage sale (usually from the county sheriff's department). Track down and subscribe to all publications in your area that publish the foreclosure listings.

• **Networking in the neighborhood to find leads on preforeclosure opportunities:** Although you may want to focus exclusively on buying properties at auction, I encourage you to work the preforeclosure arena, as well. With preforeclosures, you contact the homeowners prior to auction, present their options, and encourage them to choose whichever option they find most attractive. Develop a referral network of real estate professionals who can work with people in foreclosure. Your referral network should include the following:

- Loan officers

- Bankruptcy attorneys

- Title insurance companies

- Financial advisors or credit counselors

• **Following foreclosure notices published in your area.** Subscribe to any publications in your area that carry the county foreclosure notices and read them every week for leads.

• **Researching documentation on foreclosure properties, including the title and any liens against the properties.** Head down to your county courthouse and research the public records for your home as practice. Inspect the mortgage, title, and any other documentation that is in the public record.

• **Inspecting the properties with your own two eyes before making an offer or bidding on the properties at auction.** Visit any property prior to purchasing it and at least walk around it to inspect all four sides. If you can convince the homeowners to let you look around inside, that's definitely a bonus.

• **Networking with loan officers, bankruptcy attorneys, title insurance companies, and other real estate professionals who can assist homeowners facing foreclosure.** Other professionals who work with distressed homeowners may be eager to find an investor like you who can purchase the home quickly for cash, so their clients can get out from under a home they cannot afford.

• **Preparing a foreclosure packet informing distressed homeowners of their rights, options, and deadlines:** The more options you have, the better your chances of putting a deal together. Consider offering the following options:

- Listing and selling the home at market value

- Selling the home to you for cash

- Selling the home to you for cash and buying it back on a land contract

- Selling the home to you for cash and then leasing it with the option to buy later under a lease-option agreement

- Reinstating the mortgage with the lender, by bringing the payments up to date

- Negotiating a forbearance (a payment plan) with the lender (a payment plan)

- Negotiating a short sale with the lender, in which the lender agrees to accept less than full payment of the mortgage balance

- Referring the person to a loan officer to refinance out of foreclosure

- Referring the person to a bankruptcy attorney for further legal assistance

Tip: Even if you earn no money helping a homeowner in foreclosure, as long as you treat that person with respect, act with integrity, and do what is truly in the best interest of all involved, you earn a customer for life and a wealth of positive word-of-mouth advertising. If the homeowners are ever in a position to purchase another property, they're much more likely to call you.

After you learn the laws, figure out which options your organization can offer, and collect data on all the homes in foreclosure, you simply have to get out there and start contacting prospects. You can do this through general advertising, direct mail, or actually going out to the houses and knocking on doors. Just remember that because the foreclosure process has definite beginning and ending points, you're racing against the clock on every single deal. After you make contact with someone, you have to move quickly to make things happen, or there's a very good chance that the customer will actually lose his house and whatever equity he has in it.

Optimizing success

The one common thread running through nearly every foreclosure case is that those in trouble desperately need good advice from someone they can trust. People in foreclosure are usually besieged by disreputable opportunists looking only to profit from their misfortune. They need an upstanding, understanding person who will simply discuss the situation with them and present their options in a nonthreatening manner.

By being knowledgeable in your area's foreclosure laws and procedures, you can quickly become the homeowners' confidant. You can build trust in a manner of minutes when you help them to regain even a small amount of control over their situations by explaining the rights and options that may be available to them.

Remember: Let people tell their stories and lend them a sympathetic ear. At the same time, be brutally honest about their situation. Don't sugarcoat anything—doing so is like setting a time bomb to blow up in your face later. Tell them the truth about their situation; let them know what options you think are best; explain what you're going to do to try to make those options become reality; and honestly assess the chances you believe they have of successfully getting out of foreclosure. Even though it might be painful for them to hear at the time, most people will be better off in the long run because of your candor. Plus, when you're able to put a deal together, no hidden surprises will surface and mess things up.

It is also important to admit when a deal is dead. Sometimes, homeowners have unrealistic expectations or refuse to list and sell when that is the only real option available to them. In these cases, admit to yourself that there is nothing more you can do, wish the homeowners good luck, and move on to the next deal.

Investing in preforeclosure and foreclosure properties can be very profitable and rewarding, but it can also be frustrating and risky if you don't know what you're doing. For additional details on investing in foreclosures and preforeclosures, check out *Foreclosure Investing For Dummies* by Ralph R. Roberts, with Joe Kraynak.

Other departments

You may also want to consider creating departments such as your own mortgage company, title insurance company, and building company. But because laws vary greatly from state to state, we can't offer a great deal of guidance that applies to all real estate businesses in every state. Needless to say, having these types of companies under your umbrella allows you to make more money on the same transactions you're already making as well as generate new business.

Tip: If you decide not to invest the money and resources into developing these divisions within your organization, consider developing close ties and partnerships with owners of these types of companies in your area that are similar in size and focus to your organization. Creating productive synergies can increase the flow of business and boost your bottom line.

Adding a New Department to Your Business

Whenever you grow your business, you want the growth to be natural and organic. When you add a new department, you're essentially starting an entirely new business, so plan well in advance. Carefully choose a manager for the new department, and make sure you have the proper personnel in place before launching. This section shows you how to proceed and offers some additional suggestions.

Drawing up a new business plan

When you have an idea of the direction you need to go to grow, set up your business plan. We won't go into the specific details of your business plan, because all plans are different, but we can highlight various areas that your business plan needs to address:

- **Description of your new department:** Write down your vision for the department—what will it do, who will it serve, how will it generate revenue? List the services it will offer.

- **Goals and milestones:** State the goals of your new department. What do you want it to accomplish? When do you want it to be fully operational? Then, list milestones, so you can ensure that the development of the new department remains on track. Regular weekly meetings should keep goals and guidelines well within your sight.

• **Obstacles: Identify potential obstacles.** Do you have the skills and talent on staff to run the new department competently? Do you have sufficient office space and the required equipment and other resources?

• **Descriptions of potential competition and ways you'll rise above them:** If other agent teams in your area have similar departments, do some research to find out how they operate and the types of services they offer. Brainstorm ways to make your department superior.

• **Staffing:** Draw up a list of positions you need to fill in the new department, and estimate the amount of time you need to fill those positions.

• **Financing for training and discovery:** When you spot a promising team member, set aside the training, counseling, time, and money that person will need. In addition, always plan time and money for the discovery portion of an endeavor. Instead of taking a stab at new challenges, educate yourself about that business—all the pros and cons and what to expect.

Warning: Keep in mind that current team members may not be right for the new department. Choose the best people for each position; don't use the new department as a tool for promoting team members who aren't qualified for those positions.

• **Marketing plan and budget:** A new department usually means offering new services to clients. Draw up a marketing plan and budget to get the word out about your new department. Keep in mind that marketing new services may mean that you are marketing to a different target audience. Be realistic when developing your marketing budget; you're better off overestimating costs to cover hidden or unexpected expenses.

• **Breakeven point:** How much will the department need to earn to pay for its operations?

• **Profitability goal:** Set a date on which you expect the department to achieve its breakeven point and begin to generate a profit. When starting a new construction business, for example, it might take a builder up to a year to finish the first home. Make sure you have sufficient cash reserves to cover expenses while the new department is getting on its feet. Set realistic goals for both income and expenses.

• **Earnings estimate:** Your business plan should include an estimate of earnings showing how much you plan the new department to earn monthly, quarterly, or annually after it begins fully functioning.

A business plan doesn't have to be 20 pages long. Two to four pages should do the trick. You can also modify your business plan on the fly as conditions change. Consider consulting a mentor or coach—someone who has developed business plans before—to help you out. And of course, check out Chapter 4, where we cover business plans in detail.

Establishing a mission statement

It's important to adhere to a foundation for each of your new endeavors. Oftentimes, complex diversification leads to pandemonium if not planned carefully. Each division or company should have a separate and distinct mission statement that functions as a guide to bring you back from the brink of changing directions in the middle of your journey.

The mission statement should be a clear and succinct description of the department's purpose and the manner in which it will seek to achieve its goals. The mission statement should be worded in such a way that it appeals to prospective clients, making a commitment to serve in the client's best interest. Following are some sample mission statements:

Agent team: Our mission is to be the highest quality, most respected, assertive, innovative, and successful provider of real estate services in the country, while providing a genuinely enjoyable and fun place to work.

Foreclosure department: To provide homeowners who are facing foreclosure with all the information and guidance they need to make the best choices while earning a reasonable profit for our services.

Cash-buy department: To identify potentially lucrative cash-buy opportunities, purchase properties, repair and renovate them to bring them up to market value, and then sell or lease the properties for a profit.

Property management department: To manage and oversee repairs and renovations, make sure that team-owned properties are either being sold or rented in a timely manner, and manage client-owned properties as if they are our very own.

Finding a team leader for your new department

Within your local area, if you're in touch with your local agents, you know of specific people who stand out in your mind. They're the local professionals who have made it to the summit in their field. Often, they're excellent at what they do but play the lone wolf. They've hit a plateau in their business, and though it's a nice and comfortable plateau, they'd love to move up and bring in new challenges to their business. Approach them! Don't be shy. You'd be surprised how many people might be ready for a different concept such as a team.

Here are some of the qualities to look for in a team leader:
- Knowledgeable and highly skilled in her field
- Passionate about what he does
- Take-charge personality with an ability to delegate
- Ability to get along with others
- Well aware that by serving the team's best interests, everyone earns more money

Staffing up for your new department

Recruiting talent for your new department doesn't necessarily mean that you have to limit yourself to people who have experience in real estate. Most real estate agents have come from other walks of life. Keep an open mind and recognize talent, assets, and personality wherever you go. You might consider hiring a waitress to sell new construction homes because she can sell a soufflé like no one else! Sometimes a person with a clean slate is better than a seasoned expert. Training for a new person is easily obtainable in today's world, so don't let a lack of knowledge and experience discourage you from taking on a promising candidate.

Here are the qualities you want to find in a team member of your new department:
- Eagerness to work with others
- Proactive
- Creative
- Energetic
- Passionate
- Organized
- Professional
- Optimistic
- Experience in the field is a bonus, but not essential

Maintaining a Lucrative Multi-Faceted Business

After you get your new department(s) set up, keeping everything running smoothly can become a bit of a challenge. Here are a few things you can do to make sure your organization doesn't start spinning out of control:
- **Keep yourself informed, but don't micromanage.** Have regular meetings with each department, during which you discuss the department's

progress, set goals, and solve problems. Schedule meetings often enough to keep things moving forward and keep you informed—this may mean having daily, weekly or monthly meetings. Resist the urge to throw yourself into the middle of every deal that comes through your organization. If you choose the right people and train them properly, they should be able to capably handle normal, nonproblem transactions with only minimal input from you.

• **Hire and pay good people.** When it comes to staffing, think long-term. The more solid your staff, the more deals they'll put together, and the more money everyone will make. In many cases, giving away a bigger piece of the pie to a talented department manager, though painful at first, will lead to many more pies to divvy up, because the manager is happy and working hard.

• **Cross-train everyone.** As you grow, have key personnel learn the ins and outs of every job within your organization. Don't allow any employee to hold you hostage because he or she is the only person on your staff who knows how to do a particular job. No one should be irreplaceable.

• **Know what's going on with your books.** Salespeople generally have the attitude that if they're low on money, they simply need to sell more. You have to lose this attitude as you build your organization. Have a bookkeeper or CPA help you keep track of the income and expenses of each department. That way, when finances get tight, you'll know where you have to cut. Also, when your business is thriving, you'll know which department deserves more marketing dollars.

Chapter 16

Overcoming the Top Ten Challenges to Operating a Successful Agent Team

Building and managing a top-producing agent team is no easy feat. It requires the right attitudes, careful preparation, constant motivation, and careful and sustained growth. Most team leaders learn by trial and error—the most costly and frustrating way to obtain an education.

In this chapter, we asked Char MacCallum of the Char MacCallum Real Estate Group of Olathe, Kansas (www.char4homes.com), to highlight the top ten challenges that agent teams are likely to encounter. She also provides advice on how to steer clear of common mistakes by confronting these challenges head-on.

As you run your business, think of challenges not as obstacles or hurdles but as opportunities to grow and create a positive experience for everyone involved. Implementing an agent team approach introduces fundamental changes to the way you do business. Embracing these changes gives you and your team the opportunity to soar to new heights.

Challenge #1: Nurturing a Team Mentality and Presence

A group consisting of one or more agents and staff isn't necessarily a team; to qualify as a team, all members need to share values and work toward a common goal. If you simply add members to your team to take care of jobs that you don't have the time to do yourself, you aren't exactly creating a team. You are a boss with employees who have no emotional bond or feelings of loyalty toward a common goal, which typically results in a high turnover.

When everyone on the "team" acts independently in service solely to his or her own interests, the culture you create is that of every man for himself. What you want to strive for, rather, is an "all for one and one for all" culture. Otherwise, you end up with a team that has a Viking mentality—pillaging and plundering their way to fleeting success. Someone on the team will decide that he can do what you do, take your team, and hang his own shingle. And that person will likely suffer the same fate when a disgruntled team member decides that he or she can do a better job of running things.

Your number one priority as a team leader is to nurture a sense of family among team members. Through weekly meetings, training sessions, mentoring, personal partnerships, shared goals, and team activities and events, you can create strong bonds that hold the team together through good times and bad. For tips on forming a cohesive team, check out Chapter 12.

Your team also needs to decide which values it wants to present to the public. How do you want your team to be perceived by clients and prospective clients in terms of value and commitment? Jot down a list of core values. For the Char MacCallum Team, the core values are as follows:

- Compassion
- Integrity
- Joy
- Honesty
- Achievement
- Vitality
- Bounty
- Loyalty
- Orderliness
- Passion

From this list, the team developed its mission statement: "Helping people experience ultimate service when buying or selling real estate through Integrity, Honesty, and Joy." Your mission statement can help you identify the values you want all your team members to embrace, including a sense of team spirit and the need to take initiative and believe in themselves.

Tip: People pretty much fall into three categories: givers, takers, and those who give and take. When bringing new team members aboard, steer clear of the takers. They'll drain your team's time, energy, and resources, all of which you need to better serve your clients and maintain a positive work environment.

Challenge #2: Setting Up Systems
To ensure reliable service while allowing you to add team members without any reduction in that level of service, your team should operate like a German train system. To achieve that goal, you need to create systems for everything, including:

- **Answering the phones:** Have a policy in place so that everyone in the office greets clients and prospects in a tone that's happy and excited. You may even want to have scripts in place, so the receptionist knows exactly what to say in common situations.

- **Managing leads:** To transform leads into clients, construct a system that ensures each lead is contacted on a regular basis starting within minutes (not hours) of when you first receive the lead.

- **Listing presentations:** Although you should customize every listing presentation for each client, all listing agents should have a clear idea of the types of information the presentation should contain and the level of quality you expect.

• **Placing a home on the market:** As soon as a seller signs the listing contract, you should have a system in place for putting up the For Sale sign, adding the property to the Multiple Listing Service (MLS), delivering a lockbox, and producing and distributing marketing materials.

• **Managing showings:** A showing requires more than just letting prospective buyers into a home. You want to be able to present the people with a flyer, estimated utility bills, and highlights of the home's unique features. Have a system in place to ensure that all showings are handled consistently.

• **Hosting open houses:** Hosting an open house is like throwing a party. Get the best party planner on your team to draw up instructions on how to plan, announce, and host a successful open house.

• **Handling closing documents:** Have a system in place that ensures a smooth closing. The system should commence as soon as the buyer and seller come to terms on the purchase agreement and continue through to escrow.

Tip: Through careful planning and by setting up systems, your team can overcome one of the main challenges to success—success itself. Success can threaten your profitability in two ways. First, it can cause your team to become complacent and lose the ambition and commitment to customer service responsible for the success. Secondly, it can compromise your team's ability to provide excellent customer service if it comes at a time when you're ill prepared to handle it. Careful planning and an unrelenting pursuit of business can help you avoid this trap.

Managing Leads Case Study: The Char MacCallum Team
By Char MacCallum

We have systems in place to service the listings and track the sales through to escrow. The first 10 days we have a property listed, we launch a daily letter and contact program. The seller receives letters, post cards, and phone calls that provide them with tips on selling, preparing the house for a showing, and understanding the feedback comments they are receiving.

On one home we listed, we had an offer within 14 days. On one visit to the house, the buyers started talking negatively about real estate agents and the level of service they had received. My seller quickly spoke up and defended my team by saying her real estate agent was very attentive, that they've never had such great service, and that she hears from us every day.

We received this endorsement because we have a system in place for keeping in touch with clients on a daily basis. I wasn't the person calling them or sending them letters—my team did it all, and because we had an automated system in place, the efforts seemed effortless.

Challenge #3: Eliminating Negative Forces

Every day your team will likely be bombarded with negative attitudes, whether from the news media, family, friends, clients, or coworkers. How this negativity affects you and the rest of your team is up to all of you to decide. You can't control what other people say or do, but you can control your responses to them. Your best bet? Establish a No-Negativity policy on your team and nip any negativity in the bud. Even one negative person on a team can drag down the entire team. If you can't turn a negative team member into an optimistic one, then you may need to let that person go.

According to Char MacCallum, her biggest challenge is keeping negativity out of the team. She tells the story of a team member who was the team's closing manager: "After talking on the phone to a client, she hung up and said 'Bite me.' Now the person she was talking to never heard what she said because the phone was disconnected, but the rest of the team heard it, and it affected us in a negative way."

You and the rest of your teammates must make a concerted effort to shut down gossip and negativity. You can confront the person directly, joke about it in a way that lets the person know you didn't approve (by saying something like, "Wow, that was certainly a positive thing to say."), or highlight the positive side to coach the person back into thinking and speaking more optimistically.

Warning: As the leader goes, so goes the team. If the team leader isn't a strong role model, motivator, visionary, manager, and mentor, the team is likely to flounder. As team leader, you need to remain a positive role model, especially when other team members are having trouble remaining positive. See Chapter 6 for tips on how to become an effective leader.

Challenge #4: Training, Training, and More Training

A comprehensive training program is the key to the success of individual team members and to the team as a whole. With appropriate training, you cut down on the number of questions, mistakes, and interruptions; give team members a greater sense that they can accomplish daily tasks independently; and demonstrate your commitment to each team member's success. You can implement your training program in any number of ways, including the following:

• **Do it yourself.** Develop your own training program, write the instructions, and train team members internally.

• **Hire an outside coach or trainer.** You can offer input and develop systems to make team members accountable, but you leave the rest up to the trainer or coach.

• **Buy a training system.** You can purchase a real estate training program from a third party, follow the program step-by-step, and develop your own system to hold team members accountable.

Although whatever training program you use should cover all the basics, training should be continuous. When issues arise, look for opportunities to train your staff on how to deal with those issues more effectively in the future. Char MacCallum tells the story of a team that refused to learn from its mistakes:

"I phoned an agent friend of mine to list my mother's home. My friend took the listing—we just needed to agree on the price and make sure my mother felt comfortable with the agent and my friend's team.

"The team sent its listing partner to the house, and after showing this person the property, we discussed and agreed upon the asking price. My mother asked a couple of questions that are fairly common before signing the listing contract, and then I asked whether the agent would put flyers out on the sign in a flyer box.

"The agent answered 'No,' that wasn't something they do. The team preferred to have people call into their office, so they could speak with them directly. I objected, explaining that in my experience, eliminating those flyers would mean a loss of my #2 and #4 lead sources. The agent then closed the binder and said something like, 'Well, we don't do that. Thank you very much, but it looks like we can't help you.'

"I was stunned. I e-mailed my friend to tell her that my mother was looking to use another agent, but I would like to explain why. My friend e-mailed me back and said that there was no need to discuss, because her listing partner had already told her that the problem had to do with the fact that they don't place flyers on the For Sale sign.

"My friend missed an excellent opportunity to coach her listing partner and the rest of the team. Her team didn't lose the listing because of a flyer—they lost it because they didn't ask for the order. All the listing partner needed to say was 'Char, I respect how you market your homes, but in this area we sell a lot of homes and don't use the flyers. Do you think we can sell the house?' I would've said 'Yes,' and the agent could then have said, 'Great—let's sign the papers and get your house on the market.' Simple as that.

"Don't miss those golden opportunities to coach and train your team to greatness beyond formalized training programs."

Tip: Having a solid training program in place can enable your team to manage its growth. Growth is usually a positive thing in the long term, but in the short term, it can actually set your team back, especially if you don't have the training and infrastructure in place to support a new member of the team. Grow your team at a steady pace, and always make sure you have systems and training in place to accommodate new team members.

Challenge #5: Holding Team Members Accountable

One of the key reasons why the Weight Watchers® program is so successful is that it holds members accountable. Every week, members meet for a public weigh-in, the scales tell the story, and members hold one another accountable for meeting their weight-loss goals.

The same is true for agent teams. On the most successful teams, team members hold each other accountable. An accountability system reinforces the training you provide and gets team members in the habit of following up with leads, past clients, and scripts. See Chapters 12 and 13 for details.

Warning: Some agents have a difficult time handling success. If you tell them that they are on track to surpass their goal for the year, they may unconsciously hold back for the remainder of the year. You have to find a way to keep agents motivated even when they're highly successful, or you'll lose valuable additional business.

Challenge #6: Making Team Members Feel Appreciated

All workers need to feel that what they do is rewarding. They need to feel appreciated. Your compensation package should be structured in a way that rewards achievement, but the compensation mostly covers only the monetary aspect of work. Even more important, you need to address the emotional needs of your teammates.

The trick is to show your appreciation in a way that the other person values. In his book *The Five Love Languages: How to Express Heartfelt Commitment to*

Your Mate, Gary Chapman reveals that people give and appreciate what others give them in different ways (love languages):

- Quality Time
- Words of Affirmation
- Physical Touch
- Acts of Service
- Gifts

Chapman points out that couples often get into trouble when one partner gives what the other partner doesn't value receiving. For example, a husband may paint the house (doing an act of service) thinking that his wife will love him more for it, only to find out later that she's angry because what she really values is spending time with him, and he took that away from her.

The same is true when you're rewarding team members. Some team members may prefer having a weekend off (quality time) over a big bonus (a gift). Others may prefer being thanked and recognized during team meetings (words of affirmation). By building close relationships with team members, you can find out what their individual love languages are and respond accordingly. You can often tell what a person likes to receive by what they like to give. Someone who gives gifts, for example, usually likes to receive gifts in return.

Tip: Nurture an entrepreneurial atmosphere. Each and every person on your team should feel personally responsible for his or her own success as well as the success of the entire team. Consider setting a production minimum that all agents must meet in order to remain on the team. When agents complain, remind them that they're not simply salespeople but entrepreneurs earning commissions. Set up the system in such a way that the more they sell, the more they earn.

Challenge #7: Creating a Productive Office Space Layout

Your office floor plan can have a significant influence on how your team functions. If you're working in a traditional brokerage, you may have little input on how offices are arranged and how the conference rooms are shared. If you do have input, however, make sure you have a large conference room or an open area that is large enough to accommodate your entire team. Also make sure that agents have a space where they can meet privately with other team members or clients should the need arise.

The team leader and others who play managerial or administrative roles should each have an office with a door on it for confidential meetings and to block out office noise that can cause distractions. However, the team leader should always remain accessible to answer questions and deal with any issues that might arise.

Tip: Colors and lighting can have a strong effect on production, in addition to the office ambience. Choose warm and inviting colors that energize people, and make sure the office is well lit. Some teams have hired Feng Shui designers to help increase the energy and harmony of the workplace by redesigning the layout.

Challenge #8: Paying Team Members Well without Overpaying

Whenever we speak about agent teams, some of the most popular questions center on what to pay team members—buyer's agents, the listing manager, closing managers, marketing directors, receptionists, assistants, and so on. We address this topic in Chapter 6, but you need to keep in mind that when you overpay for a position, you set a precedent that's tough to escape. Char MacCallum fell into this trap by not thinking ahead:

> I spent a lot of time considering a compensation package that would be fair for my first administrative assistant. The person would be taking on a reasonable portion of my work, so I offered $1,000 a month guaranteed salary plus 10% of my earned commission.
>
> I was terrified at the thought of how was I going to pay someone $1,000 a month minimum, so I asked my broker to write a check to her for $500 out of every commission check I earned plus 10% of my commission. Within four months, I had a year's worth of her base salary checks made out to her sitting in my desk drawer. By the end of the year, she was the second highest paid person in the office, behind me. Office morale took a nosedive. My administrative assistant was earning more than the other agents in the office. Overpaying also brought a sense of entitlement to someone whose position normally would receive only about a third of what she was making.

To avoid making the same mistake, Char suggests that you research your market before making an offer. Find out what companies are paying for clerical workers, administrative assistants, sales positions, and general labor. Look into how much brokers are paying their agents—buyers' agents and sellers' agents. Then calculate a fair amount to pay each person. Take into account the fact that you're covering many of the expenses that each agent would be responsible for paying if he or she was working independently—marketing costs, office space, equipment, supplies, and so on. Your agents may make less in commissions as a percentage, but given the fact that you have a support system in place, they're likely earning much more than if they were working independently.

Challenge #9: Unifying Sales and Administration

Division often occurs between sales and administration. Agents may start to believe that they are generating all the revenue and start to treat the administrative staff as second-class citizens. Likewise, the administrative staff may think that the agents have the "cushy" jobs—talking on the phone, meeting clients, and showing houses—while the administrative staff is doing the real work of managing the transactions. However it begins to happen, that resentment can quickly spin out of control and drag the whole office down.

To prevent such divisions from occurring, demonstrate your appreciation for the entire team and foster a culture that makes the team feel more like family. Keep the dialog open so that everyone on the team is well aware that every other team member makes a significant contribution to the team's success. Everyone needs to feel the love, because when crunch time hits, you want to know that your back is covered and the team is there to support your efforts.

Tip: Consider sending out surveys to your clients asking them to share their experience of working with your team, and to describe the level of service you provided. When you get the surveys back, route them around to all team members, and have each team member sign off on them. If the surveys are positive, team members can celebrate the fact that everyone did a great job. If the surveys highlight shortcomings, the team can rally to correct any problems.

Challenge #10: Convincing Clients to Buy into the Agent Team Concept

Although agent teams are popular among agents, home buyers and sellers tend to be a little less enthusiastic about the concept at first. When you break the news to your buyers or sellers that they may be working with someone other than you, many of them instantly feel cheated. They feel as though you pulled the old bait-and-switch on them—selling them a top-producing agent and then sticking them with an assistant.

Warning: Other agents who work independently in your area are likely to try to use your team approach against you. If prospective clients mention that they talked with you, an independent agent may tell them something like, "Well, so-and-so works on a team, so you're likely to get stuck working with her assistant rather than directly with her." Be prepared to counter this argument.

To overcome this challenge, be proactive in your marketing and listing presentations:

- Assign meaningful job titles to everyone on your team, so clients don't feel as though they're getting stuck with a lowly "assistant."

- Market your team as a full-service real estate business consisting of qualified specialists.

• Inform clients that your team has the added advantage of having someone always on call.

• Highlight your success as a team.

• Use testimonials from past clients to prove that you deliver outstanding service.

Selling the Team Concept
By Char MacCallum

To sell the team concept to prospective clients, I compare the situation to having major surgery: If I needed major surgery, would I want the surgeon to greet me at the reception desk, take my blood, perform the lab analysis, wheel me down to the operating room, administer and monitor the anesthetic, and operate on me? Of course not, because I would want a surgeon who was very skilled at performing the type of surgery I required and had plenty of experience performing that surgery. I would want a team of other specialists to handle all the other tasks, including processing the paperwork for my insurance company.

It's the same way with agents. Multiple tasks demand attention at any given stage in the process of buying or selling a home. Being able to pass those tasks along to other people who specialize in performing them gives me the freedom to focus on finding homes for buyers and marketing homes for sellers. I make my clients well aware of the fact that they'll receive more personal attention from my team than they'd receive if I were working without that support. Instead of having one stressed-out agent who's attempting to do it all, they have a team of competent, skilled experts all focused on meeting each client's needs. We have a higher success rate because each person on the team can specialize in what he or she does best.

Appendix

For Brokers Only:
Supporting Agent Sales Teams in Your Office

Real estate power teams benefit not only team leaders and team members, but also real estate brokers who support agent teams in their office. Many brokers, however, are unaccustomed to the real estate power team approach. In fact, some brokers view agent teams as a threat. They fear the possibility that a strong team leader might steal agents from the firm or that the team will function as an informal union, forcing the broker to pay higher commissions and a larger share of expenses.

Remember: Although such fears are justified to a certain extent, they shouldn't discourage brokers from embracing the real estate power team approach. Properly managed power teams deliver a substantially higher return on a broker's investment than a broker can expect from individual agents. In addition, the risks inherent in a team-based system are no greater than the risks posed by independent agents.

In this chapter, we explore the pros and cons of real estate power teams and then explain what you, as a real estate broker, can do to make your office real estate power team friendly.

Considering the Pros and Cons of Agent Teams

Prior to launching any new venture, most business owners analyze the cost-to-benefit ratio of the prospective venture. They want to know whether the expense is worth the potential payoff. Before you embrace the real estate power team approach in your office, you should perform a similar analysis. In this section, we reveal the pros and cons of the team-based approach so you can decide for yourself whether the potential return on your investment is worth taking a chance on teams.

Pros

In Chapter 1 we describe many of the benefits that the team approach delivers to agents. As a real estate broker, you're likely to receive the same benefits, such as:

- Increased number of listings
- Increased sales and profits
- Increased agent productivity
- A more efficient office
- Better customer service

• A host of new opportunities

Some less obvious benefits also follow. As a team grows and develops, for example, it builds its own brand within your brand. The team begins to take on the role of community leader, carrying your flag and promoting your brand. Managed properly, the team has no desire to compete with you, choosing rather to focus on selling and to let you take the lead by using your skills and experience as the broker.

One of the most important reasons to encourage the power team approach in your office is to prevent that power team from setting up shop down the block from you and launching its own brand. Supporting successful agent teams brings more value to your company while simultaneously discouraging top agents from competing against you.

Cons

Problems with agent teams usually arise when either the team itself or its relationship with the brokers isn't managed properly. When this happens, you may face the following problems:

• A team leader recruits personnel from your office to launch his or her own office in competition with you.

• A team provides poor customer service, which reflects poorly on your brand.

• The team tries to run your business or dictate the terms of your relationship with the team.

• The team calls upon you to provide an inordinate amount of training in order to make the team successful.

Warning: Before allowing an agent to form a team, make sure the team leader has a detailed plan in place that spells out exactly what you are responsible (and not responsible) for providing. A team leader can become high maintenance very quickly if he or she has no plan or a defective plan. By being more involved early on, you can set the team on the right path and invest less time and fewer resources later.

You may also encounter some minor drawbacks and setbacks that, fortunately, the benefits of the team-based approach typically outweigh:

• Higher phone and utility bills, due to the needs of increased personnel and office traffic

• A busier office that could increase the level of stress

• Longer operating hours

• A bigger initial investment on your part to train new team members

<u>Why Agent Teams are an Overlooked Gem</u>

The concept of real estate power teams is relatively new, and, as with all new things, the concept has met some resistance. Real estate brokers and agents are often reluctant to embrace the agent team approach even when they're well aware of the potential benefits. Why? Mostly because of fear and ignorance in the following areas:
- Fear of losing control
- Fear of sharing
- Fear of success
- Lack of knowledge

Just think back to the early days of the Multiple Listing Service (MLS), when agents weren't allowed to share their knowledge because they were afraid that if the listings were publicly accessible, they'd lose their jobs. Now look at our industry. If you aren't on the information superhighway openly providing listing information, you just might be out of business.

It's my firm belief that the agents, franchises, companies, and brokers that embrace the team concept today are going to be the industry leaders tomorrow. They'll be the survivors in a rapidly changing industry in a rapidly changing world.

Hopefully, this book will eliminate your fears and provide you with the information you need to make a rational decision. With the right preparation, you can begin adding agent teams to your brokerage and reaping the many benefits of the agent team approach. *–Ralph R. Roberts*

Understanding Your Role in the Team's Success as Well as Your Own
As a real estate broker, you play a unique role in the success of each team that works out of your office. Your job is to protect the health and well-being of your own business while providing your agents and teams with the information and resources they need to be successful. Following are some tips to help ensure the success of your agent teams:

• **Get involved in the planning stage.** When teams first start out, they are swimming with sharks. The sharks are all the distractions that can end up causing the team to self-destruct: vendors pushing their products, personality conflicts, differing opinions, power struggles, and so on. We see teams that generate millions of dollars a year in sales and still have very little profit left at the end of the year.

Many agents have problems transitioning from the role of independent agent to small-business owner. As a small-business owner, you can help them with the transition. First, you need to keep reminding the team leader that he or she is running a business. This isn't teaming up for social hour. This is teaming up to provide more and better service, to accomplish more, to raise the bar, to increase revenue and profits, and to create a business entity that will live on, taking care of its staff and clients long after the team leader retires.

Once the team leader is well aware of the need to establish a business, you can begin training the team leader on the techniques for running the business—hiring and firing, managing the accounts, compensating team members, serving clients, and so on. Review the team leader's plan and offer your advice as an experienced team leader. Make sure the team leader is well aware of his or her responsibilities to you.

• **Request a profit and loss statement.** You should have your own P&L statement as well as a P&L statement for every agent and team. This will help you spot strengths and weaknesses in your organization.

• **Remain involved in the hiring and training process.** To ensure that teams are staffed with qualified personnel, play a roll in the hiring of team members. Don't try to dictate who a team can and can't hire, but do offer some input. Also, work closely with the team leader and other team members to properly train all new team members. Again, don't take on the entire burden of training—a shared approach works best.

• **Meet with the team leader every day.** Establish a collaborative working relationship with the team leader to increase loyalty. Team leaders should seek your input on every idea, marketing campaign, and advertising plan. Collaboration is key.

Tip: Most team leaders are passionate visionaries who do not appreciate having roadblocks thrown in front of them. Be involved without being too intrusive. Don't try to play the role of team leader. As the broker, you take on the role of advisor—offering your expert opinion and insight, and encouraging the team leader to explore new ideas and opportunities.

• **Audit transactions regularly.** Real estate and mortgage fraud are all too common these days. By auditing selected transactions regularly, you can spot any signs of fraud before they become a serious problem.

• **Treat agents and teams as your clients.** Keep in mind that your clients aren't the people buying or selling homes you've listed; your clients are the agents or agent teams who are working for you. If your agents are working hard and earning good profits, then they're motivated to do more. Create an environment where work is fun, profitable, satisfying and nonthreatening.

Warning: Some brokers can't accept the agent team approach. They simply can't overcome their own egos or share the spotlight with a team leader. These types of brokers tend to squeeze the life out of the team as well as out of their own businesses. If you fall into this category, do whatever possible to turn things around. You can't exist as an island, and everyone worth keeping will eventually leave. Get in tune with your staff and your agents. Care about their goals and aspirations. As soon as you do, you'll begin to attract the best of the best.

Negotiating Mutually Beneficial Contracts

As a real estate broker, you're accustomed to hiring agents on contract. You do the same with agent teams, although the terms of the contract may be quite different. An agent team has the potential to earn substantially higher profits than an individual agent, but the team's expenses are also substantially higher. The terms of the contract need to account for this.

Remember: Your goal is to achieve TT+WBB success: Tremendous Team Without Busting the Broker. Work toward developing a compensation package that motivates and rewards team members for their successes while increasing your sales and net profit. Compensation for the team doesn't have to center solely on money; the guidance and training you offer can be a valuable perk.

In this section, we discuss compensation in greater detail, breaking it down into commissions-based compensation, resources, and support.

Setting reasonable commissions

Negotiating splits with your agents is no new thing for you. With a novice agent, for example, you may offer something in the range of a 50/50 split, whereas a seasoned, top-producing agent earns an 80/20 split. The more revenue an agent brings in and the less time and fewer resources the agent requires, the more you can afford to pay the person.

The same is true for agent teams. If a team is a top producer and basically runs itself, giving the team a higher percentage of the sales commission may be good for both of you. It motivates the team to work harder and generate more sales and revenue for both the team and your brokerage. If the team needs you to supply office space, equipment, training, and other resources, however, you may need to pay them a lower commission, so you can cover the cost of these items.

However you choose to structure your commissions, always tie them to performance. Tie the commission percentages to gross sales or some other benchmark so that if the team falls short of its projected goal, the shortfall has less of an effect on your bottom line.

Tip: Consider offering a top-producing team a "golden handcuff" program; give them a piece of the pie that becomes substantial only upon the team's success. We know of an agent team leader who's been at the top of his game for the past 20 years. His broker pays him a percentage of the company's profits from its real estate investments. This keeps the team leader from looking elsewhere—a 5–10% chunk of the profit isn't something he's likely to get someplace else.

Too many agents and brokers worry about what the split is. The numbers they should be looking at are the net earnings, the bottom line for both the broker and the team. You don't create a team to get a higher split. You create a team to increase sales volume and create more and better business. This will naturally generate more revenue for both you as the broker and for the team.

Warning: Watch out for independent agents or team leaders who are committed to playing Beat the Broker. These agents spend a good deal of their time and talents thinking up ways to score higher earnings without actually earning them. By tying your compensation package to production, you can discourage most attempts to beat the broker.

Offering additional resources and support

Some teams pretty much run their own business, relying on the broker for office space and the broker's brand presence. Other teams may need additional resources and support in order to achieve success. As a broker, you need to remind the team leader of all the benefits you offer above and beyond the commissions you pay out. These benefits may include the following:

- Brand presence that the team doesn't need to create or maintain
- Advertising and marketing
- Web site
- Lead generation
- Accounting services
- Systems for processing transactions
- Office space and furniture
- Office equipment and supplies
- One or more receptionists

Getting what you need out of the deal

Giving teams what they need to succeed is only half the equation. You also need to secure your own best interests. What do you need to receive in order to make the deal attractive to you? How much revenue does the team need to generate? How much positive press does it need to produce? What effect do you want the team to have on your office?

Remember: How much revenue the team generates directly is only part of the equation as well. A team can indirectly generate additional revenue by increasing your brand presence, motivating other agents and teams that work for you, and opening the doors to additional revenue-generating opportunities. When the expense of supporting an agent team begins to discourage you, consider what you stand to lose by not having a highly productive team working for you.

Tip: Consider extending the agent team concept to other areas of your real estate business. For example, you can launch your own team-based mortgage company, title company, or insurance agency, each of which generates additional revenue while driving business to your other companies. For details about branching out into different areas, check out Chapter 15.

Managing Your Agent Sales Teams without Micromanaging

Agent teams don't always run smoothly. The team can wander off track and lose sight of its vision and goals. Team members may encounter professional or personal crises. Personality conflicts may develop. And a host of other issues can arise that cause difficulties. In this section, we show you when it's time to step in and step out and offer strategies for working productively with the team leader and countering any setbacks.

Knowing when to get involved and when to sit back

In baseball, the manager has to decide when to pull a pitcher who's having a bad day. If the manager pulls the pitcher too early, it could send a signal to the pitcher that the manager has no faith in his abilities. If the manager waits too long, the team could end up losing the game. A great manager knows when to step in and when to hold off and let the pitcher and the catcher work it out.

As broker, you play a similar role. You don't want to become so intrusive that the team leader feels you are overstepping your bounds, but you can't afford to have the team fail either. You need to keep your finger on the pulse of the team without keeping the team under your thumb. By their very nature, agent sales teams require very little supervision and management, because these two factors are built into the structure of the team. The team leader is responsible for supervising, training, and managing the team's agents and other personnel. Your role is to collaborate with the team leader to ensure your mutual success, support the team with training and resources, and step in when needed to make sure the team stays on track.

Recognizing situations where you should step in

Sometimes, you may need to step in and address particular situations with the team leader, such as:

- Resolving disputes and office politics

- Maintaining office policies and procedures

- Ensuring all teams are abiding by franchise rules

- Procuring cause

- Rectifying complaints from clients about the team

- Maintaining quality control on files

- Making sure all escrow deposits are turned in

- Ensuring that your teams and independent agents are supporting your brand and business culture

- Addressing any situation that could negatively affect your E&O (Errors and Omissions) policy

- Ensuring that independent contractors and employees are treated fairly so your business isn't negatively affected

Tip: When you step in, avoid stepping on any toes. Discuss the situation in private with the team leader, and let the team leader take the lead. If you undermine the team leader's authority in front of other team members, you could cause long-term damage. Allow the team leader to carry the image of leader while encouraging him or her to accept your constructive criticism and advice.

Warning: Do immediately send packing any agents who are trying to beat the broker. They'll always choose the easy route and beat someone out of something. In the process, they'll beat themselves and everyone around them out of everything. It doesn't take long to spot them. Here are some of the most common signs:

- Agents scheming together to figure out ways to negotiate a higher split

- One agent recording his or her deals in the name of another agent who's earning a higher split and then dividing up the money on the side

- An agent who refuses to kick up the volume but is demanding a bigger piece of the pie

Discerning when to let the team leader take the lead

A strong team leader with the cooperation of loyal team members can often weather the storm without your assistance, so be prepared to step out when needed and let the team work out its own problems. Following are some situations in which you'd probably be better served taking a hands-off policy:

• Daily schedule of the team

• Daily activities of the team

• Team meetings, unless you're invited (you can schedule your own separate meetings with the team and team leader)

• Human resource issues that apply to team members who aren't your employees (if one of your employees also serves as a member of a team, you can handle human resource issues together)

Joining forces with the team leader

Always stay in contact with the team leader. Establish a solid relationship in which you treat one another as equals who are dedicated to one another's mutual success. If you're concerned about something the team is doing or not doing, first find out as much about the situation as possible before offering your guidance, and then approach the team leader and voice your concern. The team leader may already be aware of the situation and working on a solution. If not, the two of you can work together to develop a suitable solution.

The following are five key areas where you can offer valuable assistance:

• **Finances:** Keep track of the team's financial well-being. Monthly and quarterly P&L statements can keep you informed of the team's progress. If the team seems to be slipping, contact the team leader to brainstorm possible solutions.

• **Goal setting:** Based on the team's past performance and future vision, you can assist the team in setting monthly, quarterly, and annual goals.

• **Meetings:** Meet with the team leader at least once a week and make sure the team meets on a regular basis. You may even want to sit in on the team meetings to ensure that they remain as productive as possible, assuming, of course, that you're welcome at these meetings.

• **Rewarding the team and team leader:** Celebrate the team's and the team leader's success. Offering bonuses, catered lunches, or other perks when the team meets or exceeds its goals communicates your appreciation to the team and its leader.

• **Promoting the team leader to partner:** There's no better way to ensure a team leader's commitment to the success of your company than by giving the team leader a bigger name—a small percentage of the net profit, a piece of a real estate investment opportunity, or the piece of a new affiliate business, such as a title or mortgage company.

Whenever you introduce a new agent, a new team, or a new concept to your business, you're liable to run into a host of new challenges, as well. You're likely to encounter some issues that are unique, but most issues are fairly standard—things that others have had to deal with in the past. Here are some of the more common issues you're likely to encounter, along with suggestions on how to best deal with them:

• **Office politics:** Office politics are historically one of the most nagging problems for small businesses. Implement a no-gossip, no-talking-behind-someone-else's-back policy, and you should be able to curb the office politics to a great extent. Be sure to enforce the policy or it will have no effect.

• **Competition between agent teams and individual agents:** Individual agents may feel threatened by an agent team, especially if these agents perceive that you are playing favorites. Do your best to give both individual agents and teams ample time, resources, and praise. Otherwise, jealousies are likely to arise.

• **Recruitment from within:** Set a recruitment policy to prevent your agent teams from actively recruiting your independent agents. Each team should be responsible for recruiting its own agents and staff from outside of your company.

• **Overblown egos:** Both the broker and team leader need to be well aware of the mutual benefits of working for one another. The "you would be nothing without me" attitude must go. You and your team leaders need to team up to do what's best for your clientele, which is ultimately what's best for both of your businesses.

• **Absentee leader:** A team leader who simply sets up the team and then tries to sit back and collect the proceeds is no leader. Make sure the team leader is well aware of his or her responsibilities and is an active member of the team.

• **Inaccessible team leader:** A team leader who is unavailable to team members or to you as the broker of record is equivalent to an absentee leader. The team leader should be holding weekly meetings with the entire team as well as with individual team members and with you.

• **No troubleshooting strategy:** When challenges arise (and they will), have a system in place for identifying the challenge and confronting it.

Your plan may be as simple as holding a meeting to discuss the challenge and your options.

• **No exit strategy:** No matter how successful you think your agent team will be, always have an exit strategy in case things don't work out. Your exit strategy should cover who gets to keep the clients and current listings and how profits will be split on current transactions. Develop the exit strategy early on; when relationships sour, agreeing on an exit strategy is nearly impossible. As the broker/owner, put yourself in the shoes of the team leader and try to be as fair as possible.

RE/MAX Professionals: From Agent to Team Leader to Broker/Franchisee

RE/MAX Professionals, with office locations in Glendale, Surprise, and Avondale, Arizona, is co-owned by business partners and friends Nate Martinez (www.nateshomes.com) and Frank Russo. "When I first started selling real estate over 21 years ago," Martinez says, "I never dreamt that someday I'd be the co-owner of a thriving RE/MAX franchise with three offices, our own mortgage company, and a full-service property management department. We now have 27 employees and 160 licensed associates."

In the beginning, Nate and Frank had a vision for a new kind of real estate office, one with the agent in mind, with training, support, and advanced technologies. Says Martinez: "I have been a die-hard RE/MAX fan since the day I joined the company back in 1991. I wanted our offices to model the vision Dave Liniger had over 30 years ago when he founded RE/MAX."

The two men set out to make their dream a reality: RE/MAX Professionals. They knew they needed quality help if they were going to make this a successful brokerage. They sought out top agents and professionals around the city and recruited them to work for the new company. "Frank and I are not great at paperwork or the day-to-day details of running an office, and we were okay admitting that early on," says Martinez. "We knew it was really important to create a strong support staff from the very beginning." They also knew they needed a strong broker to help them with the legal aspects of a brokerage. Although both of them are extremely knowledgeable about contract law, real estate rules and ethics, neither of them felt it would be their best contribution to the company. They hired a broker to manage the sales associates so they could focus on what they do best—selling the RE/MAX way of life to new recruits.

Nate and Frank still continued to manage their individual teams and depend on those key players even more now than before, during the start of the franchise. "It was hard to juggle both in the beginning because my team needed me, but so did my new office. I really had to delegate and empower those people working for me at that time to help me run the team and still continue to be profitable. Both our teams helped fund the office project, and sometimes their roles bled into the office administrative needs. We really wanted them to remain separate entities, so it was a delicate process for the first year or so."

Because of their reputations and market share, they had some concerns about how the prospective recruit may feel about coming to work with the competition. "We have always been of the mindset that sharing is the way to get ahead in this business. You exchange ideas with your fellow comrades and help each other prosper. We put ourselves out there with this company as an opportunity for new and seasoned agents to come work in an environment where they could learn from us and each other." So far that philosophy has worked for RE/MAX Professionals; having a separate, designated broker, the agents no longer fear the competition. Here are a few of the routines they follow:

- Nate and Frank hold company meetings once a month, during which they share important information about changes in the market and provide their team members with an opportunity to talk about their own challenges. They also highlight the accomplishments of associates with peer recognition.

- Once a week they have one-hour training classes that vary from outside speakers to Nate and Frank getting down and dirty with scripts and dialogue role-playing. RE/MAX International provides RSN, a satellite network broadcasting dynamic guest speakers and trainers delivering the latest and best industry tools.

- Unfortunately, not everyone has RSN at home, so Nate and Frank decided to bring RSN to their agents. Every month, one of the office locations hosts an RSN night, with food and drinks, and agents are given the opportunity to watch the program. "I am a firm believer in continuing to educate yourself in this industry. You can't stop learning and trying new ideas. Education is power, and that is why we go above and beyond to make sure our affiliates have all the opportunities we can provide as owners."

The interoffice functions of RE/MAX Professionals are a little different from the average setup. Frank and Nate co-own the RE/MAX Professionals franchise, but they have an acting general manager as well as the designated broker. They also co-own a joint business venture with Wells Fargo Home Mortgage, Professional Financial Services of Arizona. "We currently have three offices, and each office has its own Director of First Impressions. We have a Recruiter, Office Managers for two of the locations, two Transaction Coordinators, a Human Resources and an Accounting Department, a Broker Assistant, and an IT person. Frank and I really try to stay out of the management part of the business. We attend only one management meeting per month because we realized that things run better when we aren't in the middle," says Martinez. "I am a visionary, and the biggest challenge I have is getting people to see what I see for the future. Not only do I have to pave the way, but I have to instill courage and confidence in my management team to follow me down the path, a tough feat when you're stuck in micromanagement mode. It's hard to trust people with that much control of your business, but the bigger question is, if you can't trust them, then why are they working for you in the first place?"

Of course, Nate and Frank still make the final decisions and oversee major changes that come into play. They focus on recruiting and building relationships with their affiliates. On an agent's anniversary date every year, Nate and Frank invite that person to a special lunch to thank him or her for being a part of RE/MAX Professionals. "We are grateful for the success we've had, and we couldn't have done it without the agents making the decision to not only join our company but also to stay year after year. We never want to take that for granted. This is just one of the ways we can continually remind them how important they are to our success."

So what is the future of RE/MAX Professionals as they head

into their seventh year of operation? More agents and more offices! "Frank and I just launched a company-wide recruiting contest because we want everyone to share in our vision for the future. We have a goal for 2008 to recruit a net of 60 more high-quality agents to our company. In order to do that, we are going to need help, so why not reward those who have been loyal to us?"

Nate and Frank are making real estate history every day with their hybrid offices, equipped with an on-site lender and title company and state-of-the-art technology. Their collaborated efforts, combined with their individual genius and immeasurable drive for success, could easily bring to life the next great trend in the industry.

Contributor Bios

Martin Bouma, team leader of The Bouma Group (**www.bouma.com**), Keller Williams Real Estate of Ann Arbor, Michigan, graduated from the University of Michigan with a degree in biochemistry before ultimately launching a successful career in real estate. To best serve his clients, Martin and his enthusiastic team create a customized marketing plan for each seller and buyer they represent. Thorough market knowledge, exceptional follow-through, and good old common sense are the hallmarks of The Bouma Group's continued success. Martin Bouma is actually the #1 Realtor in Ann Arbor and Washtenaw County and has been for several years. In Chapter 6, "Handling Team Member Compensation," Bouma discusses the importance of avoiding the temptation of overpaying your buyer's agents.

Howard Brinton, creator of the STAR POWER® Systems, Inc. (**www.gostarpower.com**), and mentor to top-producing REALTORS® across the country, is a generous, knowledgeable, experienced, wise, and entertaining educator. Brinton has a pulse on the heartbeat of the real estate industry from first-hand experience; having been an agent and broker for 17 years and closing 470 transactions his peak year, he's no stranger to the challenges and demands of the job. In Chapter 11, "Handpicking Your Workforce," Brinton leads you step-by-step through the process of using the DISC assessment to ensure that you place the right people in the right positions. Howard also makes cameo appearances throughout the book, where other contributors reference the lessons they learned from him.

Paul Corona, a listing partner at Ralph Roberts Realty, attributes the success of his 22-year career to his close family, solid middle-class values, and the game of golf. In Chapter 13, "Taking on the Role of Mentor and Motivator," Paul shares his personal account of the training he received to make him a productive member of the Ralph Roberts Realty Team.

David Crockett left management in 1994 to form The Crockett Team, Ltd., a minibrokerage within Howard Hanna Smythe Cramer in Concord and Painesville Townships of Cleveland, Ohio, with his wife, Judie, daughter, Melissa Crockett Willis, and son, Todd. Together they built a market-dominant real estate business based on the team concept by using effective systems, cutting-edge technology, and a proactive marketing approach. In 1995, the Crocketts were selected as STAR POWER® "Stars" by Howard Brinton. _REALTOR® Magazine_ has honored The Crockett Team as being among the Top 100 Realtors in the country. Chapter 1, "Grasping the Power Agent Team Concept," introduces the Crockett Team, while Chapter 6, "Handling Team Member Compensation," reveals the Crockett team's unique approach to compensating team members for success, the Casino Game.

Judie Crockett launched her career in 1978 and quickly rose to her status as the top REALTOR® at Smythe, Cramer Co. (now Howard Hanna Smythe Cramer). She's an effective marketer with a real street sense, which makes for a powerful combination. These talents help her not only in real estate but also in her consulting business, because she can read situations and people almost instantly and then cut to the chase. Judie has spoken at many state and national real estate conventions in addition to being a Senior Instructor for STAR POWER University, specializing in marketing and listing. Chapter 1, "Grasping the Power Agent Team Concept," introduces the Crockett Team, while Chapter 6, "Handling Team Member Compensation," reveals the Crockett team's unique approach to compensating team members for success, the Casino Game.

Brandon Fairbanks (**www.mymaderacountyrealestate.com**) is president and CEO of Montecino & Associates Real Estate and Go Platinum Lending in Coarsegold, California. Fairbanks has built his business based on a team concept to better serve his clients; he enjoys training and educating the members of his team. He also enjoys building and renovating homes to sell. Chapter 1, "Grasping the Power Agent Team Concept," introduces the Fairbanks team, which consists of several family members including Fairbanks' mother, Patty. In Chapter 12, "Establishing a Firm Foundation," Fairbanks offers guidance on how to properly train and equip team members with the tools they need to succeed.

Bryan Felder is a lifelong resident of Northern Virginia and the guiding force behind the highly successful agent team The Virginia Realty Group (**www.varealtygroup.com**) of Chantilly, Virginia, named one of "The Top 25 Teams to Watch in 2007" by RISMedia's *Real Estate* magazine and one of the Top 25 RE/MAX teams in the state of Virginia. Felder built his team within the RE/MAX Gateway firm, which allowed him to cobrand his operation with one of the largest international real estate companies. Felder believes that building long-term relationships in real estate is the key to success, so he centered his team on the vision, "Building Clients for Life." In Chapter 3, "Transitioning from Independent Agent to Team Leader," Felder shows how his team achieves its goals by carefully assigning tasks to team members who have the specialized training required to perform those tasks.

Kandra Hamric (**www.kandrahamric.com**) is a professional virtual assistant and CEO of Hamric Enterprise, LLC, a virtual assistant company with professional experience in the field of real estate and a positive track record of increasing productivity, profits, and efficiency. Kandra's knowledge and experience in real estate is extensive, and real estate professionals frequently call on her for advice and assistance with real estate transactions, marketing online and offline, and a host of other routine and atypical tasks related to real estate. Kandra holds a degree in arts and is certified by the NATIONAL ASSOCIATION OF REALTORS® as a Real Estate Professional Assistant. In Chapter 12, "Establishing a Firm Foundation," Kandra offers her insight on how to communicate effectively in the digital world.

Curtis Hicks is president and CEO of the Center for Computer Resources, a Metro Detroit–based technology services firm that has been one of Southeast Michigan's most trusted and experienced full service systems integrators for over 26 years. Hicks brings over 25 years of experience to this collaboration, providing quality technology solutions to the market, and he delivers a unique set of skills as president for CCR, having both the technical knowledge of computers and computer networks and an extensive sales and marketing background. In Chapter 10, "Equipping Your Team with the Tools and Technologies to Succeed," Hicks shares his insights into online communications tools that are ideal for real estate agent teams.

Ashley Leigh (**www.ashleyleighteam.com**) of Linton Hall REALTORS® in Gainesville, Virginia, is one of the most successful real estate agents in the country. He has produced over $1 billion in sales in his first ten years and has been featured in the book *Billion Dollar Agents* by Steve Kantor. His innovative marketing programs have been the subject of articles in *Fortune* magazine. He's been featured in RISMedia's *Real Estate* magazine and *Power Team Report* and has been recognized by *REALTOR® Magazine* as one of the Top 100 Sales Agents in the U.S. Ashley produced a top volume of $183 million in sales in a single year and sold over 400 homes in 2004. He is the founding owner of the innovative electronic lead capture kiosk company Lead Gorilla. In Chapter 8, "Managing the Money," Leigh offers guidance on how to manage the office finances.

Rob Levy of The Rob Levy Team (**www.roblevy.com**), Prudential Northwest Properties in Portland, Oregon, has been a licensed REALTOR® with the same firm and in the same office since 1988 and has been a Portland resident since 1984 after having lived all over the world. The first eCertified Prudential real estate agent in the world, Levy is very tech savvy and is a well-respected speaker on the topic of using the latest technologies to run real estate businesses more effectively and efficiently. In Chapter 10, "Equipping Your Team with the Tools and Technologies to Succeed," Levy highlights some of the top technologies for equipping your team to compete successfully in the increasingly digital world of real estate.

Char MacCallum of the Char MacCallum Real Estate Group, Inc., of Olathe, Kansas (**www.char4homes.com**), has been a REALTOR® for 30 years and was one of the first agents to introduce the team concept to the Kansas City area. Char was listed by *REALTOR® Magazine* as one of the Top 100 REALTORS® in the nation. Char commits time and resources to ensure that her clients always receive the highest level of service and knowledge from her team. The whole intent behind opening her own company and keeping it a team-only firm was to preserve the integrity of service. In Chapter 6, "Handling Team Member Compensation," MacCallum shares her insights on how to manage expenses and compensation to team members, while in Chapter 16, "Overcoming the Top Ten Challenges of Operating a Successful Agent Team," she reveals the biggest challenges that real estate agents are likely to face when building and managing an agent team.

Domenic Manchisi (**www.domenicmanchisi.com**) of Prudential Town Centre Realty in Milton, Ontario, is an accomplished REALTOR® who is recognized as leading one of the top three teams in all of Canada in 2006. Manchisi believes that providing the very best service is essentially about putting his clients first, and it's this quality that has led him through an award-winning career as a consistent top producer. Through hard work and strong leadership, Manchisi and his team of three buyer specialists, two administrative assistants, and a marketing specialist have earned the respect of not only his clients but also his colleagues. In Chapter 1, "Grasping the Power Agent Team Concept," Manchisi shares his experience of building and managing a successful power agent team.

Nate Martinez (**www.nateshomes.com**) of RE/MAX Professionals, located in Glendale, Arizona, runs his team as an equal partnership with his colleague Frank Russo. His team consists of three full-time Buyer Specialists along with three full-time Administrative Assistants. In addition to being a coowner of RE/MAX Professionals, Nate is a director for the state and national Association of REALTORS® as well as the incoming 2008 president for the Phoenix Association of REALTORS®. Nate's personal and professional philosophy is a quote from the great Wayne Gretzky: "Skate to where the puck is going, not where it's been!" In Chapter 1, "Grasping the Power Agent Team Concept," Martinez shares his experience with forming a partnership team. In Chapter 2, "Taking Stock: Is an Agent Team Right for You?", he reveals the benefits of having a customer service rep who functions more as a "director of first impressions." And in Chapter 6, "Handling Team Member Compensation," he weighs in on the topic of how to fairly compensate team members.

Chip Neumann of Neumann Real Estate (**www.chipneumann.com**) in Ridgefield, Connecticut, is quite familiar with Ridgefield and its real estate. His success in the business has earned him local and national recognition as Ridgefield's most active home seller. He was featured in Pat Zaby's real estate book, *Profiles of Top Producers*, and was 1 of only 12 REALTORS® in the United States to be chosen by Howard Brinton for his "Star of the Month" yearly interview series. He continues to receive numerous national awards for his real estate achievements. In Chapter 13, "Taking on the Role of Mentor and Motivator," Neumann shows how he uses bonuses rather than raises to motivate and reward team members.

Faye F. Rispoli operates the Rispoli Team (**www.ffrispoli.com**) of Latham, New York, under the internationally renowned RE/MAX brand, with her own agents and administrative staff. Faye is the top producing agent in her office, with over 10% of the company sales volume. A New York State real estate agent for 36 years, Faye is a recognized industry leader, ranked in the top 1% of REALTORS® in the United States. In Chapter 3, "Transitioning from Independent Agent to Team Leader," Faye shares her experience of transitioning from an independent agent to power agent team leader.

Bill Ryan, a native of Chandler, Arizona, entered the real estate business in 1974. In 2004 and 2005, The Ryan Team (**www.billryanrealtor.com**) earned the distinct honor of being the number one RE/MAX Team in Arizona. Ryan has been managing teams and using personal assistants in his business since 1981. His team manager, Kerri Wade, is responsible for overseeing all team activities, goals, stats, and marketing from her home in Idaho, performing all her job duties via the Internet. A transaction coordinator and listing coordinator, along with two property management employees, round out Ryan's administrative staff. In Chapter 12, "Establishing a Firm Foundation," Ryan shares his insights on the importance of team communication and weekly meetings.

Jeannie Sample has over three decades of successful real estate experience as a new construction expert, licensed REALTOR®, professional real estate trainer, and team leader. Over the years, Sample and her personally trained team members have dominated the Michigan market. The proof hangs on her office walls in the form of countless awards. The culmination of her experiences, leadership mentality, college background in writing and marketing, tenacity, work ethic, and genuine kindness to others makes her a unique and valuable REALTOR®. Jeannie and her husband are also committed providers for hundreds of sick, wayward, and once-abused horses and other animals. In Chapter 15, "Identifying New Opportunities and Adding New Teams," Sample shares her insights and experiences with adding a New Construction division to Ralph Roberts Realty (**www.ralphroberts.com**).

Marylyn B. Schwartz (**www.marylynbschwartz.com**) is a noted expert in real estate, corporate sales training, and team development. She is president of her company, TEAMWEAVERS, and is a Master Trainer for the most successful real estate sales training program to come along in more than 20 years, Leader's Choice®. She's also an author, real estate monthly columnist, meeting facilitator, and business/life coach. In 1999 the National Speakers Association awarded her the prestigious designation of Certified Speaking Professional; fewer than 7% of the 6,000 members worldwide achieve this level of excellence. In Chapter 1, "Grasping the Power Agent Team Concept," Schwartz describes the predictable stages of a team's development: forming, storming, norming, performing, and, when needed, adjourning. You can contact Marylyn via e-mail at **teamweaver@aol.com** or by calling 203-798-8031.

Alan Shafran of The Alan Shafran Group (**www.alanshafran.com**), Prudential California Realty in Carlsbad, California, is consistently in the top 1% of the nation's real estate professionals. His sales have repeatedly earned him top producing and selling agent awards from some of the nation's largest real estate firms, and he earned recognition as high as the #3 Highest Producing Agent Nationwide. In addition, he's received several awards, including Top Volume Salesperson, Multi-Million Dollar Producer, Top Selling Agent, and Top Listing Agent. In Chapter 10, "Equipping Your Team with the Tools and Technologies to Succeed," Shafran shares his insights and expertise on technologies that can help your team succeed.

Jean Shine of the Shine Team (**www.shineteam.com**) is an award-winning, multimillion-dollar-producing real estate agent with Coldwell Banker United REALTORS® in Killeen, Texas. Jean and her team specialize in providing clients with the most professional, top-notch service and experience, allowing them to have the best quality and most stress-free move they can imagine. Jean's strength as a team leader lies in her ability to honestly assess the strengths and weaknesses of all team members, including herself. In Chapter 1, "Grasping the Power Agent Team Concept," she shares her team's secret for effectively managing the office by keeping her out of it.

Teresa Lazazzera Strohmeyer of The Teresa Team (**www.theteresateam.com**) at ERA OakCrest Realty in Winchester, Virginia, is a seasoned REALTOR® and team leader who is well aware of the challenges of building and managing a team. Teresa's team includes a marketing director, transaction coordinator and client services coordinator. In Chapter 4, "Assembling Your Real Estate Agent Team," Strohmeyer shares her experience and insights on identifying the positions you need to fill on your team and finding the right people to fill them.

Wayne Turner (**www.wayneturner.com**), of the Wayne Turner Real Estate Company in Hendersonville, Tennessee, is a real estate broker who has been recognized as one of the leaders in residential home sales in the state of Tennessee and ranked among the top 0.5% of all REALTORS® in the nation.

Wayne and his team consistently sell over 210 homes annually, placing the team among the top for home sales. Embracing technology every step of the way every passing day, Wayne understands and teaches the meaning of Leads, Listings, and Leverage. Knowing that time is one of his most valued commodities, Wayne redefines the meaning of using systems and techniques and having an exceptional team. In Chapter 3, "Transitioning from Independent Agent to Team Leader," Turner shares his techniques and strategies for smoothing the transition from agent to team leader. In Chapter 9, "Teaming up with Your Broker for Your Mutual Benefit," he offers a tip on how to work with your state's real estate commission to ensure compliance should you ever decide to create your own brokerage.

Julie Vanderblue, president of the Higgins Group (a Christie's-Affiliated, 15-office, Fairfield County, CT-based brokerage in Fairfield, Connecticut), has created what she refers to as a Green Beret, special-task-force team within her company that has become synonymous with superior innovation, technology, world-class marketing, and, most of all, *results* in the supremely competitive Connecticut Real Estate market. Forming a team has allowed Julie and company founder Richard Higgins to pioneer many forward-thinking systems by incubating them first within Julie's skillful, creative, and unified group—The Vanderblue Team (**www.vanderblueteam.com**). In Chapter 2, "Taking Stock: Is an Agent Team Right for You?", Vanderblue answers a series of questions related to the early stages of building a team. In Chapter 13, "Taking on the Role of Mentor and Motivator," she weighs in on the importance of having team members communicate with one another. In the same chapter, she offers her insight on how to prevent and resolve conflicts among team members.

Marsha Waddelow, a top producer with RE/MAX Associates of Arlington, Texas (**waddelowteam@hotmail.com**), continues to receive top production awards. She and her team are consistently ranked in the Top 5 by RE/MAX of Texas for Tarrant County. She is a charter member of Success Partners, a select group of RE/MAX Top Producers who meet quarterly to focus on business and personal growth. A member of RE/MAX's Hall of Fame, Chairman's Club, RE/MAX Elite 500, and "Top 10" Referral Group, Marsha enjoys sharing her formula for success with other agents and is a regular speaker at RE/MAX conventions and events. In Chapter 11, "Handpicking Your Workforce," Waddelow reveals the advantages of behavioral interviews over traditional interviews. In Chapter 6, "Handling Team Member Compensation," and Chapter 13, "Taking on the Role of Mentor and Motivator," she offers guidance on how to compensate team members in ways that improve motivation and job satisfaction. And in Chapter 5, "Establishing Office Policies and Procedures," she shares her team's office policies.

Steve and Nancy Whitfield opened the doors to Whitfield Properties Team (**www.whitfieldproperties.com**) in Burlington, North Carolina, in 1999. Steve has been a top producing real estate agent since 1974, and Nancy has been working with Steve since 1995. Whitfield Properties Team is the only company in its market that uses the "Total Team Concept": All the duties of the buying and selling process are broken down into specializations—first-time buyers, new home sales, selecting the right builder, upsizers, the over-55 market, and the upper-end properties. Whitfield Properties' mission is to fulfill its clients' needs with commitment, integrity, and creativity while having fun. In Chapter 4, "Drawing Up a Business Plan," Steve and Nancy share their team's organizational chart.